LIVING
NAME

ESSAYS ON AMERICAN POETS

LIVING NAME

MARK HALLIDAY

LOUISIANA STATE UNIVERSITY PRESS

BATON ROUGE

Published by Louisiana State University Press
lsupress.org

DESIGNER: Michelle A. Neustrom
TYPEFACE: Calluna

COVER IMAGE: *Méros*, 2021, by Nick Carter. Mixed media consisting of dyed polycotton, thread, and nails.

LIBRARY OF CONGRESS CATALOGING-IN-PUBLICATION DATA

Names: Halliday, Mark, 1949– author.
Title: Living name : essays on American poets / Mark Halliday.
Description: Baton Rouge : Louisiana State University Press, 2025. | Includes index.
Identifiers: LCCN 2024048623 (print) | LCCN 2024048624 (ebook) | ISBN 978-0-8071-8310-6 (cloth) | ISBN 978-0-8071-8400-4 (paperback) | ISBN 978-0-8071-8433-2 (pdf) | ISBN 978-0-8071-8422-6 (epub)
Subjects: LCSH: American poetry—History and criticism. | LCGFT: Literary criticism. | Essays.
Classification: LCC PS305 .H35 2025 (print) | LCC PS305 (ebook) | DDC 811.009—dc23/eng/20241206
LC record available at https://lccn.loc.gov/2024048623
LC ebook record available at https://lccn.loc.gov/2024048624

CONTENTS

vii   Preface

1   Poetry and the Rescue of Particulars

46   Whitman and the Rescue of Particulars

64   Dear Friend, Sit Down: On Helen Vendler's *Invisible Listeners*

83   Damned Good Poet: On Kenneth Fearing

112   Kenneth Fearing and Human Lifetimes

126   Kenneth Koch and the Fun of Being a Poet

139   Kenneth Koch and Elegy

172   Robert Pinsky and Forgetting

190   Art against Loneliness: On Rachel Wetzsteon's *Sakura Park*

205   Courageous Clarity: On Tony Hoagland's *Unincorporated Persons in the Late Honda Dynasty*

225   Tony Hoagland and Second Thoughts

242   Ludic Spiritualism: On Claire Bateman

260   Dean Young and the Madding Flood

277   Dean Young, Prince of Our Lostness

291   Acknowledgments

293   Index

PREFACE

Living Name collects essays on American poets whose work has especially engaged me. Most of the poets are recent or contemporary, though I include also an essay on Walt Whitman and two essays on Kenneth Fearing, who died in 1961. In gathering these essays, I have not made any effort to "cover the field" of contemporary poetry; in such a vast literary culture, any effort to present a thorough survey tends toward blandness and looseness in the comparisons proposed, and inevitably, the critic writes about some of the many poets without palpable enthusiasm. Instead, throughout the last thirty years, I've looked for poets I could write about with excited admiration.

The poets I've chosen have in common a belief in the lyrical voice; they try to evoke a sense of the human reality of a poem's speaker. Commitment to creating the impression of a real individual speaking in a poem has been called "Romantic" by some theorists who seem to believe they are exposing an illusion, but the commitment characterizes the work of Alexander Pope as well as William Wordsworth, and it is central to what has always seemed to me crucial in poetry. I have not been interested in "experimental" poets who consider the lyrical voice to be an illusory or repressive idea. On a day of emotional or moral crisis in their real lives, I assume such experimentalists speak lyrically—that is, with presentness and convincingness of feeling and with intense seeking of clarity. I love poems that imitate the idiosyncrasy and the intensity of such speaking.

We mortals are always challenged to appreciate one another more. My great teacher Frank Bidart used to tell me "You have to love what you love." He meant that each of us should realize what we really love and then try to devote ourselves to that—to love vigorously and generously and bravely, not shyly or passively. "Love what you love"—it is not a tautology but a challenging principle. I've tried to be guided by it in writing my essays. It has pulled me toward often offering a close reading of an individual poem. If I claim that a poem is good,

I should be ready to try to convince you by discussing all of the poem. Admittedly, a book is too short—and life is too short!—for full close reading of *every* poem brought up. Still, I think it is disturbing to see how often critics neglect or disdain to offer close readings of poems, preferring to notice only certain lines or phrases and to generalize about the rest. (I bet they, as professors, disapprove of this approach when undergraduates try it.) The reader of *Living Name* is invited to go along with my frequent efforts to consider all of a given poem.

Throughout the book, I praise poems much more often than I point out shortcomings in them, but I've tried to be alert to phrases and passages that fail to rise to a poet's best level. There are, after all, many ways for a poem to disappoint us. For example, a poem can meet my criterion of presenting a very convincing speaker but without giving that speaker interesting thoughts or allowing the speaker to pursue understanding vigorously. In my favorite poems, we see a speaker striving to express or imply something deeply true about human life. The striving is dramatic; the poem is a drama.

Living Name includes two pieces not focused solely on a single poet. One is an essay-review of Helen Vendler's book *Invisible Listeners,* which led me to ponder what poets hope for from readers. The other is "Poetry and the Rescue of Particulars"—this is the first and longest essay here, the one in which I most directly and extensively theorize about the essential nature of poetry. The driving idea is that the impulse to write a poem is inherently elegiac: the poet wants to rescue some piece of past experience from oblivion.

As I've said, enthusiasm was the main force prompting me to write each essay, rather than any sense of encyclopedic responsibility; thus, my table of contents may look odd to some readers. Let me say that I've written nearly enough essays on other poets to make *another* book, and I will dream of a world that asks me for that book!

LIVING
NAME

POETRY AND THE RESCUE
OF PARTICULARS

We are poor passing facts,
warned by that to give
each figure in the photograph
his living name.
—ROBERT LOWELL

Human beings respond to mutability and mortality—the changing and the disappearing of ourselves and everything we love—in many ways. We can accept our losses grimly and bravely, or we can try to accept them joyously, either because all change is a wondrous spectacle or because our losses clear the path to a better world, or we can affirm that something transcendental (God or Love or Beauty or Peace or Nation) matters supremely while the poor passing facts of our earthly lives don't matter, or we can anticipate supernatural salvation of persons, whereby our mortality is revealed to be an illusion or a misleading interruption.

I believe that the impulse to write poetry involves a basic dissatisfaction with any of those responses to loss. Many motives may be in play when a poet undertakes to write a poem, but always he or she is lured by the notion that to represent in poetry a piece of human experience is *in a way* to keep it in the world; in poetry, a trace of the vanishing thing can be retained, and thus the honored thing has some transcendental lasting reality. Representational art, while it undertakes to fulfill other purposes as well, always attempts such keeping.

But the attempt to confer permanence upon loved objects by representing them is endlessly threatened with absurdity. One reason for this is the awful difference between the actual present thing in life—a loved person, for instance—and the trace that is keepable in art (a likeness, a description, a name).

Another reason why the project of keeping tends to feel imminently absurd is that there is enough experience (lovable, fascinating, revealing) in one day of one person's ordinary busy life (like Leopold Bloom's) to deserve huge heaps of representation. One cannot write *Ulysses* every day; the representer has to choose, with monstrous disregard for the countless particulars (including persons) not selected. Most items, indeed most persons in the flow of one lifetime, will wash away unrecorded.

For some religious poets, and for a transcendentalizing poet like Walt Whitman, this condition is an outrage that cannot be tolerated and so must be denied (except in rare brave admissions of fear and doubt)—the "keeping" done by art must be shown as ultimately unnecessary, since there is to be a transcendental keeping for every sparrow that falls.

Lacking such faith, other poets facing the inevitability of unrepresented losses have to express grief and fear; meanwhile, they may also undertake the strategic response of selective representation. Perhaps by describing or evoking certain splendidly well-chosen particular facts (persons, events, objects, places), a poet can hope to limit, resist, offset, control, or even erase the emotional harm inflicted by our losses of beloved things. The very familiar idea is that a poet selects certain things for representation because they are representative of large groups or classes; the selected item is typical or emblematic or symbolic of many things in a category of experience, and so everything in that category can be understood to be respected, honored, even in some sense *saved* thanks to the artistic image of the selected item. Robert Herrick, praising the liquefaction of Julia's clothes, reminds us of the commendability of all splendidly dressed women. We have all often felt that a poet in this way renders a particular observed reality "universal" and that this is highly satisfying.

But some poets sometimes (my examples are mostly from the age of anxiety, the twentieth century, but examples can be found as far back as Horace) feel that such judiciously representative representation—so prudently defensible, so artistically justifiable—fails to alleviate the sensation that too many worthy particulars, too many individual truths of experience, remain unbearably unattended to, uncherished. And then a poet may resort to less obviously justifiable acts of specific recording, acts of naming. In such cases, the preserved particular does not neatly offer itself as symbolic or typical. It is somehow odd, awkward, clunky, unlovely—unpoetic. It can be a person's name, but it can also be another proper name, or date, or an insistently specific identification of an object, a fact, or an event. Insofar as poems aspire to "universal" significance (significance for all imagined present and future readers), the inclusion of such a gnarly particular tends to pull a poem toward artistic failure. I know this—and yet I've often felt intensely attracted to poems that attempt such unlikely saving and have wanted to deny that the attempt is merely naive.

It is where an act of specific recording or specific naming becomes peculiar, stubborn, transgressive, defiant, willfully insistent, even desperate, that a poem best fits my subject. In the short poems I'm thinking of, the unexpectedness of rescue creates the exciting sensation that *anything*—every lovable thing at least—could be rescued at any moment. The specificity involved tends to push toward the unique instance: not only (for example) the specificity of "a dachshund" as opposed to "a dog" but the further level of specificity in referring to a particular dachshund named Geist.

The appearance of "unpoetic" specificities in poems may serve several purposes, but the purpose at issue here is a desire to *save* the favored thing due to some un-displaceable value perceived in that thing *as itself*, without reliance on its handiness as a symbol or typical example. Moreover, this saving is attempted without reliance on the magnificence or demonstrable excellence or social salience or historic importance of the favored thing; indeed, a quality of obscurity of the favored thing (in the eyes of the world) can even seem crucial in the poet's defiant inclination to seize this small fact and honor it within a poem.

To think that the particular has thus been "rescued" in some permanent and transforming way makes sense, of course, only to people for whom a sentence in a poem has a radiance, indeed an ontological status different from the same sentence in prose. To lovers of poetry, the inclusion of a proper name or other highly specific fact in a poem is in itself already a unique kind of durable honoring, even if the poem does not contain further expressions of praise for the specified thing.

Meanwhile, poetry seriously undertaken exerts severe pressure on the poet to include only what "works" poetically, only what can participate in meanings larger than the private, larger than one's tiny individual life. When my students want to pour their diary-like scraps of personal information into poems, I challenge them with this familiar and traditional idea. (Actually, half of one's students go wrong in the opposite way, with colorless universalisms about justice or love or heartbreak.) But as a poet, and thus forever a student, I feel stimulated to rebellion by the command to rise above the microscopic unimportance of details in my life. Hence, I want to be able to claim that some poets successfully resist the requirement—or that they *try* to resist it with such appealing defiance or insouciance that the effect is delightful or moving—and thus poetic! Admittedly, the defiance or insouciance has become, in such a case, itself a meaning larger than private meaning, by representing a common human impulse.

All elegies, of course, are relevant to the subject of poetry's opposition to oblivion, and all the poems I'll discuss could be called elegiac. But I look for poems whose oddly insistent elegiac references are less generically sanctioned than, say, the names that appear in Yeats's "In Memory of Major Robert Gregory." One much-honored poem that achieves the kind of unexpected rescuing of particulars that I seek is Frank O'Hara's "The Day Lady Died." O'Hara's poem can be called an elegy for Billie Holiday, but it arranges to preserve from oblivion several specificities besides "Lady" herself. This poem has been so much written about in the last forty years that I hesitate to ask the reader to consider it yet again, but I hope to say an untypical thing about it.

The Day Lady Died

It is 12:20 in New York a Friday
three days after Bastille day, yes
it is 1959 and I go get a shoeshine
because I will get off the 4:19 in Easthampton
at 7:15 and then go straight to dinner
and I don't know the people who will feed me

I walk up the muggy street beginning to sun
and have a hamburger and a malted and buy
an ugly NEW WORLD WRITING to see what the poets
in Ghana are doing these days
                              I go on to the bank
and Miss Stillwagon (first name Linda I once heard)
doesn't even look up my balance for once in her life
and in the GOLDEN GRIFFIN I get a little Verlaine

for Patsy with drawings by Bonnard although I do
think of Hesiod, trans. Richmond Lattimore or
Brendan Behan's new play or *Le Balcon* or *Les Nègres*
of Genet, but I don't, I stick with Verlaine
after practically going to sleep with quandariness

and for Mike I just stroll into the PARK LANE
Liquor Store and ask for a bottle of Strega and
then I go back where I came from to 6th Avenue
and the tobacconist in the Ziegfeld Theatre and
casually ask for a carton of Gauloises and a carton
of Picayunes, and a NEW YORK POST with her face on it

and I am sweating a lot by now and thinking of
leaning on the john door in the 5 SPOT
while she whispered a song along the keyboard
to Mal Waldron and everyone and I stopped breathing

The poem is a narrative of O'Hara's experience during an hour, his lunch hour, on July 17, 1959. The narrative culminates in his discovery that Billie Holiday has died, a discovery that precipitates the memory of a night at a bar called the 5 Spot, the last time O'Hara heard Holiday sing. The poem's power certainly involves the startling contrast between the apparent triviality or tedium of the experiences reported in the first twenty-four lines and the intensity with which, in the last five lines, O'Hara both registers the fact of Holiday's death and recalls the transcendent non-triviality of her singing. Lady Day's talent is felt by the poet to be terrifically important, and the comparative unimportance of his lunch hour errands throws into relief the cherished memory of those minutes when, with a voice weakened but still beautiful, "she whispered a song along the keyboard." The contrast between unimportant and important is, despite the rapt admiration conveyed by the poem's last words, brilliantly understated: instead of dwelling on the cherished memory, describing it further, or commenting on its meaning, O'Hara falls silent, imitating and honoring the breathless silence of Holiday's audience that night at the 5 Spot; thus, the poem remains mostly consumed—in terms of number of words—by the lunch hour busyness, and this allows readers to take pleasure in the insightful realization that the 5 Spot memory is vastly more significant than the lunch hour.

For such readers, the trivial details—dates, train schedules, names of friends, bank tellers, commercial products, book titles—can inhabit the poetic space *only* in order to be dramatically exposed as trivial. For them, the poem turns out to be in effect a wry confession of folly in which O'Hara is seen to admit that he, like us, mostly wastes his life being interested in daily matters undeserving of interest. Marjorie Perloff says of the poem's ending: "For a moment, however brief, memory and art enable us to transcend the ordinary particulars of existence." And "finally the sequence of meaningless moments is replaced by the *one* moment of memory when Lady Day enchanted her audience by the power of her art" (*Frank O'Hara: Poet among Painters* [1977], 181, 182).

That very common view misses, I think, some of O'Hara's originality in "The Day Lady Died." For the author of *Lunch Poems,* the specificities of daily life—including, for example, the fatiguing indecision about what book to buy for Patsy and the specific books considered as candidates—are not merely detritus to be forgotten and abandoned ("replaced") in a turn toward transcendent value. "The Day Lady Died" is animated by a love of the quotidian world, even of its mildly boring elements, and this love coexists with the more intense love felt for Lady Day. Moreover, the two loves are more deeply related than is implied by coexistence because they share an origin in O'Hara's spirit of caring attentiveness. To be sure, each note sung by Billie Holiday in the twilight of her career is worth more to O'Hara than any number of hamburgers or Gauloises, yet all these pleasures are ingredients of the same life, valued by the same personality. The fascinated alertness with which O'Hara listened to Holiday at the 5 Spot is related to the fond exactitude of "three days after Bastille day" and "Miss Stillwagon (first name Linda I once heard)" and "Hesiod, trans. Richmond Lattimore." If the point of mentioning the officious bank teller were only to dismiss her as trivial, her funny last name would have more than sufficed. O'Hara is interested in the humanity signified by her first name. On this particular day, Miss Stillwagon is for some reason trusting enough to assume O'Hara has adequate funds deposited, and O'Hara notes this pleasing little fact with affection—affection not so much for Miss Stillwagon as for the day, this Friday. (The word *even* in the line "doesn't even look up my balance for once in her life" makes the phrase suggest that the hour being reported is a good hour, not an absurdly empty hour.)

The point is that the lunch hour details have for O'Hara value in them-selves. They are small but not worthless, not merely useful in the service of another meaning. Thus, I think Perloff is ingenious but astray when she ar-gues that the poet includes his assorted specificities "because he wants to make us see—and this is his great tribute to Lady Day—that she embodies both the foreign-exotic and the native American" (182). Instead, what O'Hara wants us to see is that many things matter, in many ways, each day—though few can matter as much as the performance of a beloved artist, especially when the art-ist is endangered (as Billie Holiday was by poor health). The expressiveness of a great singer causes us to see some part of experience more intensely and ap-preciatively; the voice is, we feel, loaded with awareness of social life; it knows the streets. We need poems that know the streets in their own ways. O'Hara's poem delights us because the speaker who appreciates the singer has enabled us to appreciate the urban world in which he has felt that love. Honoring Billie Holiday, O'Hara has managed also to preserve bits of July 17, 1959, by the acci-dent of their connection with her death. He has caused us to take interest in those bits; he has rescued them into the light of our attention. The poem's title is a pointer: what is rescued by "The Day Lady Died" is not only the night Lady sang but the day she died.

The originality of O'Hara's loving regard for small unique facts of quotidian experience shows itself in many poems less "urgent" and less ready for con-ventional praise than "The Day Lady Died," such as "Fantasy" and "Steps" and "Poem ['Khrushchev is coming on the right day!']" and "Personal Poem" and "Adieu to Norman, Bon Jour to Joan and Jean-Paul"—and in a hypothetical end-less expansion of this essay, I would enjoy discussing such poems, along with (for example) "Fate" and "A New Guide" and "A Time Zone" by Kenneth Koch, "Dunbarton" and "My Last Afternoon with Uncle Devereux Winslow" by Rob-ert Lowell, "Filling Station" and "Under the Window: Ouro Prêto" by Elizabeth Bishop, "Salts and Oils" and "One for the Rose" by Philip Levine, "The Ques-tions" and "The Night Game" by Robert Pinsky, "Great Topics of the World" and "Powers" by Albert Goldbarth, "The King Is Dead" and "Meetings with Re-markable Men" and "Excellent Women" by David Kirby, "Mia and Darger, Ash-bery and Gina" by Denise Duhamel, and (reaching back to Victorian England) "Mr. MacCall at Cleveland Hall" by James Thomson. These are relatively cheer-ful poems, whereas here I will consider poems more explicitly shadowed by the threat of oblivion. Much as I love O'Hara, I can well imagine a serious reader feeling that he shows too little awareness of the issue of triviality, the specter of ephemerality—chirping with his back to the deluge. So I want to show how the notion of the poetic preservation of particulars comes into play in poets more obviously serious than O'Hara.

Thomas Hardy was a poet obsessed with the unlikelihood of any rescue from mutability and mortality yet still driven to imagine rescues in poetry. If you believe, as Hardy grimly did, that no afterlife awaits us, no salvation beyond the temporal sphere, and if you feel also that human lives are worthy or beautiful and should not disappear into oblivion, then you are bound to ask what sort of preservation can be trusted to human memory and to acts of recording that support and formalize memory. Perhaps no poet has expressed the pain of relying on memory as our only provider of lastingness or immortality in a more clear and sustained way than Hardy. His poem "His Immortality" relentlessly sets forth a vision of memory's sadly finite power.

His Immortality

I

 I saw a dead man's finer part
Shining within each faithful heart
Of those bereft. Then said I: "This must be
   His immortality."

II

 I looked there as the seasons wore,
And still his soul continuously bore
A life in theirs. But less its shine excelled
   Than when I first beheld.

III

 His fellow-yearsmen passed, and then
In later hearts I looked for him again;
And found him—shrunk, alas! into a thin
   And spectral mannikin.

IV

> Lastly I ask—now old and chill—
> If aught of him remain unperished still;
> And find, in me alone, a feeble spark,
>   Dying amid the dark.

(February 1899)

There is emphatically no fifth stanza proposing that the dead man's finer part has been or will be enshrined and preserved in the speaker's verse. "His Immortality" admits no possible escape routes from mortality; the dead man whose soul once shone in the souls of others is bound for sheer oblivion. Moreover, the poem's final line is made to apply not only to the memory of the dead man but to the life of the enfeebled speaker—he, too, is "Dying amid the dark." *Nothing more to be said,* the poem stringently implies.

"His Immortality" is no elegy for the partly fine man; his finer qualities remain flatly unspecified. But I want to focus—with an eagerness that may be perverse—on a remarkable little flare-up of specificity just after the last word of the poem. Hardy appends a date: "February 1899." Hardy attached a date or a place to many poems but not automatically; something in Hardy's experience linked February 1899 and the thoughts that became "His Immortality." Though biographers may guess, the date remains opaque to us as an attribute of the poem. Yet it creates an effect, I want to say, different from the effect of the poem without the date.

The link is significant to Hardy but not to us—*except* for the effect on us of this tiny implication that Hardy is thinking of a particular real man who died and that Hardy wishes to register this particular reference. Hardy's impulse touches me. He wanted the date, February 1899, to ride with the poem into the future and participate in whatever sort of lastingness the poem might attain. The notation is to us so blank and so external that we—even I—can't possibly ennoble it as a Rescued Particular. Still, the impulse is interestingly at odds with the poem's depressed argument. The poem says that no image or version of the dead man's special value can be kept in the world by memory, but "February 1899" suggests that the special value of a chronological fact for the poet can be un-pointlessly kept in the world by poetry. The date is a trace of the effort to rescue particulars of human experience that engaged Hardy often in defiance of his own proclaimed grimness.

At the end of a poem called "The Rejected Member's Wife," Hardy inscribed another date: "January 1906." The act of specifying here is less opaque because the poem makes clear that the date has a significance (however slight) in English political history. The woman, not named but clearly a certain woman, has caught Hardy's attention precisely at the moment when her obscurity or unimportance—as "merely" the wife of a member of Parliament (for South Dorset)—has become much more obvious and seemingly absolute now that her husband has been swept from office.

The Rejected Member's Wife

We shall see her no more
  On the balcony,
Smiling, while hurt, at the roar
  As of surging sea
From the stormy sturdy band
  Who have doomed her lord's cause,
Though she waves her little hand
  As it were applause.

Here will be candidates yet,
  And candidates' wives,
Fervid with zeal to set
  Their ideals on our lives:
Here will come market-men
  On the market-days,
Here will clash now and then
  More such party assays.
And the balcony will fill
  When such times are renewed,
And the throng in the street will thrill
  With to-day's mettled mood;
But she will no more stand

> In the sunshine there,
> With that wave of her white-gloved hand,
> And that chestnut hair.

> (January 1906)

The bravely smiling woman on the balcony is seen to be a terribly small phenomenon in a long series of phenomena. Most of the poem, indeed, is devoted
to anticipation of the countless human beings who will replace this woman in
this marketplace as years pass. Yet the poem arises from an impulse to deny that
this woman is sheerly forgettable and endlessly replaceable. For Hardy, what
matters, at least while he writes the poem, is not the political history of "party
assays" and the roaring ocean of partisans and "market-men" but, rather, the
tiny unique human fact, the pathetically dignified particular individual. Hardy
insists that no amount of zeal and clashing and mettled surging of other persons can change the fact, or remove the emotional force of the fact, that after
today—one day in January 1906—*she* will be gone from the balcony. She is felt
by him, in one moment, in one situation, to be irreplaceable:

> In the sunshine there,
> With that wave of her white-gloved hand,
> And that chestnut hair.

The tenderness of this notation conveys a sense of this woman's beauty in that
moment. Whether her beauty is sexually attractive to Hardy remains discreetly
unspecified; perhaps there is more elegiac pity in the acknowledgment of "that
chestnut hair" than sexual admiration. The discretion is part of what makes the
end of the poem so touching. Hardy seems respectfully intent upon the delicacy
of the image he records.

At the same time, we must note how limited Hardy's notation of the woman's existence is. He could tell us her name, but he doesn't. Of course not, a
reader may reply: such specificity would be excessive, intrusive, distracting, unlyrical; it would pull the poem from the universal toward the trivially local. Admittedly, a proper name like "Madeleine Brymer" would alter the tone and effect
of the poem, perhaps for the worse. Given the poem's topic, such explicit identi-

fication of the rejected Parliament member's wife might seem rude. But would it also be essentially unpoetic and trivializing? Not necessarily, I want to say.

My point is not to express a wish that Hardy had written "The Rejected Member's Wife" differently, not at all, but to reflect that the poem's choices are not the only *poetic* possibilities for the topic.

"January 1906"—the specific date is a gesture in the direction of further specificity. It serves as a discreet hint that further details—including the woman's name—could be made available and are recoverable. Indeed, the date serves as a sort of diminished substitute for the woman's name, a way of saying to the reader, "This is not just a *type* of woman being recalled here, not just a symbolic figure in a tiny imaginary drama, but a certain woman, Mrs. _____." The presence of the date accords with the poem's resistance to the idea that this woman should merely merge into the forgettable nameless multitudes of past party politics and the category of "candidates' wives."

"January 1906"—Hardy's commitment to the special reality of the woman on the balcony is limited to the poignant occasion of her last appearance on that balcony. "The Rejected Member's Wife" does not turn out to be the first installment of a thousand-page verse biography of Madeleine Brymer as she gracefully deals with the decades of her husband's career and then his retirement from politics. Such a poem might be wonderful, or not. Hardy's tender interest in the woman is (or is willing to seem) only an interest in her *then*, on that day, on that balcony. Putting the matter thus sounds rather harsh, but there is another way to put it. In order for this woman to seem significant to Hardy— significant enough for a poem—it was not necessary for her to impress him by a series of hundreds of sweet deeds or delicate movements (except insofar as he may see those implied in her bearing on the balcony), nor for her to gradually achieve some historically useful participation in local politics. It was enough for her to stand briefly on that balcony bravely pretending to be cheerful "while hurt" and waving her white-gloved hand.

One person at one time can be important.

I believe that the appeal of the short poem—its essential attraction for us— consists profoundly in that idea: One person at one time—in one moment (minute, hour, afternoon)—can be important, marvelously and irreducibly valuable. This is an underlying meaning of *any* short poem. Short? Let's say, any poem that fits on three pages or less—often on a single page; any poem that offers itself to be "taken in" by what feels like one continuous act of reading (in which the reader is *one person at one time*). I avoid the term *lyrical poem* so as not to encumber my idea with limiting definitions of *lyric.*

One person at one time can be important. Whether or not a poem's images or narrative depict a person (such as a woman on a balcony) experiencing a moment or an event, the short poem is always inherently a representation of a moment or event in the life of the poet, a moment or event of observation, meditation, and composition. It is a truism to say that a poem is always in *some* sense about its speaker and, further, about its author. Behind some truisms, there is truth waiting to be articulated. When we refer to a poem's "speaker," one reason we need the term is to keep vivid our sense that the poem represents an occasion, an event of brief duration, the event of the speech represented by the poem on paper.

When we cherish a short poem, central to our cherishing is the feeling that the poem matters in itself—not merely as a brick in the edifice of an oeuvre— and that the poet matters *here* and *now,* in the "moment" represented by the poem, in a way not controlled or measured by whatever innumerable achievements or follies or routine behaviors may have preceded or followed the poem in the poet's life.

There is—emotionally, psychologically—a profound similarity linking the following twelve things:

1. A woman on a balcony, dignified and graceful in a moment of stress

2. A person somewhere in the crowd on the street, thoughtfully observing that woman

3. A good poem about that woman

4. A name invested with love or with respect for the person or thing named, and therefore cherished as meaningful

5. An athlete in a moment of unexpected glory, for instance a bicycle rider in 1888, smiling because he has just ridden a hundred miles in six hours, twenty-five minutes, and thirty seconds

6. A doo-wop group getting its harmonies right in a recording studio on a certain day in 1957

7. You in a moment of profound grief or joy or fear or sympathy or gratitude

8. Each of your good short poems

9. A poet reading his or her good poem aloud

10. You at the moment when you appreciate a good poem

11. Wordsworth crossing a bridge over the Thames early one morning in 1802

12. A dachshund trotting awkwardly and cheerfully across the snow

We feel that each of those twelve things is beautiful, and valuable, in a terribly limited and fragile yet irreducible way, so that it should not disappear into dust or a generalization. Resistance to such disappearance is a fundamental reason why we keep reading, and writing, poems.

"The Rejected Member's Wife" memorializes not only a moment of tribulation in the life of one woman but also a moment of gentle observation in the life of one man—Hardy himself. By writing the poem, and particularly by attaching the date, Hardy tries (against the tide of his own stern pessimism) to rescue from oblivion not only the woman then but also the particular fact of his own contemplation of her on a certain day.

Twenty years before Hardy's birth, a tiny event occurred in the life of John Keats: in September 1820, the ship that would carry him to Rome landed briefly on the Dorset coast, near where Hardy would grow up. A hundred years later, in September 1920, Hardy wrote a poem imagining a moment when Keats stood on that shore and looked up at a star. Like many Hardy poems, "At Lulworth Cove a Century Back" transcends its own stubborn awkwardness with a beautifully moving final stanza. The impulse of the poem is to honor Keats not simply in general but in a particular obscure moment of his short life—defiantly affirming that this small and shabby and unhealthy young man at *that* moment in *that* place was terribly important.

At Lulworth Cove a Century Back

Had I but lived a hundred years ago
I might have gone, as I have gone this year,
By Warmwell Cross on to a Cove I know,
And Time have placed his finger on me there:

"*You see that man?*"—I might have looked, and said,
"O yes: I see him. One that boat has brought
Which dropped down Channel round Saint Alban's Head.
So commonplace a youth calls not my thought."

"*You see that man?*"—"Why yes; I told you; yes:
Of an idling town-sort; thin; hair brown in hue;
And as the evening light scants less and less
He looks up at a star, as many do."

"*You see that man?*"—"Nay, leave me!" then I plead,
"I have fifteen miles to vamp across the lea,
And it grows dark, and I am weary-kneed:
I have said the third time; yes, that man I see!"

"Good. That man goes to Rome—to death, despair;
And no one notes him now but you and I:
A hundred years, and the world will follow him there,
And bend with reverence where his ashes lie."

   (September 1920)

The commonplace brown-haired youth gazing up at a star over Lulworth
Cove is apparently doing only what many do. But this appearance of insignificance is misleading. Hardy believed that Keats wrote the sonnet "Bright star!
would I were steadfast as thou art!" the very evening he walked at Lulworth
Cove. (Research has since shown that the poem was composed earlier and re-
copied by Keats during his voyage to Italy and that the ship may have anchored
at a different spot. This brings up the disturbing point that poems, like other

acts of recording, can be wrong about the facts of human experience they propose to preserve. I love to think of the rescues performed by poems as accurate. However, even where they turn out to be inaccurate, they may still have given readers the sensation that something real and valuable has been honored and that such honoring is *possible* for any beloved fact of experience.) At any rate, the young man there stargazing was in fact the man capable of writing a poem addressed to a star that readers of English have cherished for more than two centuries. Hardy is fascinated by the discord between Keats's outward obscurity and his inner—spiritual, poetic—significance and fascinated especially by the idea that this discord obtained at each moment of Keats's life. Hardy's poem implicitly rejects the suggestion that Keats was, most of the time, just an ordinary man like countless others, while Keats's poems were and are all that matters about him. "At Lulworth Cove a Century Back" asserts, instead—emotionally, irrationally perhaps, but with the truth of a depth of feeling—that the unhealthy young man himself was, at many distinct moments of his life, *like* one of his poems, a marvelously valuable particular of reality worthy of the kind of time-transcending rescue that poetry sometimes claims to confer. The urgency of this assertion—with a sense of the outrage of its being ignored—is expressed by the impolite persistence of the voice (whether we imagine it as the voice of Keats's friend Joseph Severn or of Time or of the spirit of poetry itself) that says three times, "*You see that man?*"

The effect of "At Lulworth Cove a Century Back" is not only to make us think of the unobvious importance of John Keats on a certain evening but also to make us consider—despite the absurd overwhelmingness of the challenge—that countless other "commonplace" individuals might deserve our intense respect and intense interest on any given evening or day of our lives. This is not to say that every individual is in some way just as interesting and important as John Keats, but rather, the implication is that such interestingness and importance may not be obvious and may be located in persons who seem at a glance trivial—"So commonplace a youth calls not my thought"—*and* may inhere in such persons not only in the cumulative weight of their achievements but at any obscure moment of their lives.

Many of the poems that engage the issue of the rescue of particulars by poetry—whether they hopefully attempt such rescue or find it to be terribly tenuous or sheerly impossible—concern themselves not with a moment or event in time but with the whole of a person's life, which is felt to be itself a particular threatened (as in Hardy's "His Immortality") with utter disappearance. Such poems prompt reflection on the relation between elegy and names. Hardy did not choose to include the *names* of the honored persons in "His Immortality," "The Rejected Member's Wife," or "At Lulworth Cove." (In the third of those, Hardy counted on the literate reader to supply the name of John Keats, and the reader's readiness to supply the name is part of the poem's meaning.) A large proportion of poetically successful elegies do not include the name of the mourned-for person in the body of the poem—and often not in the title either. In the elegiac tradition that includes "Lycidas," "Adonais," and "Thyrsis," the proper name of the deceased person (Edward King, John Keats, Arthur Hugh Clough) is felt to be unpoetic; where a name is used, the elegy offers an idealizing substitute for the person's actual name. An elegy traditionally seeks to elevate the lost beloved from the flux of temporality into the transcendent realm of poetic permanence, and a syllable like *Clough* may be felt to be too difficult to hoist aloft or too specific, since the dead beloved should represent all dead beloveds. To be rescued, some readers would say, a particular must undergo a sea-change, must shed its sweaty earthy substance and become a higher signifier, a trope (how I hate that word), so that a person's actual name then will mean something no less broad than "the admired lost friend." This is why (they'd say) so few good poems include the kind of proper name specificities I watch for.

Emotionally resisting that sober warning, I like to remind the warners that real-life proper names show up frequently in Horace and Catullus. Horace and Catullus sometimes avoid real-life names for social and political reasons but not because such names were considered inherently "unlyrical" and inappropriate for inclusion. Horace affirms the special power of poetry to give a kind of immortality to selected persons—by identifying them specifically.

> Many brave men have lived before Agamemnon,
> but, unwept and unknown, they are all crushed
>   under eternal night
>   because they have no sacred poet.
>
> Courage unseen differs little
> from cowardice dead and buried. I will not leave you

unsung, Lollius, in what I write,
  nor easily suffer all your great labors

to be gnawed away by envy and oblivion.

(*Odes* 4.ix; translated by David West)

Nevertheless, it is true that when I wander the orchards looking for good short poems that attain the effect I attributed to O'Hara's "The Day Lady Died"— whereby several proper name specificities are lifted into the special kind of preservation that good poetry affords (unless such preservation is a mythic delusion)—without shedding their particularity of reference—I don't find hundreds tumbling into my basket. I find dozens and dozens but not hundreds. There are, of course, countless attempts, but poems in which certain peculiarly insistent particulars become radiant for the reader are rare. The kind of rescue I celebrate cannot be done easily or routinely.

Indeed, the next thought—frighteningly cogent in the teaching and writing of Allen Grossman (one of my mentors)—is that, in his terms, fame must necessarily be scarce. Most people must always be commoners who can't be promoted into the aristocratic nobility of poetic registration. In *Summa Lyrica*, Grossman writes: "At present, inclusion is obtained by exclusion, the seen thing by reference to the unseen thing, the acknowledged soul by reason of the unacknowledged. The central obstacle to egalitarianism is the fact of the foundation of the culture of visibility and acknowledgment upon the metaphysics, politics, and economics of difference (that is to say, differentiation through hierarchy). Nonhierarchical differentiation is inimical to the nature of personhood itself" (in *The Sighted Singer* [Johns Hopkins University Press, 1991], 301).

The implication is that the poetic effect of elevating one fact above the mob of facts must necessarily be unusual, not only because of artistic difficulty in the writing but because for it to count, it must impress us as extraordinary, unexpected, unlikely. It can't happen on every page of a book; it can't become common because then each rescued thing would not glow with being singled out, the way we single out from a crowd a person we love. To this dour point, my reply must be: "True, but it *can* happen; it does happen; the possibility is in the air."

A woman or a man dies. People who love the deceased person want to use language to honor her or him. Words may be carved on a tombstone. Elegies are spoken at a memorial service. Obituaries are written and published. In some cases, an entire biography is written. What is enough? When my father died, my brother and I paid $862 to publish a very brief statement about him in tiny print on the Obituaries page of the *New York Times,* the newspaper my father loved. The statement was absurdly insufficient, and very few readers noticed it at all, yet we were glad to have published it. In some irrational nook of my mind, the *New York Times* is eternal and confers permanence on whatever is "fit to print."

HALLIDAY, Ernest M. Known to his friends as Hal. Died August 1 at home in Manhattan, at age 89. Editor of *American Heritage* magazine for many years. Author of *Understanding Thomas Jefferson,* and *John Berryman and the Thirties,* and *The Ignorant Armies.* Hal was one of the first important critics of Ernest Hemingway. Passionate lifelong advocate of civil liberties and the separation of church and state. Memorial service to be held in Graduate Lounge of Philosophy Hall, Columbia University, at 4 p.m. on Saturday, September 20.

In another unreasonable part of my mind, which I want to imagine as deeper and wiser than the *Times* nook, good poetry confers a greater permanence. Who is to decide which poems are good enough to save certain facts from oblivion? The serious reader is to decide; the calmly attentive, deeply reflective, maturely empathetic reader; let it be you, and let it be me.

I've written poems about my father and used his first name in a few of them, but mostly I have the sensation of being too close to the subject, unready to gain a calm, clear perspective on my father's life. He is so huge in my mind that my terms in this essay hardly seem to apply to him. In all the poems discussed here, the distance between poet and "the particular" is much wider than the distance between son and father. Poetic rescue of the sort I'm examining seems to require a sense that the beloved thing is separate from the poet and relatively small.

Robert Herrick felt affection for his loyal servant Prudence Baldwin and mentioned her in several poems. The most memorable is an epitaph poem, "Upon Prew His Maid," which Herrick apparently wrote anticipating her death. (Herrick died in 1674 at the age of eighty-three, and Prudence—Herrick's spelling of her first name varied—outlived him by more than three years, according to Emily Meader Easton's biography of Herrick.)

Upon Prew His Maid

In this little urn is laid
Prudence Baldwin, once my maid,
From whose happy spark here let
Spring the purple violet.

There are in the world millions of rhyming epitaphs on tombstones that are not very different (their composers might say) from this poem by Herrick, yet this one is preserved in a way that all those stone-carved epitaphs are not: this one is in the library, in anthologies; I noticed it more than three centuries after Prudence Baldwin's death in *The Norton Anthology of Poetry*. In the life of print, Herrick's tiny poem is a rescued particular surviving apart from millions of specimens in its genre that wait scattered in thousands of cemeteries to be appreciated by the occasional mourner or passerby. Wit may be exercised in an analogy between a book of poems and a cemetery, but we who love literature feel the analogy's inadequacy; we feel there is something eternally vital and communal about literature whereby it can offer a kind of immortality to individuals and works not provided by marble or the gilded monuments of cemeteries.

Why has Herrick's miniature poem escaped oblivion? Because of a beauty in the writing, no doubt; what I want to insist is that a key part of the poem's beauty is its insistence on including the full name of the loved person. We sense something beautifully true in the gentle expression of tender (but not passionate) affection felt for Prudence Baldwin by the poet. The poem may be said to have earned its own rescue from the vanishment of a billion forgotten poems. Does the poem, meanwhile, rescue Prew as well?

Certainly, the poem gives us no developed portrait of this woman nor even a sketch like Hardy's sketch of the politician's wife. We have the name: Prudence Baldwin. Writing this full name, Herrick specifies a person: this Prudence, not some other Prudence. (I speak of the feeling conveyed by the poem, regardless of the annoying fact that another Prudence Baldwin could have existed in Devonshire.) We feel certain the name is accurate, not altered for artistic purposes. We feel immediately, therefore, that the woman here is different from the Corinna or the Julia of Herrick's entertaining poems of sexual romance, and she summons a different attention. If the poem succeeds, it carries into our memories the name of a woman who has become—"in a way"—less forgotten than all other serving maids of Devonshire in the seventeenth century.

The name reaches us in a miniature context that enables us to care. The context includes the indication that her personality was cheerful ("happy spark"); and an association with the idea of modesty or the idea of remembrance symbolized by the violet; and the sense that Herrick has gone out of his way—across a social class boundary—to commemorate someone whom a distinguished poet would not be expected to commemorate; and the affection audible in the informal, familiar *Prew* of the title. Calling her "Prew" emphasizes the gap between our knowledge of her and his. We don't know her, but we're made to feel she existed and mattered to Herrick. The effect is profoundly different from that of a hypothetical poem entitled "On the Death of His Maid," which would be identical with Herrick's poem except that the four syllables of *Prudence Baldwin* would be removed in favor of a phrase such as "a gentle woman." The imaginary poem might benefit from the play of *gentle woman* against *gentlewoman,* if you like, and in any case might be a fine bit of literature. But "Upon Prew His Maid" carries a different meaning, a meaning we long to believe is not hollow.

Ever since my freshman year, I've remembered the title of John Crowe Ransom's poem "Bells for John Whiteside's Daughter." Would the effect of the poem be significantly different if the title were "Bells for a Neighbor's Daughter"? A friend of mine argues that the poem would *not* be significantly different with this alteration and might be slightly improved by the less distractingly specific title. I disagree. What I feel is that by naming the father of the little girl who has died, Ransom includes in the meaning of the poem the speaker's feeling that the particular identity of the bereaved father requires to be honored in the needful elegy for the girl. The reader understands that the name John Whiteside holds irreducible emotional meaning. We are caused to infer the compassion of one John for another John. The point here need not be simply about neighborly compassion, however. A reader may warrantably wonder why the girl's mother is not named, let alone the girl herself, and may speculate that the identification of the dead girl as "John Whiteside's daughter" reflects the objectionably patriarchal orientation of Ransom in his 1920s Tennessee society. Be that as it may, what the reader carries away from the poem includes the sense that Ransom was unwilling to let it refer simply to "a neighbor's daughter." Responding to the profound vexation of the astonishing unjust mortality of a child, Ransom has chosen to lift at least one identifying fact—her father's name—into the space of art, where (it may be felt) this particular will be protected from obliteration.

Again, though, such protection is expensive; such fame has to be scarce. What if Robert Herrick followed "Upon Prew His Maid" with "Upon Stu His Carpenter" and another miniature elegy and another? Herrick did write sweet epitaph poems for his nieces and others. What if he'd written a hundred, each bearing the full name of the deceased? Would Prew's name be cheapened? Would it still be possible to speak of her name as a rescued particular? This frightening question keeps returning. How many can be saved? By saving Prudence Baldwin under the spotlight of art (even in such a tenuous way), did Herrick simultaneously, necessarily, push dozens of his acquaintances further into the shadows? Maybe we can imagine Herrick writing each of a hundred brief elegies with as much care and skill as he exercised in the case of Prudence Baldwin; if so, we could claim that "rescue" had indeed been afforded to each named person among the hundred. To turn those pages would be a moving experience but also a tiring one, more tiring than a long slow walk through a well-maintained cemetery.

Reading Edgar Lee Masters's *Spoon River Anthology* (1915) is not demanding in the same way because we never feel that the named posthumous speakers in that great book were real people; we are always aware that Masters has made up names and has fictionalized—for the sake of an artistic effect different from the artistic effect that veracity can foster. His speakers are characters, and we receive them as such; his Elsa Wertman and Hamilton Greene (for example) do make claims on our imagination, but Prudence Baldwin—who does not belong to Herrick in the sense that Elsa Wertman belongs to Masters—makes a different claim.

If Prudence Baldwin were only one among hundreds of real persons named and described in Herrick's poetry, her happy spark would be dimmed in our eyes to some extent, yes. There is an economy of available attention—as every governor, every classroom teacher, every Red Cross relief worker, knows. At the same time, there is a yearning, an appetite in us, that continually renews itself for the task of acknowledgment. We are ready to try to care about an actual individual life remote from our own experience, about someone far from fame. Something in us wants such unexpected and unpromised acknowledgment of individual lives to be as possible as possible. So we try to listen well when someone at a party speaks of a child or parent who is troubled or successful. We pick up a literary journal, and though we've encountered innumerable dreary poems, we focus on a new poem—to see what the poets in Illinois, or Ghana, are doing these days. When we sense that an actual person is being named and honored in a poem, we want it to work. It might not work; the artist might fail to register the particular human fact in a memorable way. But we want it to work. If it can be done for a serving maid in Devonshire so that we think caringly of her more than three centuries later, then it could be done for anyone— for ourselves.

As Andy Warhol famously pointed out, in postmodern society, fame has become at once common and evanescent. Now, as before, though, there is a deep difference between the naming in poetry of someone presumed to be already known by name to the reader (Ben Jonson, Oliver Cromwell, Napoleon, Queen Victoria, Douglas Fairbanks, Rita Hayworth, Margaret Thatcher, Michael Jordan) and the naming of someone unknown to the reader. Insofar as a person named in a poem was famous at the time of composition, the case is less relevant to my discussion, though it may still be viewed as a kind of guarding of the famous name ("MacDonagh and MacBride") from the abrasion of time. For those of us in love with poetry, there is a kind of lastingness that poems can confer that is less noisy but more reliable than historical fame.

Standing among rural graves in the 1740s, Thomas Gray was generous enough to speculate that "The rude forefathers of the hamlet" buried nearby may have included a few individuals of great talent or of great potential at least:

Perhaps in this neglected spot is laid
Some heart once pregnant with celestial fire;
Hands that the rod of empire might have swayed,
Or waked to ecstasy the living lyre.

However, "Elegy Written in a Country Churchyard" is firm in its assumption that "the unhonored dead" must remain forever unknown, mutely inglorious, forgotten, because poverty prevented them from fulfilling their talents, and the poem is an effort to accept this state of affairs and even to find that it is good. William Empson, in *Some Versions of Pastoral*, noted that many readers "have been irritated by the complacence in the massive calm of the poem"— nevertheless, "what is said is one of the permanent truths; it is only in degree that any improvement of society could prevent wastage of human powers; the waste even in a fortunate life . . . cannot but be felt deeply, and is the central feeling of tragedy." Gazing upon tombstones, Gray is not at all inclined to salvage any of the names by re-presenting them in poetry—"the passing tribute of a sigh" is all any of the dead can expect. Gray's mood rules out the idea that elegy might supply what could not be supplied by fame, and his tone is dismissive as he glances at each countryman's tablet:

> Their name, their years, spelt by the unlettered Muse,
> The place of fame and elegy supply:
> And many a holy text around she strews,
> That teach the rustic moralist to die.

Gray's tone might remind us of Hardy's tone in "His Immortality" except that Hardy does not try to convince himself that the inevitable process of the erasure of selves is all for the best. Gray concludes his poem with an epitaph for himself that sternly discourages any rescue of particulars by human minds, relying instead (though tremblingly) on transcendental rescue by the God in whom Hardy could never trust:

> *No farther seek his merits to disclose,*
> *Or draw his frailties from their dread abode*
> *(Though they alike in trembling hope repose),*
> *The bosom of his Father and his God.*

But I think the reason we still cherish Gray's poem (with whatever reservations involving his social class complacency) centers in our feeling that the resignation he recommends at the end does *not* suffice as a response to the unjust obscurity he has so memorably called to mind. We are moved by the solution being inadequate to the problem.

In his brief catalog of conceivable achievers among the local dead, Gray imagines "Some village Hampden, that with dauntless breast / The little tyrant of his fields withstood." Here Gray seems unaware that (unlike the names of Milton and Cromwell in the same famous stanza) the name of Hampden—briefly a hero in the political opposition to Charles I, as a footnote nowadays needs to inform us—might less dauntlessly withstand the tyranny of time. For those of us who embrace the quasi-religion of poetry, John Hampden (1549–1643) has a foothold in eternity thanks more to Thomas Gray than to historical accounts of the English Civil War.

As punishment for the Easter Rebellion of 1916, the British authorities executed sixteen men. William Butler Yeats referred to these martyrs in his poem "Sixteen Dead Men," but in his most successful poem commemorating the rebellion, "Easter 1916," he named only four of them.

> We know their dream; enough
> To know they dreamed and are dead;
> And what if excess of love
> Bewildered them till they died?
> I write it out in a verse—
> MacDonagh and MacBride
> And Connolly and Pearse
> Now and in time to be,
> Wherever green is worn,
> Are changed, changed utterly:
> A terrible beauty is born.

Ostensibly, the assertion here is that the Dublin rebels have, through their astounding history-making action, ensured their eternal fame in Ireland. The "terrible beauty" of their sacrifice has removed them from the status of motley fallible mortal creatures and won for them a glory as indestructible as stone. Accordingly, the ostensible role Yeats plays in writing about the heroes is to recognize something already taken care of, to acknowledge an immortality rather than to create it. In this light, the naming of heroes in "Easter 1916" is not a rescue of particulars but a ceremonial citation of particulars already rescued by fame, or perhaps by a transcendental condition of which fame is merely a necessary result.

However, "Easter 1916" is haunted by the possibility that the eternal status of the martyrs is not secure. Three times the poem assures us that they are "changed, changed utterly" from their previous nature as players in "the casual comedy" of human mutability, and we may concede that the dominant tone is one of conviction, but there is an undertone of worry, suggested partly by the insistence of repetition. The poem abundantly indicates that the martyrs were rather foolish individuals prior to their magnificent alteration—they shared in "polite meaningless" conversations; the woman among them (Constance Markievicz, who would be imprisoned rather than executed) spent her days in "ignorant good-will" and her nights in shrill argument; one of the men (John MacBride) was, in Yeats's view, "A drunken, vainglorious lout." Their survivors in Ireland have a duty "To murmur name upon name," but the unforeseen tender simile for such murmuring carries an association between the hotheaded heroes and excitable children:

> As a mother names her child
> When sleep at last has come
> On limbs that had run wild.

Moreover, the poem allows the glory-threatening suspicion that the sixteen may soon be seen, as history proceeds, to have martyred themselves unnecessarily:

> Was it needless death after all?
> For England may keep faith
> For all that is done and said.

Instead of developing a picture of the Irish rebels as noble brave fighters, Yeats describes them as men fatally baffled by an overdose of passion: "And what if excess of love / Bewildered them till they died?"

The cumulative effect of these suggestions is to imply that the fallible individuals who fought for a few days against overwhelming odds and then surrendered and were executed may need something less rationally weighable than historical fame while also more definite than the mystical condition of being "Enchanted to a stone," to safeguard their surprising but flawed specialness. The "what if" question can be heard as calling for a saving generosity in defiance of the fate likely to await any bewildered dreamer.

And the answer to this call comes promptly in the next line: "I write it out in a verse—." In this line, pointing to the difference between poetry and historiography or patriotic talk, Yeats is conscious that he does something for the dead men that they could not do for themselves. To "write it out" is to do something more laborious and deliberate than simply to write and more determinedly purposeful than to "murmur name upon name." To announce "I write it out in a verse" is to admit that under pressure of emotion, the poet insists on writing something the reader would not have expected to find in poetry. There is nothing unexpected about the poem's last lines, which revert to the declaration that "A terrible beauty is born." What is unexpected is the names: "MacDonagh and MacBride / And Connolly and Pearse"—four names rescued from mere history and hereby painted with the preservative shellac of art.

Four names. But there were sixteen men shot by the British. We may say that the four names represent all sixteen, but if specific individual presence in poetry makes the kind of difference—emotionally, to the poet and to readers— that I keep trying to affirm, then Yeats has created an inequity. Should he have "written out" the names of all sixteen patriots in "Easter 1916"? Surely such a long roll call would have sounded obligatory, programmatic, merely reportorial, uninspired and uninspiring—unpoetic? Yeats chose the ingredients he could fit into poetry—a matter partly of formal convenience: *MacBride/died, Pearse/verse.* He wanted an act of naming that would not diminish poetic vigor.

"Wherever green is worn"—Yeats couldn't have realized how quaint this phrase would sound to non-Irish readers many decades later. If you stand outside a group of people passionately interested in something—Irish nationalism or bicycle racing, or poetry!—their notion of what is "famous" can seem awfully parochial, even pathetic. This thought arose grimly in Frank Bidart's mind when he wrote a poem marking his thirty-fourth birthday (in 1973).

Happy Birthday

Thirty-three, goodbye—
the awe I feel

is not that you won't come again, or why—

or even that after
a time, we think of those who are dead

with a sweetness that can't be explained—

but that I've read the trading-cards:
RALPH TEMPLE CYCLIST CHAMPION TRICK RIDER

WILLIE HARRADON CYCLIST
THE YOUTHFUL PHENOMENON

F. F. IVES CYCLIST
100 MILES 6 H. 25 MIN. 30 SEC.

—as the fragile metal of their
wheels stopped turning, as they

took on wives, children, accomplishments, all those
predilections which also insisted on ending,

they could not tell themselves from what they had done.

Terrible to dress in the clothes
of a period that must end.

They didn't plan it that way—
they didn't plan it that way.

The repetition of the poem's zero-option ending suggests that awe has devolved into depression. If so, the poem's title is flatly ironic—though the "sweetness" of a happy birthday, if experienced, would in this poem's vision be as thoroughly fated to dissipate as "all those / predilections which also insisted on ending." Bidart's sensation of vanishing human significances has been triggered by some nineteenth-century trading cards that honor bicyclists. By not bothering to explain why he happens to focus on these, of all things, Bidart stealthily implies that any other realm of prowess and glory may be seen as similarly obscure, including whatever activities you or I might deem self-evidently important and productive of fame. Bidart has seen these images of champion bicyclists as symbols of the even-less-famous accomplishments and predilections of his own past—things that seemed important at the time. Ralph Temple, Willie Harradon, F. F. Ives: each rider was once a big deal in a certain context. But the trading cards—outdated and observed by a person not at all obsessed with bicycling prowess—unintentionally present the heroes stripped of their context, and their glory appears abjectly ephemeral. CYCLIST, CYCLIST, CYCLIST—the attitude that would find satisfaction in such images, *or* in the exploits they represent, is felt to be naive, sweetly foolish at best, a fetishizing connoisseurship blind to larger truths.

Nevertheless! There is a sense in which "Happy Birthday" does find satisfaction—for the poet and for the right reader—in the facts of the three trading cards and creates a context in which cherishing, or carefully noting, the champions' names is not pointless. The context is the poem. The particulars—three names, three cards—have helped Bidart to make the poem, and the poem has enabled him to honor them, in a limited and anxious way, by including them. Ralph Temple, Willie Harradon, F. F. Ives: these three persons (in representation) caught the poet's attention precisely for their ironic obscurity in his eyes, and he has contrived to reverse their vanishing.

What if we were to discover that the names of Temple, Harradon, and Ives were invented by Bidart? I admit I would be dismayed—naively, you may say—to learn that the names were fictional. (They're not. You can Google them.) In this, I diverge from conventional sophistication that habitually affirms art's need to "transform" everything for the sake of artistic truth. However, even if men named Temple, Harradon, and Ives were never champion cyclists, still it would be true that the poem deliberately causes us to feel that the names are historically authentic, and the poem's lines would thus still express a profound impulse to rescue true particulars from oblivion. But the poem would have a more muddy relation to my subject than it does when I know it has recorded specificities without transforming them.

Naming the cyclists, Bidart wants to gain control over the exact irritants that have induced his unhappy state of mind. There is a healthy impulse to isolate and deal with certain distinct painful stimuli as a strategy for escaping or mitigating a pervasive dismay. In this way, the effort to include certain facts intact in a poem may spring from an intention less plainly benevolent than verbs like *rescue, save,* and *cherish* imply. In an extensive inventory of poems that insist unexpectedly on particulars, other verbs such as *capture* or *quarantine* or *detoxify* or *impound* might be useful to evoke shadings of motivation.

In "Happy Birthday," the seizure and recording of particulars does not rescue Bidart from unhappiness. The real satisfaction of making the poem does not erase the depression it expresses. Depression begins to reveal itself where

Bidart includes wives and children in the category of "predilections which also insisted on ending"—he seems unwilling to admit that marriage and child raising can be commitments fundamentally different from an athlete's commitment to his sport and unwilling to suppose that a spouse or child can be a source of meaning that continues, when it must, even after the death of spouse or child. The idea toward which "Happy Birthday" gravitates, grammatically as well as psychologically, is frightening: "they could not tell themselves from what they had done." Depression shows not necessarily in the idea itself but in Bidart's refusal (on his thirty-fourth birthday) to question the idea.

One response to the feeling that we cannot tell ourselves from what we have done is silence—awed, stunned, or helpless—as at the end of "Happy Birthday." Another response could be frantic activity to create new present versions of identity. Another could be earnest efforts to retain records or preserve traces of what we have done. Certainly, the struggle to rescue past particulars involves the feeling that one's identity is profoundly related to them—and profoundly similar to them in its susceptibility to disappearance. However, Bidart's frightening line should push me to realize that despite my campaign on behalf of the retention of specific details, I don't finally feel that "I" am indistinguishable from a thousand or million little facts of my past. I cherish my large box of diaries, but I don't finally feel that my reality depends on them. I think I feel that my essential reality depends on, and consists in, a compounding of kinds of love: love for my son and daughter, love for my wife, love for my brother, love for my deceased parents, love for my friends, love for myself, love for humanity, love of language and poetry, love of life. Saying this, I realize I open the door to a basic challenge to all the fretting about accurately retained details in my discussion: "Let the details fall away, significance consists in the pervasive and continuous realities we call love, integrity, dignity, kindness, courage, imagination." My reply must be that those underlying realities inspire some people— including some poets—to retrieve certain glowing facts from the flux of experience and that such retrievals, in poems especially, foster and facilitate those great qualities—love, integrity, dignity, kindness, courage, imagination—in our lives, by honoring certain specific situations and connections in which they have revealed themselves.

Turning thirty-four, Frank Bidart felt frighteningly similar to the terribly forgettable and mortal cyclists, and he used a few particulars about them bravely and imaginatively, to express and control his fear as best he could. Robert Lowell, in his poem "Remembrance Day, London 1970's," is similarly sensitive to the relation between his own anxiety about lastingness and the obscurity of others around him.

Remembrance Day, London 1970's

Flipping the *Sundays* for notice of my new book,
I lost my place to a tall girl, a spine and ribs;
she bought every paper, even *News of the World*—
she had reason, her face on every front page:
Olympic runner, Lillian Board, and twenty,
told yesterday she is a cancer victim. . . .
In my coat I found a leaflet: "Our beloved
Ruth Fox . . . her first and last book, *Catch or Key,*
Journeys to far off lands or strolls at home,
was read by Frances Mintern Jones at the service
last Friday in the New England Poetry Club. . . ."
The remembered live, bagpipers in tan kilts,
their old officers in black suit, bowler and poppy,
their daughters on the sidewalk keeping their step.

Lowell's poem is especially useful for this essay because it confesses explicitly the similarity between the poet *as a poet* and other persons (athletes, soldiers, parents) who yearn for rescue from the sensation of having been forgotten, tossed aside, wiped out by inexorable time and history. Lowell here calls to mind the triple analogy that underlies my discussion: a specific fact of human experience is *like* a poem, and both are *like* an individual person, in relation to the tides of literary history and all history; all three are luminous small things in danger of disappearing all too soon beneath the waves.

"Remembrance Day" arranges a deceptively casual gathering of juxtapositions to evoke a world in which the threats—to putatively special individuals—of triviality, forgottenness, and disappearance are everywhere. The poet goes to a newsstand in London, on a holiday officially devoted to recognition of England's military veterans, searching for recognition of his own prowess and valor in the campaigns of literature. He is so busy "Flipping the *Sundays* for notice of my new book" that he loses his place in the line of customers to a tall thin woman who is, he suddenly realizes, Lillian Board, victim of one of life's outrageous twists: an internationally famous athlete in the prime of youthful vigor, she has suddenly learned she has cancer, which threatens to destroy her before she can win Olympic glory. Her chance for one kind of so-called immortality thus cruelly spoiled, Lillian Board is nevertheless fascinated by her sudden fame of another kind, the fame of her bad luck—"her face on every front page"; "she bought every paper." She must know that she will not appear on tomorrow's front pages, let alone those that report the next Olympics. But she seems to want to examine every instance of "notice" earned by her misfortune. Lowell suspects that Lillian Board on this Remembrance Day wants to repudiate oblivion and would not tolerate the cold comfort A. E. Housman offered to an athlete dying young:

> Now you will not swell the rout
> Of lads that wore their honors out,
> Runners whom renown outran
> And the name died before the man.

Housman implies that early death is better than the typical fate of outliving one's own fame, but Lillian Board is not accordingly relaxed; as one kind of fame recedes from her grasp, she reaches out for another kind.

Alerted by the disturbing similarity between himself and Lillian Board, both seeking notice in the papers, Lowell notices a third instance of human yearning for recognition: the leaflet in his pocket, which tries to win attention for a poetry presentation by one Frances Mintern Jones, who in turn wished to win attention for a deceased poet named Ruth Fox. Lowell does not mock the effort of Ms. Jones to honor Ms. Fox or Ms. Fox's effort to preserve her musings in her one book of poetry, but Lowell knows how hard it is to imagine that Ruth Fox's poetic renown will ever extend beyond the members of the New England Poetry Club, who listened on a certain Friday. Ruth Fox seems as obscure as Lillian Board will be four years hence or Ralph Temple twenty years after his tricks or perhaps Robert Lowell a hundred years after his new book. Therefore, there is not only humor but respect in Lowell's scrupulous notation of the particulars concerning Ruth Fox's book and the occasion of its honoring. The notice Lowell thus gives may be called "minimal"—we don't imagine he will make an effort to find and read *Catch or Key*—but it is still an act of careful attention to someone's attempt to signify, and as such, it represents the larger and more complicated acts of attention that Lowell hopes his own books will attract. Lillian Board and Ruth Fox have reminded Lowell that the line of customers is long and one may lose one's place.

As in the case of Bidart's "Happy Birthday," Lowell's poem seems to intend that the reader will take the mentioned names as accurately recorded facts; thus (despite our learned sophistication about the difference between life and art), if we were to discover the names were "just made up," an odor of duplicity would inform the poem. But we could still admire the poem for *imitating* and *dramatizing* the possible poetic rescue of true particulars. Lowell sometimes did alter facts for poetic purposes; in my opinion, he underestimated the connection between poetic power and trustworthiness. "Remembrance Day" conflates a few memories in a way less reliable than we feel on first reading. The odd reference in the title to "1970s" instead of a certain year signals this. Lillian Board was indeed a famous Olympic runner who won a silver medal for Britain in 1968; she was popular enough to be nicknamed "Britain's favorite girl"; you can find dramatic finish line photos of her on the Web; she died in December 1970 at the age of twenty-two, of colorectal cancer, which was diagnosed in the summer of 1970. As for Ruth Fox, a note in Lowell's *Collected Poems* (edited by Frank Bidart and David Gewanter) identifies her as Ruth Berrien Fox, who published *A Catch or Key* and died in 1969.

"Remembrance Day" ends beautifully by noticing a fourth instance of the yearning for notice. With the leaflet of the Poetry Club in his pocket (as we imagine it), Lowell watches the holiday parade of World War I veterans. Dressed up in their significant imagery, marching rhythmically, the veterans publish themselves on Remembrance Day: the parade is their brief poetry against the power of forgetfulness. The old officers carry poppies, which symbolize the graves of fallen comrades in Flanders—lost particulars who have, here, no more specific representation. The wry humor that has informed the poem so far, along with the (arguable) silliness of parades, might imply quite a grimly sardonic conclusion about human hopes for lasting honor. Instead, Lowell allows the poem to come to rest with the idea of a kind of victory over death different from those victories dependent upon, and registered by, public acclaim. The life of each veteran father continues, in a way, as genetic inheritance and paternal influence in the life of his child. In this sense, the "remembered" men "live" beyond their own mortal bodies, not in their ceremonial music and pomp but in "their daughters on the sidewalk keeping their step." This gently understated suggestion of the *keeping* of at least some aspect of mortal selves does not come across as Lowell's answer to the worrying about fame and recognition, but it does wonderfully afford some relief from that worrying. By writing the poem, though, Lowell implicitly testifies that genetic "immortality" is not enough. The spirit craves some other mode of preservation.

There are many poems that accept—whether despairingly, stoically, or with bemused or amused helplessness—in their main current of meaning the obliteration of all human particulars, while making room for a subversive undercurrent in which one or more particulars are smuggled into the eternity of art. We glimpsed such an impulse in the dates appended to Hardy's "His Immortality" and "The Rejected Member's Wife," and we saw it more clearly in the cyclists in Bidart's "Happy Birthday."

A poem could hardly accept the universality of obliteration more explicitly than "The Hearts" by Robert Pinsky, yet what keeps the poem vividly alive in my mind is its inclusion of several particulars, and especially of a particular song. These things are presented as examples, yes, but my claim—the claim I keep cherishing—is that we don't feel they are, for Pinsky or for us, *merely* examples.

At eighty-seven lines, "The Hearts" is too long to quote in full here, yet the poem lives in my mind as one luminous whole thing, like the shorter poems I've discussed, like a speech by a person on one occasion, like a song, like a beloved object you wouldn't be willing to see cut up, something you want to keep forever, a human creation that ought to be carried intact into the eternity (if any!) of literature.

"The Hearts" is a meditation on the helpless and beautiful repetitions of human desire. Like many of Pinsky's most impressive poems, "The Hearts" brazenly engages a vast topic directly, in defiance of the seeming impossibility of doing so without banality, and finds its success through odd juxtapositions of metaphor. From the cosmic perspective solicited by the poem, the forms taken by stubborn human desire are absurdly ephemeral, absurdly recurrent, and often absurdly self-harming as well—like the heroin addiction of jazz saxophonist Art Pepper (1925–82), one of the desirers cited by the poem. And yet, Pinsky feels, "the turns / Of these illusions we make become their glory." This affirmation is what we would expect the poem to reach; indeed, it is the essential affirmation that a poem in a secular world—a world without God waiting as the Great Recognizer after death—radically needs to reach or imply. Developing his panoramic vision of the sheer ephemerality of human desires and the constructions arising from those desires, Pinsky desires to mention specifically certain instances: Art Pepper, two of Shakespeare's tragedies, a clay cup from Benares, India ("I keep one here," Pinsky writes, "Next to me: holding it awhile from out of the cloud // Of dust that rises from the shattered pieces"), and a 1957 doo-wop song called "Teardrops."

In a poem of high seriousness, it is one thing to honor Shakespeare and another thing to honor Lee Andrews, lead singer on "Teardrops." Can a doo-wop song at all withstand the deluge of dissolution seen by Buddha, who called the desirous heart a foolish ape?

> Over the poor beast's head the crystal fountain
> Crashes illusions, the cold salt spume of pain
> And meaningless distinction, as Buddha says,
>
> But here in the crystal shower mouths are open
> To sing, it is Lee Andrews and The Hearts
> In 1957, singing *I sit in my room*
>
> *Looking out at the rain, My tear drops are*
> *Like crystals, they cover my windowpane,* the turns
> Of these illusions we make become their glory:
>
> To Buddha every distinct thing is illusion
> And becoming is destruction, but still we sing
> In the shower. I do.

Every distinct thing may be illusion to Buddha, but to Pinsky, one particular song of 1957 is manifestly distinguishable from others and worth distinguishing. He identifies the singing group and quotes the song's opening lines in the teeth of the superhuman view that every little song is infinitely unimportant. He has decided to "sing" in poetry of this loved song, as Lee Andrews has insisted on singing, in a formally elaborate way, of his (or his persona's) disappointment in romance. The singer's impression that his tears cover his (rain-spattered) windowpane is obviously (with intentional comedy of hyperbole) an illusion, in which meteorological events mirror human wishes and values. The singer's irrational insistence on the central importance of his caring is a metaphor for every human insistence of this kind—including Romeo's protestations to Juliet and Pinsky's own avowal of devotion to the song.

However, "The Hearts" is a poem that ostensibly undertakes to transcend naive deluded confidence in the significance and durability of our romantic devotions, so it presses on past the passage quoted here (which comes at midpoint) into a barrage of metaphors emphasizing that our hearts' creations (ideas, beliefs, works of art) are dispersible as dust, ephemeral as clouds. But something returns at the end of the poem, unforgotten, and it is "Teardrops," the end of the song:

> The Hearts in a shifting velvety *ah*, and *ah*
> Prolonged again, and again as Lee Andrews
>
> Reaches *ah* high for *I have to gain Faith, Hope*
> *And Charity, God only knows the girl*
>
> *Who will love me—Oh! if we only could*
> *Start over again!* Then The Hearts chant the chords
>
> Again a final time, *ah* and the record turns
> Through all the music, and on into silence again.

By constructing "The Hearts," Pinsky has found a way to rescue into poetry the vocal group and its lead singer. For me, for readers like me, and surely for Pinsky, one salient element of what he achieved in the poem is his specific and extensive honoring of "Teardrops." The poem did not arrange to include the names of all the performers, but their names await some future poem. In October 1957, Lee Andrews (whose original name had been Arthur Lee Andrew

Thompson) was the lead singer for The Hearts: Royalston Calhoun, first tenor; Thomas "Butch" Curry, second tenor; Ted Weems, baritone (replacing Jimmy McCallister); Wendell "Breeze" Calhoun, bass (replacing John Young); and Gerald Thompson, piano (replacing Kenny Lowe). Pinsky can feel to *some* extent that he has repaid the music and the musicians for the gift of lovely expression of romantic yearning; the poem—named after the group!—exerts its sacramental power against the vanishing of this particular beauty from the world. By the grace of poetry, Pinsky can feel he has done this even while at the same time the poem admits we will never be satisfied or finished in our negotiations with the beauties we perceive.

If you love a song and you indicate this in a good poem, what about the next time you think of a great song? It happens the very next day! Can you come up with another good poem for each great song of the 1950s? The 1960s? . . . Someone needs to get to work honoring songs of 2010 and 2020—not just in blogs but in eternal poems. Convincing rescues are always unlikely but always possible. There will always be another candidate for rescue, *and* another attempt at rescue, calling for your attention.

(All the poems I've discussed are by male poets. Why? If you imagine someone obsessively cataloging and describing hundreds of popular songs from a past decade, the person you imagine is male. Why? I'm frightened by an answer that comes to mind, which is that a man is less willing than a woman to face the insignificance and the accidental nature of one's own particular cherished facts, experiences, perceptions; that a woman more realistically accepts the reality that our little adventures and impressions are fortuitous, shaped by vast currents and forces we can't choose or control; that there are no absolutes [best song, perfect lover, immortal poem]. Somehow I sense a truth in this gender generalization notwithstanding the absolute devotion of most mothers to their particular children. But in my attempt to earn your interest and respect, reader, so that your interest and respect will stand between me and eternal night, I don't offer myself as a gender theorist! Having brought up the issue, I quickly set it aside.)

When a band records a song, the recording captures (or at least represents) the valued presence of certain performers in *one* place at *one* time. Instead of turning now to another poem honoring a song, I want to emphasize the essential lyrical wish to rescue a moment or event by turning to Hardy's "At Castle

Boterel." When Hardy's wife Emma died in November 1912, he was released from a marriage that had grown unhappy since their wedding in 1874, but he also felt a remorseful desire to honor the happiness of their first years. To resist the way death threatened to freeze the definition of the marriage in its recent sad form, Hardy revisited the Cornwall region where he had met Emma Gifford in 1870, when she was twenty-nine. "At Castle Boterel" comes with "March 1913" at the end of the poem and narrates an experience from that nostalgic expedition. On a rainy day in March 1913, Hardy rides up the same hill that he climbed with Emma on a dry March evening more than forty years past. Here are the first three of the poem's seven stanzas:

> As I drive to the junction of lane and highway,
>   And the drizzle bedrenches the waggonette,
> I look behind at the fading byway,
>   And see on its slope, now glistening wet,
>   Distinctly yet
>
> Myself and a girlish form benighted
>   In dry March weather. We climb the road
> Beside a chaise. We had just alighted
>   To ease the sturdy pony's load
>   When he sighed and slowed.
>
> What we did as we climbed, and what we talked of
>   Matters not much, nor to what it led,—
> Something that life will not be balked of
>   Without rude reason till hope is dead,
>   And feeling fled.

"At Castle Boterel" could be more thoroughly appropriate to my purposes than it is: it could include the name Emma Gifford, and it could incorporate the two dates into the poem, and it could insist on including some of "What we did as we climbed, and what we talked of." Admittedly, it's hard to imagine the poem staying afloat with all those facts in it. Still, its emotional power depends on Hardy's determination to assert the irreducible value—"such quality"—of certain human events that would seem trivial to any objective historian of, say, Cornwall or Boterel Hill or even of Hardy's own life.

If we bear in mind the title, and the subscribed date (and the poem's context among other poems about Hardy's courtship of Emma), "At Castle Boterel" does attain considerable particularity about the events described. We can't feel the poem would be better entitled "On a Rocky Hill" nor that the date "March 1913," which strikes a chord with the poem's reference to an earlier March, should be dropped as an unpoetic distraction. In the third stanza, Hardy nods to the perspective—objective, impersonal, unromantic—according to which his experience with Emma one day long ago "Matters not much," but no sooner has he done so than he claims (with his characteristically endearing awkwardness) great significance for what that experience led to: romantic love. To justify a focus on an event by stressing its large long-term results, though, is reasonable and explicable in a routine way that this poem yearns to transcend. What Hardy wants desperately to say is that his uphill walk with Emma that night mattered and still matters *in itself,* not for what it led to but for what it was. (We saw the same impulse expressed on behalf of John Keats in one place at one time, in "At Lulworth Cove a Century Back.")

In the fourth, fifth, and sixth stanzas, Hardy acknowledges the obliterative effects of time and of multiplicity (thousands of people have done more or less the same thing on Boterel Hill that he and Emma did), and he balances against this his defiant assertion that those forces cannot remove the unique value of one fact: "that we two passed."

> It filled but a minute. But was there ever
> A time of such quality, since or before,
> In that hill's story? To one mind never,
> Though it has been climbed, foot-swift, foot-sore,
> By thousands more.

> Primaeval rocks form the road's steep border,
> And much have they faced there, first and last,
> Of the transitory in Earth's long order;
> But what they record in colour and cast
> Is—that we two passed.

And to me, though Time's unflinching rigour,
　In mindless rote, has ruled from sight
The substance now, one phantom figure
　Remains on the slope, as when that night
　　Saw us alight.

Hardy knows he is being irrational; to be merely rational would be to betray the truth of feeling. The emotion of those three stanzas is the essence of the yearning for a *rescue of particulars* in poetry; moreover, I believe it is the essence of our attraction to short poems as such, because they embody and honor moments of feeling, moments of vision, moments of human being.

In the final stanza of "At Castle Boterel," Hardy laments that he will never again see the "phantom figure" that has appeared to him on the hill. But this lament belongs to the drama of his nostalgic expedition and his anticipation of his own death (though in fact he lived another fifteen years), and its effect does not shrink the claim he has made for the unique and lasting value of a certain experience in dry March weather. He has labored to make his phantom figure visible and has succeeded in the way poetry permits.

I look and see it there, shrinking, shrinking,
　I look back at it amid the rain
For the very last time; for my sand is sinking,
　And I shall traverse old love's domain
　　Never again.

(March 1913)

"March 1913"—the poem gives an account of a rainy day in the present as well as a dry night in the past. Hardy uses "At Castle Boterel" to record in language's "colour and cast" some particulars of two very different times and to ensure that *neither* experience will shrink into oblivion; both are inscribed in a poem that may conceivably outlast primeval rocks. Any act of specific observation in a poem is always partly an implicit testimonial to the worthy attentiveness of the observer who was in the right place at the right time. "At Castle Boterel," with its explicit superimposition of past and present, is an unusually clear illustration of this general truth.

There is a frightening perspective from which one's entire life will turn out to have been but a moment, a fleeting phenomenon disappearing into the past, shrinking amid the rain. The elegiac response is to declare that although a life may seem, in a heartless empirical sense, drastically brief and small, in another sense it has a transcendent, time-defying value that can be both recognized and protected by poetry—indeed, by a poem empirically brief and small. In many proudly short poems, Emily Dickinson teaches us that the most important kind of scope is not physical; "The Outer—from the Inner / Derives its Magnitude—." Her poem "If anybody's friend be dead" beautifully expresses the haunting force of particular details—outwardly trivial—from the life of a lost beloved.

But my final example of elegiac rescue will be a poem of several pages, Matthew Arnold's "Geist's Grave," an elegy for a life brief and small.

Is there a kind of dog more obviously trivial and silly than a dachshund? It depends on your perspective and on the dachshund. (Is there a kind of person more obviously trivial and silly than, say, an American professor of English in 2025? It depends on your perspective and on the professor.)

In November 1880, Arnold, who had written almost no poetry since publishing a volume in 1867, undertook to write an elegy for his son Richard's dachshund Geist, who died in October. Most of Arnold's earlier poetry had struggled to chasten unwisely romantic sentiment and to rise austerely above the self-indulgence that seemed to him a threat to human dignity. Such intentions, unless richly complicated with ambivalence, are not apt to generate much poetry. Arnold regretted his poetic silence, as he indicated as early as 1867 in a grim little poem called "The Progress of Poesy," but his regret couldn't overcome the attitudes that caused his silence. Yet in 1880, the death of a dog provoked him to write a poem more moving, I think, than his more famous poems.

The apparent triviality of the topic seems to have freed Arnold's imagination from the fetters of austere seriousness. By being so obviously a small thing, Geist excused Arnold from the dreary obligation of stressing yet again the smallness of particular human concerns in the cosmos. But an elegy for a dachshund? Is the project not doomed to be silly or at best microscopically forgettable?

Eighty lines long, "Geist's Grave" defies the idea that it is too big for its subject. (It was followed two years later by a much longer elegy for a canary named Matthias!) Arnold begins "Geist's Grave" with stanzas expressing amazement that the dog's charming life comprised only four years and then writes:

Yes, only four!—and not the course
Of all the centuries yet to come,
And not the infinite resource
Of Nature, with her countless sum

Of figures, with her fulness vast
Of new creation evermore,
Can ever quite repeat the past,
Or just thy little self restore.

Stern law of every mortal lot!
Which man, proud man, finds hard to bear,
And builds himself I know not what
Of second life I know not where.

But thou, when struck thine hour to go,
On us, who stood despondent by,
A meek last glance of love didst throw,
And humbly lay thee down to die.

Yet would we keep thee in our heart—
Would fix our favourite on the scene,
Nor let thee utterly depart
And be as if thou ne'er hadst been.

And so there rise these lines of verse
On lips that rarely form them now;
While to each other we rehearse:
Such ways, such arts, such looks hadst thou!

We stroke thy broad brown paws again,
We bid thee to thy vacant chair,
We greet thee by the window-pane,
We hear thy scuffle on the stair.

We see the flaps of thy large ears
Quick raised to ask which way we go;
Crossing the frozen lake, appears
Thy small black figure on the snow!

It would be hard to find a more earnestly specific and insistent effort to rescue from oblivion a beloved particular. Particular of human experience, I almost
said—and of course, the subject *is* in part the human experiences of Arnold's
family: watching the dog's ways, arts, and looks in the past and mourning the
dog's death in the present. Later stanzas of the poem make more clear that the
dog's is not the only life Arnold wishes to save from oblivion.

But note first Arnold's effort to "fix our favourite on the scene." He achieves
a degree of vividness not typical of his poetry. The poem is unapologetic about
its undertaking; Arnold does not require himself to say that a pet's death is unimportant or to acknowledge defensively that readers might think so. He writes
under the spell of tender emotion—not passionate perhaps but not moralis-
tically repressed either—trying to protect Geist from disappearing "as if thou
ne'er hadst been." Arnold doesn't want a poem about bereavement in general
nor a poem that might as well be about any dog. The uniqueness of the beloved
has its grip on Arnold's heart. The family can buy another dachshund, but not
even Nature herself can "just thy little self restore."

Concomitantly, this elegy wants to express and record the grief not of some
generic mourners but particularly of the Arnolds. Here is the conclusion of
"Geist's Grave," beginning with an awkwardly touching stanza that specifies the
grief of Arnold's son Richard, who was in Australia when Geist died:

Nor to us only art thou dear
Who mourn thee in thine English home;
Thou hast thine absent master's tear,
Dropt by the far Australian foam.

Thy memory lasts both here and there,
And thou shalt live as long as we.
And after that—thou dost not care!
In us was all the world to thee.

Yet, fondly zealous for thy fame,
Even to a date beyond our own
We strive to carry down thy name
By mounded turf, and graven stone.

We lay thee, close within our reach,
Here, where the grass is smooth and warm,
Between the holly and the beech,
Where oft we watch'd thy couchant form,

Asleep, yet lending half an ear
To travellers on the Portsmouth road;—
There build we thee, O guardian dear,
Mark'd with a stone, thy last abode!

Then some, who through this garden pass,
When we too, like thyself, are clay,
Shall see thy grave upon the grass,
And stop before the stone, and say:

People who lived here long ago
Did by this stone, it seems, intend
To name for future times to know
The dachs-hound, Geist, their little friend.

Arnold notes a difference between human beings and animals: the human mourners are "fondly zealous" for some preservation of their beloved, and of their love for the beloved, beyond their own mortal remembering (that evanescent power whose defeat Hardy faced in "His Immortality"), whereas the dog Geist was too simple (or too realistic!) to worry about fame, the attention of unknown others: "In us was all the world to thee."

The poem's closing stanzas describe a very human effort to guarantee the permanence of Geist's name by establishing the dog's grave with "graven stone." Specifying the grave's location "Between the holly and the beech," Arnold makes sure that one of the particulars identified—rescued—by the poem is the grave itself. The poem's title, meanwhile, has a deeper meaning: for this poet who lacks faith in any "second life" in heaven, there is still a transcendental sense in which Geist's "last abode"—last and lasting—is meant to be the poem itself. In "Geist's Grave," the dog is relinquished as flesh and blood while also—in poetry's terribly limited way—kept. Kept more memorably perhaps than Herrick's Prudence Baldwin, another figure of humility and loyalty whose poetic trace has not been extinguished. The sweet insistence of Arnold's effort appears where he pauses one last time to describe the living dog when he was "Asleep, yet lending half an ear / To travellers on the Portsmouth road."

At the end of the poem, Arnold imagines other travelers, unheard by Geist and unseen by the poet and his family, travelers "who through this garden pass"—the unknown travelers of posterity who will see the grave and imagine a certain dog and imagine also "People who lived here long ago." Meanwhile, Arnold must be thinking that other travelers, those who wander the roads and gardens of literature—you and I—can read the poem and call to mind certain worthy lives long ago, including that of a man named Matthew Arnold. To be available for such calling to mind, however limited, still seems different from being merely gone, "as if thou ne'er hadst been."

Why do I focus on "Geist's Grave" and ignore countless other poems about dead pets? Admittedly, Arnold's fame, and the ironic contrast between his famous concerns and a dachshund, attracted me, but I prefer to think I would have cherished "Geist's Grave" for its inherent value even if I'd never heard of its author. Like anyone in love with the art of the short poem, I need to believe that such a piece of writing—done well enough—can all by itself resist the titanic forces pulling everything we love toward darkness.

WHITMAN AND THE RESCUE
OF PARTICULARS

Are individual lives completely destroyed by death? Walt Whitman, not a true believer in any one religion that guaranteed an afterlife, found this question endlessly troubling, and in his poetry, he tried a variety of answers, which may be sorted out this way:

1. Human beings do not cease to exist when their bodies die; they survive with an improved kind of individuality in a next realm.

2. Human beings live on after death in a spiritual mystery that may not preserve their individuality but is wonderfully good.

3. Individuals are destroyed by death, yes, but this is not bad; it is perfectly all right because the record of their lives is preserved by some spiritual power, some version of God.

4. Individuals are destroyed by death, yes, but this is perfectly all right because to have participated in the ongoing story of humanity is infinitely good.

5. Individuals die and vanish, and this *is* a frightening loss, though it is mitigated somewhat by the ways in which succeeding generations remember them.

6. Ordinary remembering by survivors is not enough to mitigate the fear and pain of the obliteration of individuals; mortal individuals *need* a special kind of acknowledgment that preserves a precious trace of their individuality; and the specially powerful machine that produces this special acknowledgment is poetry.

Whitman was someone who never wanted to say no, always sought ways to say yes no matter how his affirmations might contradict each other. As *Leaves of Grass* evolved across the decades, he kept all six of the responses to mortality afloat, using his incredible charm and bravura to dodge having to choose one of the answers at the expense of the others.

My own focus—tilting toward obsession—is on the sixth answer: the idea that poetry can provide a specially valuable and comforting kind of acknowledgment that significantly compensates for (without undoing) the removal of individuals from earthly life. Like most nonreligious poets, I find this idea marvelously alluring, even if it leads toward delusion. I want to consider the extent to which Whitman was tempted by this idea—an idea that obviously elevates the importance of poetry and the poet—though he repeatedly rediscovered the danger of relying too entirely on poetic commemoration as humanity's answer to death.

In his most sweeping surges of optimism, Whitman assures us that death is no problem and therefore poetry performs no *necessary* service in response to death. In section 13 of "Starting from Paumanok," Whitman proclaims:

> Of your real body and any man's or woman's real body,
> Item for item it will elude the hands of the corpse-cleaners and pass to
>   fitting spheres,
> Carrying what has accrued to it from the moment of birth to the moment
>   of death.

There Whitman devotes his rhetorical flair to one of his favorite poetic effects, the dissolving of differences: the binary distinction between body and soul is rejected in favor of the insistence that the "real" body *is* the soul—or it is the individual aspect of ourselves that survives the destruction of the physical (and unreal?) body. A few lines later, Whitman declares that the human body "includes and is the soul"—a phrase characteristically evasive, preferring not to choose whether body contains soul or precisely equals soul. Here, as almost everywhere, Whitman is unconcerned with satisfying any logical philosopher. As he says in "Song of Myself," section 25,

> Writing and talk do not prove me,
> I carry the plenum of proof and every thing else in my face,
> With the hush of my lips I wholly confound the skeptic.

Insofar as he can sustain the mood of visionary optimism, Whitman presents himself as a bringer of good news, rather than as a supplier of something painfully lacking in human existence. Indeed, sometimes he suggests even more modestly (though admittedly, the adjective *modest* sounds very odd applied to Whitman!) that he is simply a reminder of good news, reminding healthy persons of the wondrous good fortune they already recognize intuitively. More often, though, he feels he must bring his good news loudly, to wake people up from their debilitating illusions and lethargy.

Yet even in such a superhumanly ebullient and encouraging poem as "Song of Myself," there are glimpses of the notion that poetry can offer mortals something crucial that wondrous life cannot provide—namely, a transcendent kind of individual acknowledgment.

> Through me many long dumb voices,
> Voices of the interminable generations of prisoners and slaves,
> Voices of the diseas'd and despairing and of thieves and dwarfs . . .
> Through me forbidden voices,
> Voices of sexes and lusts, voices veil'd and I remove the veil,
> Voices indecent by me clarified and transfigur'd.

In such a grand account of his own service to humanity, does Whitman promise to manifest and in some sense preserve the *individuality* of each oppressed voice? Not explicitly; often he is willing to imply that what he celebrates in poetry is the shared humanity of everyone, the common denominator (including vigor, courage, comradeship, desire, hope) found in all persons. But I will try to show that Whitman also felt the pull of the idea that individuals in their uniqueness *deserve* particular recognition in poetry and the further idea that such particular recognition could give mortal individuals a kind of rescue from the obliterations of change and death.

A short poem of 1860, "Once I Pass'd through a Populous City," is haunted by the notion of such rescue.

Once I Pass'd through a Populous City

> Once I pass'd through a populous city imprinting my brain for future use
>   with its shows, architecture, customs, traditions,

Yet now of all that city I remember only a woman I casually met there
    who detain'd me for love of me,
Day by day and night by night we were together—all else has long been
    forgotten by me,
I remember I say only that woman who passionately clung to me,
Again we wander, we love, we separate again,
Again she holds me by the hand, I must not go,
I see her close beside me with silent lips sad and tremulous.

Whitman remembers that he encountered countless vivid stimuli in the bustling city (New Orleans, in 1848, according to the biographers) and that he tried to retain in memory their details, yet now he can't recall those "shows" and instead retains only the uniquely valuable memory of one person. The poem's emotional power depends on this contrast between the forgettable multitude and the unforgettable individual. The poem focuses our attention on the remorseless elitism whereby the soul selects its own society and then shuts memory's door, finding sufficient focus for its attention in the single beloved.

Concomitantly, the reader is called upon to note that the poet feels his assertion of the uniquely memorable specialness of one passionate woman is fully sufficient to constitute the burden of a poem. No further discussion of the city, no further elaboration of ideas about memory or love, is required; the assertion of the woman's mattering to him can stand alone, as the sorrowing woman stood alone when Whitman left her. It can endure as an independent entity of art amid the crowd of other poems, bigger and louder poems, as the image of the woman has endured in Whitman's mind amid the shows of New Orleans (or Brooklyn or Boston). To notice this poem in the multitudinous pages of *Leaves of Grass* is to cherish one small thing despite the distracting claims made by many more burly things (and some even smaller things) and to deny that it is only an interchangeable blade of grass in a huge field. What I'm suggesting is that "Once I Pass'd" provides a particularly useful illustration of the deep relation between short poems as such and the cherishing of the uniqueness of human individuals. Like a lover, a poem is something that always yearns for special attention.

That analogy between poem and person, a favorite idea of mine, may not reappear explicitly in what follows here, but implicitly, it colors all my thinking about the purpose of poems.

Why has Whitman devoted a poem to affirming the unique memorability of a certain person? What is the motive to speech? One answer involves a feeling of debt: the poet left the forlorn lover behind, for some reason, against her will, and now, long afterward, he owes her something: acknowledgment of her importance, which has become more clear through the years as the kaleidoscopic shows of society have proven ephemeral in his mind. Her importance, we feel, is in one respect her importance to Walt in his story of himself, but more essentially, it is a matter of her dignity as an individual.

(Editors and biographers point out that in the poem's original manuscript, the lover was male. If the love acknowledged in the poem is imagined as secret homosexual love, the poem's undertaking to acknowledge the once-loved person has an extra dimension of anxiety.)

If the poem wants to pay a debt, how adequate is the payment? The poem is tender, and we may say the long-lost lover is honored by the tenderness, but tenderness is not identical with affection, and we can't quite say the poem is a love poem. The unforgotten lover is remembered in a rather impersonal and generic way. Her trembling lips allow the poem a haunting close-up for its ending, but what about her face as a whole, her distinctive manner, her self?

The question sounds ungrateful in response to such a gentle poem, but we can imagine that the special woman in the populous city might feel more lovingly acknowledged, more respected, if her specialness were more specifically represented. Her clothes, her dwelling, her age, her voice, her gestures, her eyes—and her name?

Why should her name not be given in the poem? This would surely be a decisive way of acknowledging her. True, in the vast traditions of love poetry and elegy, real-life proper names are omitted far more often than included. We can supply plenty of reasons for Whitman to have omitted her name. There is the possibility of a wish for secrecy, a wish perhaps shared by the lover (male or female) even many years after the affair. The tone of tender discretion in referring to a deeply private relationship serves this poem's particular effectiveness. At the same time, although Whitman says he returns imaginatively to the immediacy of being with the lover—"Again she holds me by the hand"—nevertheless we sense a distance between him and her, a distance implied in the poem's first word, inflected with the storytelling tone of "Once upon a time . . . ." We sense that the unforgotten lover has by now become for Whitman an example of something: she is an example of the insistent, unappeased yearning of a lover left behind; moreover, she is the occasion for Whitman to ponder the romantic selectivity of memory. His affair with her has become an instance. Their interaction is reenacted every day by thousands of lovers who must separate—and the poet sounds conscious of this as he composes his deliberately archetypal description. We may even suspect that he was "imprinting my brain for future use" with the shows of the lover whom he briefly knew in the populous city. We note that the vivid energies of love—detaining, clinging, holding—come from the woman in the poem, while the speaker seems passive. We suspect that he meant more to her—as uniquely valuable individual—than she meant to him.

That point does not cancel the poem's appeal, but it does help us think about the question of individual acknowledgment in poetry. Whitman's poem "Once I Pass'd" has consented to leave the sad lover undistinguished among the thousands of possible lovers in a city such as New Orleans; *she* has not been rescued from the teeming democratic mass.

But how could she be "rescued" in a poem? By including her name? By recording every detail of her life and character that a loving observer could possibly collect? Is there something a poem can do that can't be done by an obituary or a biography? What would ever be adequate acknowledgment of your unique self or mine? The question haunted Whitman.

His poem "Yonnondio" (1887) confesses this hauntedness. It is one of those poems in which an agonized honesty rises up in Whitman and presses him to admit the impossibility of the infinite superhuman assignments he gave himself. "Yonnondio" is a poem by an old man who has wanted, in his moods of sublime afflatus, to be the adequate acknowledger of *everything* and who now feels his powers waning while too much remains undone. In the cornucopian Songs of the early editions of *Leaves of Grass,* he was able, by means of his manically energetic lists of persons and places and objects and activities, to generate the sensation of a vision in which indeed everything, and especially *every* American person, was recognized and respected in its/his/her individual essence. But the unfinishability of this task troubles the bard as he slides toward silence—five years from death when he writes "Yonnondio." He has to admit that some human lives will never get their rightful poetic acknowledgment; they will never be adequately *named.* What jolts him into this awareness is itself a name, as he explains in his note on the poem's title.

Yonnondio

(The sense of the word is *lament for the aborigines.* It is an Iroquois term; and has been used for a personal name.)

A song, a poem of itself—the word itself a dirge,
Amid the wilds, the rocks, the storm and wintry night,
To me such misty, strange tableaux the syllables calling up;
Yonnondio—I see, far in the west or north, a limitless ravine,
    with plains and mountains dark,
I see swarms of stalwart chieftains, medicine-men, and warriors,
As flitting by like clouds of ghosts, they pass and are gone in
    the twilight,
(Race of the woods, the landscapes free, and the falls!
No picture, poem, statement, passing them into the future:)
Yonnondio! Yonnondio!—unlimn'd they disappear;
To-day gives place, and fades—the cities, farms, factories fade;
A muffled sonorous sound, a wailing word is borne through the air
    for a moment,
Then blank and gone and still, and utterly lost.

Contrary to his more typical inclination, Whitman here refrains from offering some compensation or comfort for the disappearance of human selves from all record. In the mood of the poem, there can be no compensation: the American poet realizes that the first Americans are utterly gone; they are, like the slain sailors in section 36 of "Song of Myself," irretrievable—beyond adequate acknowledgment.

However, in lamenting that the early Iroquois have "No picture, poem, statement, passing them to the future," Whitman implies that such "passing" of the dead into posterity's future *is* meaningfully feasible by means of depiction and description. But sufficient representation can only be achieved across manageable gaps of culture, space, and time; the "aborigines" of "Yonnondio" are too far gone to be limned, and therefore, "unlimn'd they disappear."

A Native American writer could easily point out Whitman's cultural arrogance in lamenting that past generations of aborigines are utterly lost simply because they are not preserved in the culture of English. Perhaps the legends and songs of Iroquois culture pass on to Iroquois descendants a "picture" of past generations meaningful enough for them, even if not for the ex-editor of the *Brooklyn Daily Eagle*. Still, this point should not obscure the pang felt by the poet in "Yonnondio." Whitman's longing to claim that no lives merely vanish confronts here an unanswerable challenge, and the poem conveys the pain of realizing this.

Let's notice that while the poem registers Whitman's inability to rescue by acknowledgment those "swarms" of warriors long ago, it simultaneously performs and registers his ability to rescue a word—*Yonnondio*—from the obscurity of its foreignness (to him). He feels the word in itself possesses the dignity and resonance of a poem, and he writes his own poem to honor and preserve something he feels is of the same nature or ontological significance as his own poem. The poem works to pull the beautiful word from the twilight of foreignness into the spotlight of poetic life.

(Ed Folsom notes, in his book *Walt Whitman's Native Representations,* that Whitman may well have misconstrued the meaning of the word *Yonnondio*— it may have actually meant "governor"! If so, I admit the poet's inaccuracy is depressing, but it doesn't render the poem's yearning less palpable or less convincing.)

Whitman includes in the poem an awareness of the cost of straining to rescue one thing from obscurity. "To-day gives place, and fades—the cities, farms, factories fade." Just as Whitman's memory relinquished the shows of a populous city while cherishing the image of one person, here, too, a price is paid for intense focus upon one particular: other particulars must fade into undifferentiated background, at least for the poem's moment. For that moment, disappearance is suffered not by the peripheral thing (the lovely word) but by the business of the contemporary scene. To love one thing deeply is to let other things slip out of sight—or so we may fear. This fear drives many of Whitman's big poems into insatiable anaphora, trying over and over to give each thing its equal place in the sun.

The last lines of "Yonnondio" cry out that the lovely word—the cherished particular—has vanished from the air, yet these lines conclude a poem that has saved the word for our caring now, more than a century later. Whitman lamented the vanishing of human beings and also the vanishing of the "wailing word"—but the latter, though no longer uttered by its original speakers, has in one palpable way not vanished; it is "borne through the air" each time we read Whitman's poem.

Are we pushed here toward the thought that words can only ever "rescue" other words? If there is a theoretical cogency in this thought, it doesn't really interest me because it doesn't account for, or help us appreciate, the emotional power of poetry, which is always, I believe, inseparable from the human longing for lasting, durable acknowledgment of individualities—of objects, experiences, events, words, speakers, persons.

A writer notices one thing in the world and chooses to write about it—and not about everything else. It might be a tearful woman; it might be a haunting word; it might be a mockingbird from Alabama; it might be a stagecoach driver on Broadway. The writer may have many purposes; among these is likely to be an attempt at adequate acknowledgment, or what I prefer to call *rescue* because rescue evokes urgency in a world where the selected thing is always crowded by other particulars and always subject to the forces of dissolution and forgetfulness.

Notwithstanding his fervent claims that all realities are at least acceptable and that death will be fine, Whitman the great acknowledger expressed, when he was most honest, the desperate difficulty in honoring the vanishing beauties of the world, along with the desperate longing to do so. The drama of this challenge can be seen in such poems as "To Think of Time," "Faces," and "Old Salt Kossabone."

In "Once I Pass'd" and "Yonnondio," Whitman's elegiac efforts have to cope with intervals of time and space. "To Think of Time" (which appeared in the first edition of *Leaves of Grass* before going through various revisions) includes an elegiac section wherein the details are readily available to the poet, and as a result, the possibility of adequate acknowledgment becomes disturbingly tantalizing, more immediate as a challenge to the survivor. Here, minus three opening lines, is section 4 of "To Think of Time" (entitled "Burial Poem" in the 1856 edition):

> Cold dash of waves at the ferry-wharf, posh and ice in the river, half-frozen mud
>   in the streets,
> A gray discouraged sky overhead, the short last daylight of December,
> A hearse and stages, the funeral of an old Broadway stage-driver, the cortege
>   mostly drivers.

Steady the trot to the cemetery, duly rattles the death-bell,
The gate is pass'd, the new-dug grave is halted at, the living alight,
    the hearse uncloses,
The coffin is pass'd out, lower'd and settled, the whip is laid on the coffin,
    the earth is swiftly shovel'd in,
The mound above is flatted with the spades—silence,
A minute—no one moves or speaks—it is done,
He is decently put away—is there any thing more?

He was a good fellow, free-mouth'd, quick-temper'd, not bad-looking,
Ready with life or death for a friend, fond of women, gambled, ate hearty,
    drank hearty,
Had known what it was to be flush, grew low-spirited toward the last, sicken'd,
    was help'd by a contribution,
Died, aged forty-one years—and that was his funeral.

Thumb extended, finger uplifted, apron, cape, gloves, strap, wet-weather clothes,
    whip carefully chosen,
Boss, spotter, starter, hostler, somebody loafing on you, you loafing on somebody,
    headway, man before and man behind,
Good day's work, bad day's work, pet stock, mean stock, first out, last out,
    turning-in at night,
To think that these are so much and so nigh to other drivers, and he there
    takes no interest in them.

This great passage shows Whitman racked with ambivalence about the worthwhileness of a thorough poetic acknowledgment of this particular dead man. Later in "To Think of Time," Whitman's insistent optimism will surge, and he will proclaim (with revealing stridency) that no soul ever vanishes, "there is strict account of all," and "You are not thrown to the winds, you gather certainly and safely around yourself, / Yourself! yourself! yourself, for ever and ever!" But while his imagination is caught in the vividness of the bleakly ordinary funeral under a "gray discouraged" December sky, Whitman's unhappy honesty finds immortality terribly dubious. He is torn between the impulse to eulogize a certain Broadway stage driver, "aged forty-one years," through a rich gathering of affectionate details—as most of us in secular life strive to honor the special qualities of someone who has died—and the opposing depressive impulse to admit that the man's death is an awfully small and awfully typical event. "He is decently put away—is there any thing more?"

There is nothing more—so says one voice in Whitman's mind. The man died, "and that was his funeral." If a story ends thus, the poet suspects, then it does not bear very much telling. How much telling is called for? The poem balances uneasily in a halfway zone as regards detail. How would the dead driver himself feel about this poem as his eulogy? Without undue vanity, the driver might wish for more particular information about himself to extend the "good fellow" stanza. Why not an anecdote or two? How did his quick temper relate to his loyalty? Did his fondness for women ever involve serious love? When he "grew low-spirited toward the last," was he able to escape despair? And what was his name? We know that eulogies and elegies cannot encompass an entire life story, but once specific depiction of the missing person is begun (as it is not in religious or transcendentalist elegies such as Milton's "Lycidas" or Shelley's "Adonais"), how far can it go?

The limitedness of detail in the stage driver passage stems from feelings different from those that we found limiting detail in "Once I Pass'd through a Populous City." Here depression inhibits detail. The scene of the funeral procession and burial becomes an objective correlative for depression, that mental condition of half-frozen mud. Not that awareness of mortality is in itself enough to explain inhibition of elegiac detail because a stabbing awareness of mortality often serves as the spur to copious recollection. But in depression, we fail to find life interesting: mortality becomes pointlessness. Ultimately, to be uninterested in life is to be spiritually dead—Whitman seems to shiver in apprehension of this danger in the last line of this funeral poem.

To a depressed viewer, particulars are interesting if at all only as examples of the world's slide toward decay and death. The first three lines of section 4 of "To Think of Time," omitted earlier, certainly don't promise a richly particularized portrayal:

A reminiscence of the vulgar fate,
A frequent sample of the life and death of workmen,
Each after his kind.

These lines concede a subordination of individual to category, as depression reduces individuality to typicality and ordinariness to vulgarity. Still, there are enough details in the funeral poem so that we don't quite feel we are reading about just *any* driver or *any* "good fellow" but a certain quick-tempered man who died in December at the age of forty-one. Something deep in Whitman resists depression and does so provisionally by means of specificity. It is a grim effort in the context of his funeral day mood, and soon Whitman will turn—in later sections of "To Think of Time"—to the easier strategy of whipping up reassurances out of his sublimely unorthodox kind of religious zeal.

Resisting depression through specific observation, Whitman devotes one solid stanza to details about the dead driver, but we note that the preceding two stanzas concern not the man himself but his funeral procession and burial and that the concluding stanza (beginning "Thumb extended . . .") describes not precisely the behavior of the individual who has died but the daily routine of his former livelihood, which will continuously be enacted by his surviving colleagues. Thus, most of section 4 of "To Think of Time" does not specifically eulogize the deceased. However, the funeral itself—minute by minute—was a particular in the flux of Whitman's experience, and this particular has been (to some extent, insofar as words can do the job) rescued from oblivion by two stanzas, perhaps more vividly than the dead stage driver has been rescued by the stanza directly about him. Further, I want to suggest that Whitman's recurrent experience of observing the behavior of such stage drivers may be thought of as a "particular" that is lifted away from forgetfulness by the concluding stanza. Seen in this way, the poem fights more than one battle against the obliteration of particulars.

But this rescue business is exhausting work, and one's responsibility will need to be limited somehow. Candidates for rescue—objects, facts, moments, events, persons—present themselves to the poet incessantly, and most seem doomed to disappear not only because of the sheer volume of the competition but also because of their own difficult-to-cherish limitations. In his poem "Faces" (one of the 1855 poems), Whitman saunters up to this problem as if daring it to alarm him.

"Faces" is one of his large-voiced poems in which he will not allow the feared truth (about selves disappearing in the unjust chaos of time) to grip his imagination for more than moments. On the streets and roads of America, he encounters an amazing array of human faces; "I see them and complain not," he assures us, "and am content with all." But he follows this assurance with a rhetorical question that reveals how this poem will cope with the worry that unlovely particulars may fail to win adequate acknowledgment. He tips away from Whitmanian immanence toward Whitmanian transcendence: "Do you suppose I could be content with all if I thought them their own finale?"

Fortified by the essentially religious sense of eventual salvation implicit in that question—a question whose bluster barely veils its anxiety—Whitman wades into the crowd and acknowledges, passingly, the most regrettable human particulars:

> This now is too lamentable a face for a man,
> Some abject louse asking leave to be, cringing for it,
> Some milk-nosed maggot blessing what lets it wrig to its hole.
>
> This face is a dog's snout sniffing for garbage,
> Snakes nest in that mouth, I hear the sibilant threat.
>
> This face is a haze more chill than the arctic sea,
> Its sleepy and wabbling icebergs crunch as they go.
>
> This is a face of bitter herbs, this an emetic, they need no label,
> And more of the drug-shelf, laudanum, caoutchouc, or hog's-lard.

The Swiftian misanthropy in these lines—and there are more in this vein—is shocking from the author of *Leaves of Grass*. What we hear (as in Swift, indeed) is the outrage of a writer who cares about all reflections of humanity and therefore cannot ignore its most disappointing manifestations. But Whitman cannot bear to linger in his dismay. The images he supplies are only snapshots taken from hostile angles; these individuals, he implies, would not deserve painstaking portraits even if there were time enough for the task. He needs to claim that the ultimate truth of humanity is not visible in this album of grotesques. He does so in the next section of "Faces," which culminates in lines that refer (according to editors Sculley Bradley and Harold W. Blodgett) to his younger brother Eddie, who suffered from physical and intellectual disabilities.

Features of my equals would you trick me with your creas'd and
    cadaverous march?
Well, you cannot trick me.

I see your rounded never-erased flow,
I see 'neath the rims of your haggard and mean disguises.

Splay and twist as you like, poke with the tangling fores of fishes or rats,
You'll be unmuzzled, you certainly will.

I saw the face of the most smear'd and slobbering idiot they had
    at the asylum,
And I knew for my consolation what they knew not,
I knew of the agents that emptied and broke my brother,
The same wait to clear the rubbish from the fallen tenement,
And I shall look again in a score or two of ages,
And I shall meet the real landlord perfect and unharm'd, every inch
    as good as myself.

Especially if the passage about "my brother" is understood to refer literally to Eddie Whitman, it is a heartbreaking passage. The older brother relinquishes the task of finding a cherishable (and poetically salvageable) particular in the present visible reality of Eddie, by claiming to know that the true Eddie waits to meet him in some transcendental future. The religiosity of this prediction matches that of Gospel songs about family reunion on the far side of the River Jordan, and indeed the poem's next line will abjectly refer to traditional religious language: "The Lord advances." Whitman has shifted from his shoulders the intolerable burden of praising all present particulars.

No emotion is more understandable and forgivable than the emotion in the stanza about "my brother." But we need to notice what work is abandoned by "Faces" as a whole. It leaves to a poet like Browning or to Shakespeare or to fiction writers like Dreiser or Sherwood Anderson or Faulkner the labor of describing and illuminating very damaged or repellent human personalities. "This is a face of bitter herbs, this an emetic, they need no label," says Whitman, moving hastily away. The revulsion he feels is both against certain particular realities and also against specific registration of them. When something in the present ("This face is a dog's snout sniffing for garbage") seems ineligible for the embrace of Whitmanian affirmation, the poet turns toward some mysterious superior future.

Sometimes he does the same in response to something in the past if it seems too far for imagination's reach and if his mood is less painfully honest than the mood in which he wrote "Yonnondio." His poem "Unnamed Lands" (1860) purports blithely to solve the problem of innumerable human disappearances, the problem that remains so hauntingly unsolved in the later "Yonnondio." In "Unnamed Lands," Whitman produces his impatiently generalized kind of listing of human achievements and behaviors in "Nations ten thousand years before these States," including "Who were witty and wise, who beautiful and poetic, who brutish and undevelop'd" and including "crimes, prisons, slaves" as well as "languages, governments" and "heroes, poets." As in "Faces" and the last parts of "To Think of Time," Whitman is determined to say that all these things "were not for nothing." He rejects the idea that a human thing can simply end and that its value can last only as long as it lasts or even only as long as it is specifically remembered. Though he could write wonderfully about physical pleasure and joy, Whitman was no hedonist. Today was never enough unless attached to infinite tomorrows. Accordingly, the idea of a "land" in ancient history without a *name* lasting into the present agitates Whitman. It is not enough that those lands must have had names in the speech of their inhabitants ten thousand years ago; if the names have not survived, it feels too much as if they were "for nothing" and the lands have become distressingly "unnamed." Whitman's solution (again) is some ideal future realm difficult to distinguish from a Christian heaven of resurrection, with only the charm of his voice to keep the lines inflated with faith:

> I suspect their results curiously await in the yet unseen world, counterparts
>   of what accrued to them in the seen world,
> I suspect I shall meet them there,
> I suspect I shall find there each old particular of those unnamed lands.

These lines don't quite decide whether the things to be met in "the yet unseen world" are the very constituents of long-ago societies or only their long-term effects. The poet equivocates "curiously." His solution is an awfully vague expectation at the end of an awfully generalizing poem; the vagueness and generality are deeply ironic in a campaign on behalf of specificities, this celebration of the endurance of "each old particular." Whitman doesn't seem at all depressed in "Unnamed Lands," yet the poem's bland generality resembles an effect we detected in the Broadway stage driver's funeral poem. Like depression, hollow exultation involves failure to be interested, and even Whitman fails to be interested in ancient lands about which nothing can be known.

Yet Whitman was capable of beautifully specific acts of acknowledgment, and their presence throughout *Leaves of Grass* reflects his feeling that to show the specific quality of something is one crucial service poetry should perform. Hundreds of intense glimpses are so sharply evoked that they may seem "enough" for acknowledgment of individual facts (persons, actions, scenes) even though the poetry rushes on past them. Whitman is "Pleas'd with the quakeress as she puts off her bonnet and talks melodiously," and his pleasure is so convincing we may almost not notice that the line is nonspecific enough to describe thousands of women on a given day; he is "Pleas'd with the earnest words of the sweating Methodist preacher, impress'd seriously at the camp-meeting" ("Song of Myself," section 33), and we may feel for a moment as if a certain preacher has been uniquely pointed out, though the line applies to many a preacher.

Occasionally, however, Whitman could sustain a particular acknowledgment for longer than a glimpse and penetrate through type or category to believable individual—demonstrating something achievable in poetry that is not undertaken by his great expansive Songs nor by the secretive "Once I Pass'd through a Populous City." His late poem "Old Salt Kossabone" (1888) gives a picture of an "old particular"—his great-great-grandfather on the day he died.

Old Salt Kossabone

Far back, related on my mother's side,
Old Salt Kossabone, I'll tell you how he died:
(Had been a sailor all his life—was nearly 90—lived with his married
    grandchild, Jenny;
House on a hill, with view of bay at hand, and distant cape, and stretch
    to open sea;)

The last of afternoons, the evening hours, for many a year his
    regular custom,
In his great arm chair by the window seated,
(Sometimes, indeed, through half the day,)
Watching the coming, going of the vessels, he mutters to himself
    —And now the close of all:
One struggling outbound brig, one day, baffled for long—cross-tides
    and much wrong going,
At last at nightfall strikes the breeze aright, her whole luck veering,
And swiftly bending round the cape, the darkness proudly entering,
    cleaving, as he watches,
"She's free—she's on her destination"—these the last words—when
    Jenny came, he sat there dead,
Dutch Kossabone, Old Salt, related on my mother's side, far back.

The claim I want to make for this poem is that it gives us the sensation of
having met this old man on his last day, *this* old man and no one else. In purpose and in impact, this limited feat of retrieval by—and *into*—representation
may not be superior to the trumpeting feats of panoramic and synoptic vision
that Whitman more famously undertook, but a poem like "Old Salt Kossabone"
achieves a kind of *saving* for which transcontinental and cosmic rhapsodies
leave us still yearning.

We feel the presence of Kossabone as an individual—not merely a stock
character, a generic "old salt," but the man who lived with Jenny and muttered
and watched ships with expert eyes. The effect is there even though the poem
does not accumulate many details. We noted omissions of detail in the case of
the Broadway stage driver, too, but here Whitman does not sound impatient,
nor does depression threaten to alienate him from the vividness of the individual life. We feel the poet has calmly and appreciatively imagined the truth of
one person at one time.

Writing "Old Salt Kossabone," Whitman was an old man near death—he
would die in 1892—imagining a man who died very old before Whitman was
born. Unable to rescue Dutch Kossabone from forgottenness through his own
memories, Whitman has to rely on an anecdote passed along by his great-aunt
Jenny, limiting his focus to the last hours of Kossabone's life. The anecdote of

"how he died" blossoms poetically in Kossabone's intuitive identification with the long-baffled "outbound brig." Conscious of his own voyage toward death, Whitman wants to imply that Kossabone, like the ship, sails into some meaningful destined fulfillment rather than merely into darkness. Thus, Whitman's interest in another person naturally involves self-interest as well as interest in his own favorite ideas.

The special value of this poem, though, is syntactically reflected by the way it begins and ends with nominative phrases not harnessed to predicates, representing the significant reality of the man described, significant in himself. By focusing on one man's special individuality, the poem makes itself special among Whitman's works. The special value of this poem is in the way the hunger for transcendental intimation ("the darkness proudly entering, cleaving") gets subordinated to an even stronger wish, the wish to honor by description a perished human particular at the outer edge of what the poet can richly imagine: "Dutch Kossabone, Old Salt, related on my mother's side, far back."

DEAR FRIEND, SIT DOWN

On Helen Vendler's *Invisible Listeners*

Since I'm going to present several objections and resistances to what Vendler does in *Invisible Listeners* (2005), let me first remember five reasons to be favorably disposed toward her and it.

1. Vendler loves poems. How strange it is to compliment a literary critic on this as a special virtue, but in the age of theory, her heartfelt human appreciations look admirably untrendy.

2. Vendler writes engagingly, and clearly. (Or with apparent clarity, anyway; she rarely flourishes any professional jargon; as you read along, you feel spoken to in a cordial human voice; although when you think carefully about her arguments, you may find her prose getting smoky at key moments.)

3. She tries nervy juxtapositions: a book about Herbert, Whitman, and Ashbery! Why not? (Vendler previously published a book on Pope, Whitman, Dickinson, and Yeats.) Three poets of drastically different periods, beliefs, styles, concerns—maybe it can be refreshing to see what they share.

4. Vendler's earlier work on George Herbert, and Wallace Stevens, was wonderfully helpful, and indeed, many of her essays have helped me understand poets better.

5. Though I've disagreed with nearly half of her judgments of contemporary poets, at least she hasn't pretended that we don't evaluate poets when we ponder and discuss them, and her opinions are always interesting; how many critics can you say that about?

Invisible Listeners is based on the observation that poets sometimes address their poems to certain "listeners"—specific audiences of one—who are "invisible" because they are irrevocably removed from the poet's real-life quotidian world. Poets do this, Vendler says, because they feel some profound inadequacy in the social relations available to them. The central examples are: Herbert addressing God (in such poems as "The Glimpse," "Perseverance," "Even-Song," "The Quidditie," "Love Unknown," and "Dialogue"); Whitman addressing readers in the future (especially in "Crossing Brooklyn Ferry"); and Ashbery addressing Francesco Parmigianino, an artist in the past, in "Self-Portrait in a Convex Mirror." In selecting her examples, Vendler looks for a sense of "intimacy" in the address to the invisible listener: not the mere fact of the address but a feeling of interactive warmth, close personal connection between poet and listener.

Thus, the category Vendler proposes for study and appreciation has three defining criteria: (1) direct address to the listener; (2) invisibility of the listener; and (3) intimacy (or the seeking of intimacy) between poet and listener. These three criteria ostensibly create a distinct category, a category fairly rare, populated perhaps with dozens of poems rather than thousands. The intimacy element, in particular, serves to set aside the countless poems addressed to God (or other supernatural beings or forces) in a spirit of traditional reverence from a great distance. The element of invisibility, meanwhile, serves to set aside all human addressees alive in the poet's present (including all romantic beloveds) *and* all individuals personally known to the poet even if they have died (such as Ben Jonson's dead son). A person known to the poet, no matter how warmly addressed and no matter how painfully yearned for (an absent lover, a dead child or parent or spouse or friend), does not qualify as an Invisible Listener in Vendler's terms.

The three criteria propose a distinctly defined topic, but there are many signs that Vendler senses the firm definition is inhibiting and also that the supposed parallels among Herbert, Whitman, and Ashbery are highly problematic; as she carries on her discussions, she blurs the edges of her topic in ways I find rather maddening because the blurring is so un-self-critical. Vendler seems ambivalent about the scope of her project. Is she arguing for an unexpected narrow similarity (of emotional orientation) between drastically different poets in a few of their poems—a task appropriate for an appealingly tendentious *essay*—or is she writing a *book* about the relation between the lyric impulse and the absence of the beloved? *Invisible Listeners* floats between those two coherent intentions.

Herbert, Whitman, and Ashbery. What is odd about this catchy lineup? Well, you don't often hear Herbert and Whitman spoken of together—but it isn't absurd, since there is a deep sense in which Whitman is a religious poet (though his religion is an inconsistent eclectic self-inventing thing often indistinguishable from a transcendental humanism). Also, you could argue that both *The Temple* and *Leaves of Grass* present a man struggling, with heroic and anxious candor, to define and endlessly redefine a spiritually healthy self—something repeatedly elusive but urgently desired. Herbert, Whitman . . . and Ashbery? What's odd is the conjunction of two great poets and one tremendously prolific and over-celebrated minor poet.

I've been fascinated (I don't want to say obsessed) by the Ashbery inflation for more than forty years, and I've written before on my sense that Ashbery's poems don't care enough about the reader. And the whole issue of any poet's relation to The Reader is something I find importantly under-pondered in *Invisible Listeners.* These two concerns (one not so big and one huge) are what prompted me to write about this short book, and I have disproportionately much to say about them.

In her chapter on George Herbert, Vendler writes convincingly and movingly about poems in which Herbert's attitude toward God does seem warmer and closer and more interpersonal than the attitudes we would expect in acts of worship. Vendler brings this out confidently and gracefully, with the attention to nuance that has always been essential to her value as a critic. Though she doesn't present herself as a Christian commentator, Vendler is imaginatively at home in Herbert's poems. Her readings may not be groundbreaking (as her 1975 book on Herbert was), but they reawaken us to unique qualities of Herbert. (I was raised as an atheist, am an atheist; Herbert is the only religious poet who has ever made me feel a profound tug of attraction toward—not faith exactly but the life of faith.) In a discussion of Herbert's "Dialogue," Vendler helps us see the interaction between human and Savior as something more like a difficult friendship (despite inequality) than like a hierarchical encounter between servant and lord.

> In this quarrel of intimates, the sinner's reluctance produced
> Jesus' logic; Jesus' logic produced the sinner's counterlogic;
> and then Jesus' emotion produced the sinner's responsive
> emotion, a synchrony allowing the participants' tones to mirror
> each other in a common poignancy, and the poem to end on a
> completed rhyme.

"Dialogue" ends with a line in which the human sinner, Herbert, interrupts Jesus, who has been arguing for the sinner's acceptance of His difficult but saving love.

> *That as I did freely part*
> *With my glorie and desert,*
> *Left all joyes to feel all smart—*
> Ah! no more: thou break'st my heart.

Vendler's way of characterizing the encounter as intimate makes emotional sense of Herbert's having the nerve to interrupt his Savior. These two speakers know each other well, even if they exist on different planes of being. Vendler observed in her 1975 book, *The Poetry of George Herbert,* that in this poem, Christ "uses all the most human of means—irony, pun, comparison with himself— to win the sinner. . . . Herbert's Jesus is credible as a projection of the self because he speaks the same language as the self, and the air of true conversation is maintained."

For Vendler, the value of such poems in which divinity is humanized, or imagined in a warmly personal way, does not consist only in their showing how to relate to God. She says that such poems also show us how to relate to each other, and she implies that Herbert intends this: "By projecting what we know of the pains and difficulties of actual intimacy onto a symbolic plane of abstract modeling, Herbert composes a manual of instruction toward better forms of intimacy in the actual world." I'm not sure that Herbert understood himself to be a teacher (in his poems) of better interpersonal interaction, but I'd like to think so; in any case, Vendler's suggestion reminds us of something obvious yet weirdly easy for some critics to forget, namely that Herbert's poems—like *all* poems, or so I want to argue—are aimed at us. They are addressed (in one sense of the verb) to us—to The Reader. The reader is always understood to be a listener, a listener with more or less of what Vendler calls visibility, depending on how confident the poet is of a contemporary readership.

To Vendler, that truth may seem so axiomatic as to be pointless to dwell on and a mere distraction from her focus on Invisible Listeners such as Herbert's Jesus or Ashbery's Parmigianino. But I think a poem's interest in the reader is a crucial formative factor in its ethical significance and aesthetic value, and to elide or smudge this obvious (yet forgettable) truth leads to some very distorted interpretations and evaluations. What bothers me in *Invisible Listeners* is that Vendler is inconsistent about whether the reader—as a poem's intended receiver—is central to her subject or not, and she seems not to notice the inconsistency. Her discussion of Herbert's intimate addresses to God or Christ includes several great poems that *narrate* episodes of interaction with God *rather than* presenting immediate addresses to Him. "The Collar" and "Love (III)" give accounts of interaction in the past; "A True Hymne" describes a recurrent interaction with God, reporting God's actions in third-person references. (Third person, yes. And who is the unnamed second person in these storytelling events? It is us.) When Herbert says, "Love bade me welcome," and concludes the narrative with "So I did sit and eat," he is telling us a story; he's not telling Jesus. Jesus already knows the story; Jesus was there. Since Vendler has been at pains to define a kind of poem in which "this sort of intimacy springs from a fundamental loneliness, forcing the author to conjure up a listener unavailable in actual life" so that the poet "must hold a colloquy with an invisible other," you'd think she would need an emphatic decisive distinction between poems (like "The Quidditie" and "Love Unknown") in which Herbert speaks *to* God and poems in which Herbert speaks *about* God speaking. But instead, Vendler glides between the two sorts of poems without hesitation, as if all were equally instances of address-to-Invisible-Listener.

The effect is a beclouding of something important. Vendler hears "the quintessential Herbertian tone" of "intimate confiding" in the first line of "Love Unknown": "Deare Friend, sit down, the tale is long and sad." The Friend in that poem turns out to be Jesus. However, fewer than half the poems in *The Temple* are directly addressed to God or Jesus (and some of those turn to address God or Jesus only at the end in a tone of reverent prayer). Of course, we may say that God is understood to be implicitly an intended listener to any poem by this religious poet. But what I want to insist on is the other truth, that the human reader is always implied as an intended listener to any poem by a human poet. Vendler says of "Love Unknown," "Through Jesus' example here, Herbert offers us a model of how to listen to an intimate friend who is suffering." Herbert *offers us*—exactly. The reason why the first line of "Love Unknown" strikes "the quintessential Herbertian tone" is because Herbert makes us feel addressed in a candidly confidential way. Vendler writes, "Herbert conceives of his reader, I think, in terms of comparable intimacy, as the poems of *The Temple* say to us, in effect, 'Deare Friend, sit down, the tale is long and sad.'" To which I want to reply Yes! and Aha! Because in this sentence Vendler has eloquently hit upon a crucial insight that ought to greatly complicate the notion of Invisible Listeners. The problem is that Vendler seems not to notice she has done so.

If *we* are addressed by Herbert with "comparable intimacy," then perhaps we, too, are, like Jesus, the poet's Invisible Listeners. If so, do we hold this privileged status by virtue of our being invisible, beyond the sphere of Herbert's social world? Do we qualify, in Vendler's terms, as Invisible Listeners because we exist in Herbert's distant future, nearly four hundred years after he writes? But to say so would be to suggest that Herbert felt a deep distinction between readers of his own day—persons whom he could imagine reading his poems during his lifetime or immediately after his death—and us in his distant future and that the implication of this distinction would be that Herbert would aim his poems at us and *not* at his contemporaries due to some imaginative or spiritual inadequacy of those contemporaries. Such a suggestion might have a limited plausibility in the case of a bitterly frustrated and alienated poet, such a poet as Dickinson is often (misleadingly) portrayed to be. But in the case of Herbert, it is preposterous. When the dying Herbert instructed Nicholas Ferrar to preserve *The Temple* if the poems would be helpful to "any dejected poor soul," Herbert did not have in mind only those of us who are spiritually needy in the twenty-first century.

Poems seek readers. Poems are social acts in relation to anticipated readers.

To insist on that is not to deny that poems arise often out of loneliness and always out of a sense of something drastically missing from the chatter and pragmatic communications and silences of our daily lives. In her chapter on

Whitman, Vendler suggests that his poetry moves from an early excitement about possible erotic companionship in the present to a later, disappointed sublimation whereby he imagines companionship with someone invisible in the future. "Only after the physical fails does Whitman become a poet of intimacy with the invisible. Sometimes unable to secure, and always unable to sustain, actual sexual intimacy, Whitman is driven to invent an intimacy with the unseen; the poet is cast toward the lover-in-futurity by the faithlessness of the lover-in-the-present."

Vendler's chronological model here is probably not simply false, if we understand the point to be about a shift of emphasis rather than the decisive turn that Vendler's phrasing implies. But obviously, in some of the Civil War poems, Whitman is still yearning toward a listener in his actual present experience—see, for instance, "O Tan-Faced Prairie Boy." Conversely, Vendler cites passages from the 1855 version of "Song of Myself" as instances of Whitman speaking—already—to someone absent from quotidian experience. She quotes these lines: "This hour I tell things in confidence, / I might not tell everybody but I will tell you," observing that "he addresses his invisible listener . . . . The poet's unseen confidant becomes one of an elect group, a group capable of infinite growth."

If Whitman's alleged chronological turn from visible to invisible addressees is so easily shown to be an unreliable claim, why would Vendler hazard it? I think it's because she is so emotionally drawn to the idea of loneliness as a generating force for poetry that she is strongly tempted to posit relatively pure, desperate, hopeless versions of this motive. (This happens also in some of her memorably persuasive but determinedly bleak readings of Wallace Stevens.) Her wish to find Whitman in certain poems yearning for contact with an unreachable absent auditor leads her to ignore or dodge the basic complexity of the question *To whom are poems addressed?* The answer, I say, is that *any* poem—or let me say any serious poem—is *always* addressed both to readers in the present and to readers in the future. The serious poet—Herbert, Whitman, Dickinson, Hopkins, Stevens, Mandelstam—always hopes the poem will find at least a few rightly sensitive, sympathetic, insightful readers in his or her present world. (Whitman hoped for thousands; Dickinson counted on a chosen few and had to imagine others.) Such readers may be geographically far away but they are not invisible in the sense Vendler defines. Some of them are friends or rivals or colleagues or critics, *and* some of them are felt to be "out there somewhere" in the poet's contemporary earthly reality. At the same time, the serious poet also always hopes the poem will reach the unseen sympathizer in ages hence, "the reader-in-futurity" (in Vendler's phrase). Poems are meant to be durable speech, speech built to last. Poems seek human readers both visible and invisible. Meanwhile, it can also be true of some poems that they address very specific listeners (explicitly addressed as "you" or "thou") who may be presently actual, even if hard to reach (Astrophel addressing Stella), *or* ontologically remote (Herbert addressing God or Death). All of these attempted communications can be attempted with less or more of what Vendler calls "intimacy."

What I've said in the preceding paragraph might be called clumsy truisms, yet this sorting out is necessary in order to clarify what Vendler has and hasn't done in *Invisible Listeners.* Insofar as she sticks with a firm definition of the kind of poems she sets up as her topic—(1) explicit address to the listener; (2) ontological unreachability of the listener; (3) personal warmth or intimacy in the address—the topic should remain quite narrow, with rather rare examples in Herbert or Whitman or any other poet. But Vendler wants the topic to be large, and this requires letting keywords become fuzzy and unstable—*address, invisible, intimacy*—and also *colloquy,* a word she uses where *dialogue* would not ring true, to mean utterance that evokes a sense of possible dialogue though only the poet is speaking. The fuzziness allows her to imply distinctions (between her selected poets and most other poets) and parallels (between Ashbery and either Whitman or Herbert) that don't finally convince.

There is no reason to deny that Vendler points rightly to the reader-in-futurity as Whitman's Invisible Listener in "Full of Life Now" and that Whitman's outreach here is eerie, eerily warm in its attempt to transcend time; you nearly feel his breath on your neck.

> To one a century hence or any number of centuries hence,
> To you yet unborn these, seeking you.
>
> When you read these I that was visible am become invisible,
> Now it is you, compact, visible, realizing my poems,
>   seeking me,
> Fancying how happy you were if I could be with you and
>   become your comrade;

Be it as if I were with you. (Be not too certain but I am now
   with you.)

Vendler comments, "Yearning toward someone who may not be born for some years or even hundreds of years hence is, as we have seen from the examples of Hopkins and Dickinson, a feeling not uncommon in lyric, but Whitman carries it further than any poet before or since." Okay, but I want to say that what Whitman does in "Full of Life Now" is to give brash epitomizing blatancy to a motive intrinsic to all lyric, rather than merely "not uncommon in lyric."

Yet it would be ingenuously misleading to suggest that in writing and publishing "Full of Life Now," Whitman is not concerned with its effect on present readers as well as on future readers. A poet's yearning for human connection through poetry never confines itself only to readers whom it would be literally impossible for the poet to meet on earth. That's why what Whitman does in poems like "To a Stranger" is to give naked epitomizing blatancy to a motive as intrinsic to all lyric as the motive to attract posterity's interest.

Passing stranger! you do not know how longingly I look upon you,
You must be he I was seeking, or she I was seeking, (it comes to me
   as of a dream,)
I have somewhere surely lived a life of joy with you, . . .
I am to wait, I do not doubt I am to meet you again,
I am to see to it that I do not lose you.

Here, manifestly addressing someone imagined to be alive in Whitman's New York, Whitman has the nerve to crystallize a message that every poem addresses (albeit less wetly, less alarmingly) to those of the poet's contemporaries who will have the sensitivity to listen.

In arguing that poems always imply both present and future human addressees, I don't want to smudge the fact that a poem may press especially toward one or the other. "To a Stranger" tilts toward present readers; "Full of Life Now" tilts toward future readers. Whitman's most compelling address to the reader-in-futurity is in "Crossing Brooklyn Ferry," and Vendler devotes several good pages to this inexhaustibly great poem. Rather than belabor my point that "Crossing Brooklyn Ferry" is also aimed at New Yorkers and other Americans of 1856 ("Consider, you who peruse me, whether I may not in unknown ways be looking upon you"), in this case what I want to question is Vendler's emphasis on Whitman's sexual longing. Having organized her topic with a stress on intimacy and having emphasized Whitman's great wishful power to evoke erotic companionship and sexual intimacy, Vendler colors Whitman's address to a future listener with sexual desire, whereas the poet's imaginative relation to later generations in "Crossing Brooklyn Ferry" is wider, more generous and complex than sexual desire; I think it's slightly condescending to Whitman to imply that what animates his imagining of future passengers across the river is sexual fantasy. Maybe Vendler's term *intimacy* promoted this dubious implication, though of course, intimacy does not have to be sexual, as Vendler indeed notes in her chapter on Herbert.

Despite all these objections, Vendler should get credit for showing a tenuous but interesting similarity between Herbert's warm addresses to God and Whitman's warm addresses to us. What about the third star in her trio?

Herbert, Whitman . . . and Ashbery? I think one impulse behind a roster like this is the impulse to reject the idea that we have no great poets in English since Yeats, Frost, Stevens, and Eliot. Appraising the generation of poets after them, you can make the case for Auden or Bishop or Lowell; I've often wanted to make the case for Jarrell; cases are made for various poets born in the late 1920s (Ashbery's generation). But I think if you have a deeply informed sense of the greatness of Yeats, Frost, Stevens, and Eliot, then there has to be a nervous strain, a tense misgiving involved in your effort to locate comparable greatness in a poet whose work has appeared since, say, 1940. Like Vendler, I love the idea of greatness, and I'm repulsed by the notion that in some politically salubrious way we have outgrown the idea of greatness. Surely, surely, with so many of us, hundreds and hundreds of poets! working so hard and publishing so much in these decades—1960s, 1970s, 1980s, 1990s, and passionately onward—surely someone must be great? Well, maybe. Time will tell. The truest assessment will be made (I hope) by readers in the mid-twenty-first century and beyond (if mega-capitalism still allows a few thousand citizens to focus their careers and inner lives on poetry). But I don't want to kid myself, and I'm wary of coronations. To my mind, several of my own mentors and friends are among the more plausible candidates if we look for greatness emerging today. Much remains to be seen. But perhaps a critic who has a genius for recognizing and advocating greatness in poets of the past—a critic like Vendler or Harold Bloom—and who moves among all the well-known poets of the day, such a critic may feel an irresistible urge to nominate a living poet as great, or nearly so, or at least to discuss the living and the great dead in similarly appreciative terms. The equipment cries out to be used. One result is clusters like "Herbert, Whitman, and Ashbery." No living poet has benefited more than Ashbery from our craving for greatness in the present.

How does Ashbery get into a book about poems that intimately address a listener who is imagined as a beloved companion? His ticket is a single poem, one of his most famous, "Self-Portrait in a Convex Mirror." Vendler calls it a "poem of colloquy." She writes about it as if it were splendidly coherent and as if the essence of this coherence were Ashbery's imagining of friendly relation with Francesco Parmigianino, the sixteenth-century artist who painted the painting that inspired the poem. There are in fact five spots in this seventeen-page poem where Ashbery directly addresses the painter, on a first-name basis. There are also long passages in which Parmigianino is referred to in the third person and even longer passages in which Ashbery meditates on, or metaphorically evokes (and evokes and evokes), the gap between one's experience and any representation of that experience. If a good Italian translation of this poem could be handed across the centuries to Parmigianino, I wonder if he would feel intimately addressed by it? Well, Vendler prompts us to hear the friendly tone of artist-to-artist comradeship in the "Francesco" passages. She finds that the painting has "fostered the solacing illusion of direct communication between a dead artist and a living viewer, so much so as to compel the American beholder to think of the artist not as the dead art-historical 'Parmigianino' but as a kindred spirit, the 'Francesco' who forsook mimetic realism—in the crucial presentation of his own body in a self-portrait—for a candid acknowledgment of the distorting optics of every enabling aesthetic."

To say that I find this only mildly convincing is not to say that I have an interestingly different interpretation of the poem. I can't bear to seek one; I don't want to wade any longer in those seventeen pages, which, all in all, give me the blur-buzz sensation that has been Ashbery's main offering for decades and decades and of which he is not only the supreme purveyor but also the supreme describer:

> You are allowing extraneous matters
> To break up your day, cloud the focus
> Of the crystal ball. Its scene drifts away
> Like vapor scattered on the wind. The fertile
> Thought-associations that until now came
> So easily, appear no more, or rarely. Their
> Colorings are less intense, washed out
> By autumn rains and winds, spoiled, muddied,
> Given back to you because they are worthless.

That's well said, though it doesn't awaken in me a craving to hear the same feeling expressed hundreds of different ways. Oh Francesco, I mean John, must the blur-buzz always paralyze us?

Rather than struggle with "Self-Portrait in a Convex Mirror," now I just want to remind us of what has often been noted, that the poem is—notwithstanding my remarks about blur-buzz—actually extremely uncharacteristic of Ashbery's poetry, as he has readily acknowledged in interviews, precisely because it deviates so much from his mainstream of extraneous vapors. (As Larissa MacFarquhar says in her *New Yorker* profile of Ashbery, "He finds its essayistic structure alien to the rest of his work.") To some extent, "Self-Portrait" does present an evolving meditation on art and life; the poem thinks in front of us—very different from ladling out a comic pastiche that imitates the sounds and gestures of thinking. The poem's thinking could perhaps be more clear without loss of beauty, but it is there, and not just in teasing eruptions. Whereas the vast majority of Ashbery's poems refuse to sustain thinking, "Self-Portrait" is an anomaly in his oeuvre. And insofar as it is addressed caringly to an identified individual Other ("Francesco"), the poem is doubly un-Ashberian.

To admit that, though, would be to highlight the flimsiness of Ashbery's inclusion alongside Herbert and Whitman. Instead, Vendler needs something besides the Francesco cordiality to justify putting Ashbery at third base in her All-Star infield. She discovers another invisible listener for him. Guess who? The reader!

Excuse me? Yes, the reader—not "in futurity" but you and me, today. But wait—are we invisible? Well, we don't attend certain parties in New York . . . .

But in Vendler's Ashbery chapter the criterion of invisibility disappears from the program (except as regards dear Francesco, who has been dead so very long)—and yet the phrase "invisible listener" doesn't disappear because, after all, it's what the book is supposedly about. Vendler jettisons the focus on listeners who are ontologically out of reach without acknowledging that she is doing so. If The Reader is the kind of Listener we're talking about, then *every* poet belongs equally in the discussion, no?

(You might suppose at this point that explicit direct address to the reader, as in Jonson's "Epitaph on Salomon Pavy" or as in Frost's poem "Not Quite Social," would become the key criterion; Vendler invokes Ashbery's riddling poem "Paradoxes and Oxymorons" as an example. But she wants to make a much wider claim about his relation to the reader.)

The claim is that Ashbery's relation to the reader is wonderfully special; "many of his poems are acutely conscious" of the reader. Vendler declares that Ashbery solves the problem of how the lyric poem can "summon into its solitary precinct a sense of our changing society at large, so as to make us, as readers, intimate not only with the author as a private fellow-sufferer but also with his social predicaments (and therefore, by implication, with our own)." He solves this problem, she says, "by his enormous lexical range." In other words, because Ashbery freely tosses anything and everything into the Rio Grande of his poetry and because he leaves it up to us to make sense of it by tremendous exertions of wit ("the loop of co-creation between Ashbery and his reader is indispensable if the reader is to follow and understand his poetry"), Ashbery speaks to us *intimately*—kind of like Herbert addressing his "Sweetest Saviour."

To me, that all seems utter balderdash. I don't mean that Vendler is insincere. Rather, I think she is trapped in the goo of an attraction she committed herself to in the 1970s and has been unwilling to stop justifying ever since.

Speaking of goo traps, I warn myself now not to try to tackle the entire old issue of Ashbery's alleged meaningfulness here. Whenever I imagine writing about Ashbery, the word that comes to mind is *quagmire:* my troops will go in there, get stuck fighting from street to street, win a series of useless skirmishes while suffering endless ambushes, and by the time I concoct an exit strategy, we'll be bedraggled and embarrassed even if God was on our side. (Don't push the metaphor—Ashbery and Vendler are both imperial powers compared to my pesky insurgency.)

Let me say that seldom have I felt less intimately addressed than by Ashbery's poetry. The waiter or waitress telling me about today's polenta dish feels more intimate. In principle, I have to grant that Ashbery's poems are addressed (in the sense I emphasized earlier in this essay) to the reader, to us, as all poems are, but among all the poets I've read extensively, Ashbery is the one who *least* gives me the sense of a serious effort to communicate, to tell me something he wants me to grasp. Every good lyric poem gives you the feeling of someone looking you in the eyes and trying to reach you. (Often by telling it slant, yes—to reach *you* in that way, as Dickinson does—*success* in circuit lies.) (I respect John Stuart Mill, but he was wrong in his oft-quoted assertion that the lyric poem should be thought of as speech overheard.) Instead, reading Ashbery in quantity is like listening to a witty Portuguese gentleman who has ingested a loquacity drug and (glancing at you very rarely) talks to you all day in Portuguese, a language you studied briefly many years ago.

Oh, but there are blips of English amid the postmod Portuguese. Ashbery is brilliant, and every few pages, he throws a gleamy fish to the credulous reader who hungers for Meaning. Usually, these morsels amount to generalizations about his basic sense of life as chaotic flow. Vendler has shown many times over the years that a passage of five or eight lines here or there, lifted out of the Ashberian floodage, expresses a curl of wry insight or sly parody or recognizable emotion with panache and even grace. What she cannot show—because even to attempt it would be utterly exhausting and would lead only into a wilderness in which *anything* always has an endless exfoliating array of metaphorical "meanings"— is that her selected passages come at importantly right moments in structures (poems) whose elements all contribute purposefully and satisfyingly to an accumulated meaning larger than that of the enjoyably graspable passage.

Ashbery thus (in eight out of nine poems) fails a test that has been beautifully passed, as Vendler has deftly demonstrated, by every great or near-great poet she has ever praised—yet in Ashbery, this failure seems to Vendler not only excusable but somehow commendable. 'Tis strange.

One of the very few Ashbery poems Vendler invokes specifically in *Invisible Listeners,* besides "Self-Portrait," is "Grand Galop" (like "Self-Portrait," it dates from the mid-1970s, many Ashbery books ago; you could almost suspect that Vendler hasn't detected any irresistible intimacies in later Ashbery). From this poem of 162 lines, Vendler quotes 6 lines, to illustrate how the poem is a "history of emotional life." I won't argue with her take on those 6 lines (must dodge quagmire!); I note, though, that the passage she selects, 7 pages into the poem, is kicked off by this line that she doesn't quote: "Ask a hog what is happening. Go on. Ask him." And a few lines after the selected passage come these lines:

> It seems only yesterday that we saw
> The movie with the cows in it
> And turned to one at your side, who burped
> As morning saw a new garnet-and-pea-green order propose
> Itself out of the endless bathos, like science-fiction lumps.

Now, if you paid me enough, I would explain how this contributes to a history of emotional life, not just Ashbery's but yours (you pulled some weird all-nighters near the end of twelfth grade, didn't you?), but I wouldn't believe it. (As for that hog, well, we are all as baffled by life as a squealing farm animal—see?)

Vendler knows better than to attempt a complete paraphrase-and-explication of a long thing like "Grand Galop" (she smells a quagmire, perhaps). She'd have to make a case for these lines early in the poem:

> Water
> Drops from an air conditioner
> On those who pass underneath. It's one of the sights of our town.
> Puaagh. Vomit. Puaaaaagh. More vomit. One who comes
> Walking dog on leash is distant to say how all this
> Changes the minute to an hour.

Do you feel the intimacy?

Maybe there could be a way to argue that Ashbery's poetry is "intimate" with us without arguing that it makes sense—without arguing, that is, that the poems as purposeful coherent wholes convey particular meanings about life. (By particular, I mean any meanings more specific than Ashbery's Ur-meaning of our endless befuddlement.) You'd have to argue that the intimacy transcends any meaning expressible in statements—as if, say, that Portuguese gentleman were endlessly nuzzling your ear or as if he had become a murmur inside your head. But Vendler doesn't want to celebrate Ashbery in any such gaga way. She has never joined the postmodern chorus that thanks Ashbery for showing how we can never really say or understand anything. What's so strange, and in a way touching, is that Vendler has persisted in praising Ashbery as if he were a poet basically like Herbert or Whitman or all the other poets who make earnest, urgent, paraphrasable declarations about life. (Such declarations are *not* the same as what Vendler has called—propping up a straw adversary for Ashbery—"the expository flatness of the assertion of doctrine or ideology.")

Vendler's critical practice everywhere implies what I believe to be true, that every good poem can be paraphrased. If the poem is difficult or deep, or both, the paraphrase will need to be much longer than the poem and will always feel somehow flat and dreary and reductive next to the poem—that's why we wanted the poem! But still you can say to someone, "Here's what I think the poem means"—you can put it into words, and what you say will be different from what you'd say about any other poem. When you encounter a wonderful poem, awed silence may be a right initial response, but then it wants to be talked about, and a necessary part of that talk is the paraphrasing.

I agree with Vendler (and every other good critic) on that, and if an enflamed line were to be drawn between formalist explicators and postmodernist blur-buzz boosters, I'd be on Vendler's side of that line. But Ashbery is a poet for the other side. Vendler's desire to claim him for our side goes way back; in her long essay on him in her 1988 book, *The Music of What Happens,* Vendler does some very selective paraphrasing and then stakes out her bold position: "I have been extracting chiefly the more accessible parts of Ashbery, but it is possible to explain his 'hard' parts, too, given time, patience, and an acquaintance with his manner." And a few pages later, she notes that Ashbery gets called a surrealist: "But surrealism cannot be parsed into sense, and Ashbery can—a process one finds laborious at first, but then increasingly natural, as one gets the hang of it (if my own experience is typical)."

That position, set forth in 1988 and still unretracted (many Ashbery books later), is some mixture of credulous wishfulness and professorial bluffing. (If we don't understand Ashbery, sentence by sentence, it must be because we haven't tried as hard as Vendler has?) It has led her into advocacy for Ashbery that is quixotically inappropriate. Larissa MacFarquhar bases the following overview on conversations with Ashbery:

> He's trying to cultivate a different sort of attention: not focused, straight-ahead scrutiny but something more like a glance out of the corner of your eye that catches something bright and twitching that you then can't identify when you turn to look. This sort of indirect, half-conscious attention is actually harder to summon up on purpose than the usual kind, in the way that free-associating out loud is harder than speaking in an ordinary logical manner. A person reading or hearing his language automatically tries to make sense of it: sense, not sound, is our default setting. Resisting the impulse to make sense, allowing sentences to accumulate into an abstract collage of meaning rather than a story or an argument, requires effort. But that collage—a poem that cannot be paraphrased or explained or "unpacked"— is what Ashbery is after. (*New Yorker*, November 7, 2005)

The meaning of the word *meaning* in the phrase "abstract collage of meaning" is an elusive elixir; it would have to be "the sensation that something very literary and suave is going on without any strings attached and nothing to worry about." The issue of Ashbery's meaningfulness is not identical with the issue raised by *Invisible Listeners* of his alleged intimate, caring relation with the reader, yet the two issues are deeply related in Vendler's mind—and in my mind as well. If someone cares about you, how can he or she use language in ways that show and enact this caring? Well, I guess someone could entertain you with nonsense; the Lewis Carroll of "Jabberwocky" seems to me appealingly affectionate. Apart from mere entertainment, though, human caring in language will show itself in rich and vigorous offerings of meaning; such offerings may be discursive, or they may be fabulously metaphorical; they may be mysterious because the truth they pursue is mysterious, but they invite understanding.

Reviewing Ashbery's book *Where Shall I Wander*, Vendler gamely stays on the horse: "I have offered these synopses to show that Ashbery does make sense if we can tune our mind to his wavelength—something I am not always able to do, but which is exhilarating when that precarious harmony of minds is reached" (*New Republic*, March 7, 2005). She is honest enough to admit that some of the new poems puzzle her—"But I remind myself that time brings about not only the fading of failed experiments but also the wonderful clarification of passages that were perplexing on first appearance."

Posterity will care enough to judge, I hope. Which brings me to an odd thing: *Invisible Listeners* has very few endnotes, but I'm in one of them! I guess I should feel honored, and yet—something is a little off. In the endnote, Vendler is mentioning, in order to set it aside, the complaint that poets don't deal enough with issues of social injustice. She cites me as someone who has objected to "the presumed poverty of social reference of the lyric." This must allude to my book *Stevens and the Interpersonal* (1991), in which I argued that the value of Stevens's poetry is limited (not spoiled) by his chaste avoidance of all problems involving difference between persons. Vendler may think my approach was naive in some ways, and she might be right. Also in that book, though, I argued at length that Stevens is admirably respectful and helpful and *sociable* (even if not intimate) in relation to the reader, and I developed this argument through an extended contrast between Stevens and Ashbery, including challenges to Vendler's view of Ashbery. (I'm not sure I'm glad to find myself paddling in the same teapot so many years later.) If room was going to be made in *Invisible Listeners* for an endnote citing Halliday, of all people, you'd think the focus would be this Stevens-Ashbery discussion. Instead, Vendler's endnote, without actually mentioning my book on Stevens, quotes from an interview in which I speculated on posterity's view of Ashbery: "I think that from the perspective of the year 2040, Ashbery will be a curiosity, an astonishingly copious curiosity, and smart people in 2040 will find it sweetly baffling that smart people in the 80s and 90s took Ashbery so seriously. His work is delicious, in small servings, as a release from meaning, giving us a playground where we feel, for awhile, that we can survive on only the whiffs of meaning" (*Writer's Chronicle,* February 2002). Since that bit doesn't focus on "poverty of social reference," why would Vendler choose to quote this of all things? Could it be because she begins to suspect I'm right?

But maybe I'm right only for *some* readers of 2040. A poet friend of mine gets tearful with joy when he thinks of Ashbery's work. (Dear friend, sit down, you're acting kind of strange.) Near the end of her Ashbery chapter, Vendler says this true thing: "Poems constitute their invisible listeners as persons who understand, who will complete the expressive circuit of thought and language initiated by an artwork, and who will engage in the imagined ethical modeling of an ideal mutuality."

Yes. *All* poems do that. An interesting comparative book could be written about how some poems and poets do that more humanly and tellingly than other poems and poets.

DAMNED GOOD POET

On Kenneth Fearing

In order to appreciate some good but narrow writers, you need to adopt a temporary acceptance of their worldview, a willingness to postpone your possible complaint about the writer's limitations of sympathy or blind spots or addiction to certain images or attitudes; you need this willing suspension, not only of disbelief but of judgment, so that you'll be able to stay alert while reading, alert enough to notice the variations, shadings, wiggles of emotion and meaning, enacted by the writer *within* his or her narrow range of effects. Well, I suppose what I've said can be applied to the task of reading *any* writer, since any writer (except perhaps the greatest—Shakespeare, Homer, Dante, Chaucer, Tolstoy?) can be described as narrow in some sense. Be that as it may, there are certain writers, writers who will be labeled "minor" by an awfully pragmatic and taxonomic posterity, who especially deserve and repay a provisional acceptance of their limited "take" on life. Kenneth Fearing (1902–61) is such a writer.

Thanks to the long-overdue publication of Fearing's *Complete Poems* (1994), edited by Robert M. Ryley, it has become easy for a willing reader to see how good Fearing was. What you have to accept, provisionally, is that in nine out of ten poems, Fearing will be relentlessly panoramic, not focusing intently on any one person's life (especially not on his own) but, rather, producing brisk montages of experience that he presents as typical in American society of the 1930s and 1940s, and pressing grimly toward the bleakest general ideas about that experience, and that he will be aggressively skeptical about anyone's notions of romantic love, heroism, artistic achievement, honor, faith, hope.

If Fearing were mediocre, those sour consistencies of his work would vitiate it or at least render it easily forgettable.

But Kenneth Fearing is a terrific poet. There must be hundreds of people who have known this for a long time, but I didn't find out till 1999, when I happened to pick up the *Complete Poems.* Before that, I'd only noticed a few Fearing poems in anthologies and sort of liked them but allowed myself to assume that Fearing was too dated, too political, too much a Depression-era cultural commentator, to matter anymore. Now I've discovered that Fearing's poetry—in most of the more than 150 poems—survives and transcends its historical period the way great or nearly great poetry does.

In his admirably informative and thoughtful introduction to *Complete Poems,* Ryley summarizes Fearing's turbulent and rather depressing life. Born in 1902, son of a Chicago attorney, Fearing attended the Universities of Illinois and Wisconsin and moved to New York as a freelance writer in 1924; he published the first of his seven books of poetry in 1929. He also published eight novels. Alcoholism contributed to the failure of both his marriages. He seems to have had trouble believing in anything, including love. He had one son by his first marriage. During the 1930s, Fearing published in leftist journals (though also in the *New Yorker* and other mainstream journals toward the end of that decade) and allowed himself to be thought of as a Communist, but he seems never to have invested serious hope in any ideology. His last book of poems appeared in 1948; he wrote very few poems after that; he died in 1961.

As Ryley points out, after the 1930s, Fearing's poetry mostly withdrew both from daring stylistic experiment and from historical and cultural specifics (nearly ignoring the Second World War, the Holocaust, and the atomic bomb). He seems to have felt increasingly jaded and skeptical about poetry's chance to participate in national life. Yet he still wrote good poems.

Indeed, some of his best poems float free from any footnote-worthy links to the 1930s or 1940s and sound as if they could have been written yesterday. Often these poems are shorter than Fearing's typical two- to three-page length. I want to start by praising a few of these "unhistorical" poems, but in doing so, I don't mean that I prefer them categorically to the many good bitter or sardonic poems that bristle with references to urban American life in the years 1926–48.

"Statistics" appeared in the *New Yorker* in 1941, a few weeks before Pearl Harbor. It contains no reference to war, but its burden is a painful awareness of the disappearance of human lives in history.

Statistics

Sixty souls, this day, will arrange for travel to brighter lands and bluer skies.
At sunset, two thousand will stop for a moment to watch birds flying south.

In five thousand rooms the shades will be drawn, with the lamps adjusted,
>   the tables prepared, and the cards arranged for solitaire.
This day, ninety-four will divorce, while thirty-three persons meet great, though
>   unexpected, financial success.
Twenty-one, on this day, will elect to die.

These are the figures, incontrovertibly; such are the facts.
Sixty, two thousand, five thousand, ninety-four, thirty-three, twenty-one.

Actuary of actuaries, when these ordained numbers shall have been fulfilled
>   at the scheduled hour,
What shall be done to prove and redeem them, to explain and preserve them?
How shall these accounts be balanced, otherwise than in personal flesh and
>   blood?

By cold addition or subtraction? And on what fiery comptometer?
Because the need for an answer that is correct is very great.

This poem, with its mathematical conceit, is even more governed by a pretense of distanced, pallid neutrality than most; most Fearing poems allow (as if against their own better judgment) a burst or two of startling, zany, or intemperate phrasing. Still, "Statistics" efficiently displays several elements typical of Fearing's work.

Above all, there is the insistence on panoramic awareness. Fearing always requires himself to register the typicality, or at least the non-uniqueness, of any individual's experience. This is a deep thing in Fearing, a severe and self-chastening compulsion. It summons him to deploy pluralizing phrases in many poems—the "statistics" about "Sixty souls" being a coldly obvious example—which call to mind similar phrases in T. S. Eliot ("the damp souls of housemaids / Sprouting at area gates"). Only fourteen years older than Fearing, Eliot influenced him deeply.

In early poems such as "Morning at the Window," "The Boston Evening Transcript," "Preludes," and "The Love Song of J. Alfred Prufrock" and in *The Waste Land,* Eliot conveyed the depression that flows from an un-dodgeable awareness—an urban awareness—of the awful similarity of millions of lives, all of them drearily present in their physical reality while weirdly absent spiritually.

Whereas Eliot tried to move from this depression toward a beatific resignation to the inevitable, Fearing often colors his Eliotic pluralizings with anger. The anger emerges as sarcasm, contemptuous reductiveness, caricature, cartoony distortion, mocking hyperbole—and this array of angry tones animates some Fearing poems with a nervous energy that Eliot abjured in "The Hollow Men," having been tortured by it in *The Waste Land*. Anger tends to imply that what is wrong in life is not absolutely inevitable. Fearing usually seems to need to declare that misery and failure and disappointment are fundamental and permanent (a view unconducive to political poetry!), yet his anger flares up and suggests that what's bad in life arises partly from historical conditions that may not be sheerly necessary. Thus, there's a fascinating tension in Fearing between his pervasive grimness and his suspicion that someone—the rich, the government, the media—is especially to blame. We might say it's the question of whether he's to be the poet of *his* depression or *the* Depression.

"Statistics" is an example of Fearing's voice attaining a tonal register not far from the gravity of Eliot's "Burnt Norton," yet there is an element of satirical anger in it, audible to the reader who knows Fearing's earlier poetry. "These are the figures, incontrovertibly; such are the facts. / Sixty, two thousand, five thousand, ninety-four, thirty-three, twenty-one." The redundant flatness here evokes the stupid complacency of minds—in government bureaucracy or in popular journalism—that suppose human experience has been adequately responded to when it has merely been tabulated. At the same time, though, such stupid complacency is the bad version of the insistence on panoramic vision and unflinching overviews of entire classes of people that is central to Fearing's originality. In the two lines quoted, Fearing is satirizing the alienated empty-heartedness that is precisely a key danger threatening his own poetic achievement. He was dangerously susceptible to the kind of grim smugness that likes to say that something—especially something regrettable—is "incontrovertibly" true.

The trace of bitterness in "Statistics" is subsumed in pathos. A kind of cool distanced tenderness is one of Fearing's most powerful effects, rendered more affecting by its seeming to have sneaked past the censors of his anti-sentimentality. He addresses a transcendent "Actuary of actuaries" (in Whom he does not believe) and calls for an accounting of human experience in a realm beyond contingency and suffering, an accounting that would provide not mere tabulation but preservation, explanation, and redemption—"Because the need for an answer that is correct is very great." To my ear, the unadorned quality of this last line is beautiful, expressing the stoicism of someone who knows the great answers will not be forthcoming but knows also that the depth of the need for an answer deserves respect. Fearing's line is in the same key as Stevens's "One would continue to contend with one's ideas" or "It can never be satisfied, the mind, never."

The lack of any permanent honoring, the disappearance of the beauties of human experience, is the anguish animating "Memo," my favorite among Fearing's shorter poems.

Memo

Is there still any shadow there, on the rainwet window of the coffee pot,
Between the haberdasher's and the pinball arcade,
There, where we stood one night in the warm, fine rain, and smoked and
        laughed and talked.

Is there now any sound at all,
Other than the sound of tires, and motors, and hurrying feet,
Is there on tonight's damp, heelpocked pavement somewhere the mark of
        a certain toe, an especial nail, or the butt of a particular dropped
        cigarette?—

(There must be, there has to be, no heart could beat if this were not so,
That was an hour, a glittering hour, an important hour in a tremendous year)

Where we talked for a while of life and love, of logic and the senses, of you
        and of me, character and fate, pain, revolution, victory and death,

Is there tonight any shadow, at all,
Other than the shadows that stop for a moment and then hurry past the windows
        blurred by the same warm, slow, still rain?

The yearning in this poem seems more nakedly attributable to the poet himself than Fearing usually allows. The poem doesn't deploy his usual satiric devices for separating the human experience in the poem from any individual lyric speaker representing him. (The dexterity of Fearing's avoidances of the lyric "I" is indeed a crucial factor in his stylistic originality.) As we shall see, Fearing's poetry is full of characters who talk about big things like "victory and death" and who wish to claim that some bit of their own antlike (or mouselike, chickenlike, lemminglike, molelike) activity filled "a glittering hour, an important hour in a tremendous year"—but in "Memo," that "glittering" is not exposed as an absurd tinsel delusion; instead, we are allowed to infer that the poet's heart is equally implied in the need for some lasting record of brief human beauties: "no heart could beat if this were not so." In "Memo," then, Fearing reveals what Wallace Stevens was much more willing to acknowledge: underneath layers of cynicism, jadedness, and negation, there is—at least in anyone who keeps writing poems— an inevitable romanticism still pulsing, watching for rescue. It's true that the question asked by "Memo" summons the realistic answer "No, there is no such shadow"—but this is a poem in which the questioning itself becomes an affirmation of value stronger than the negation of that value's permanence. In the plangency of its need to doubt that our shared glittering must totally vanish, "Memo" strikes a chord struck (in "At Castle Boterel," for instance) by Thomas Hardy, another poet who strove dourly to resist wishful thinking but could not make his mind purely a mind of winter.

The impossibility of maintaining a dispassionate, icily reasonable attitude toward life is expressed in "X Minus X," my third example of Fearing's shorter poems without topical references. In its first and third stanzas, the poem uses one of Fearing's favorite structural devices, the anaphoric elaboration of a subordinate clause that waits in limbo for its controlling statement to arrive. I think this syntactical procedure is a way of representing a life that people mostly can't shape for themselves, a world of people who can't be the agents of their experience and mostly live subordinated to great mysterious forces, whether those forces are political and alterable or—as in "X Minus X"—anthropological and permanent.

X Minus X

Even when your friend, the radio, is still; even when her dream, the
    magazine, is finished; even when his life, the ticker, is silent;

even when their destiny, the boulevard, is bare;
And after that paradise, the dance-hall, is closed; after that theater,
    the clinic, is dark,

Still there will be your desire, and hers, and his hopes and theirs,
Your laughter, their laughter,
Your curse and his curse, her reward and their reward, their dismay and
    his dismay and her dismay and yours—

Even when your enemy, the collector, is dead; even when your counsellor,
    the salesman, is sleeping; even when your sweetheart, the movie
    queen, has spoken; even when your friend, the magnate, is gone.

The poem may be said to amount to a blunt and simple generalization, yet
something in its rhythm, and in its proposed identities (radio/friend, magazine/
dream, ticker/life, boulevard/destiny, and so on), gives it an unsettling authority. It is a vision of the endlessness of desire and dismay, suggesting that they
are the essence of our lives regardless of the ephemeral forms we cherish. "X
Minus X" is a worthy cousin of other good compressed versions of this theme,
such as Hardy's "I Look into My Glass" and Stevens's "The Well Dressed Man
with a Beard" and Dickinson's "It struck me—every Day—" (#362) and Robert
Pinsky's "The Want Bone."

We may imagine that our lives consist in the struggle for X outcome—
attaining a certain lover, publishing a certain book, amassing a certain fortune,
escaping a certain disease or danger—but when that X is subtracted (due to defeat or merely due to the depreciations of time), the result is not zero: we find
ourselves still helplessly throbbing.

Neither the radio (popular culture loaded with the dubious invitations and
promises of capitalist economy) nor the magnate (capitalism itself with its pretense that every diligent worker will succeed) turns out to be a reliable friend.
By placing the word *magnate* so noticeably at the end of "X Minus X," Fearing
calls to mind the issue that was never far from anyone's thoughts in 1934, the
grotesquely unequal distribution of wealth in America. Yet the poem's clear assertion is that no rich "friend" or glamorous "sweetheart" could ever release you
from frustration and yearning.

The poems I've discussed so far are not the most typical Kenneth Fearing poems. By starting with these shorter, less satirical, less 1930s-ish poems, I hoped to discourage easy categorization of Fearing as a political poet, which can quickly become dismissal of him as a dated poet. Fearing may be, in M. L. Rosenthal's justifiable but limiting phrase, "the chief poet of the American Depression," but I'm eager to help spring him from the trap of being considered a poet interesting only in relation to one phase of history. Really, I think this would be easy if my reader had the patience (and I had the stamina) for a very long essay quoting many longer poems in full—because dozens and dozens of them feel vital and valuably disturbing more than ninety years after they were written. To quote only bits from them, I fear, would be less convincing. I realize this complaint about the injustice of brief excerpts is what enthusiastic reviewers always say, but it's especially relevant to a poet like Kenneth Fearing, who writes not in lapidary pentameters but in long lines full of demotic phrases (like Whitman) and who (again like Whitman) relies much less on metaphor than on cumulative rhetorical rhythm and nimble disorienting shifts of tone and perspective.

The inevitability of ongoing desire in "X Minus X" is a distillation of Fearing's pervasive sense of inevitable patterns in human experience—social patterns as well as psychological patterns responding to the social. Many poems evoke overwhelming forces tending to make the individual accept—and be complicit in—harmful and dishonest practices and attitudes. "Conclusion" is a poem about passivity and complacency. Here is the second stanza:

> In the flaring parks, in the taverns, in the hushed academies, your murmur will
> applaud the wisdom of a thousand quacks. For theirs is the kingdom.
> By your sedate nod in the quiet office you will grieve with the magnate as he
> speaks of sacrifice. For his is the power.
> Your knowing glance will affirm the shrewd virtue of clown and drudge;
> directors' room or street-corner, the routine killer will know your candid
> smile; your handclasp, after the speeches at the club, will endorse the
> valor of loud suburban heroes. For theirs is the glory, forever and ever.

We may say that disgust and satiric anger fuel the poem, but the underlying spirit is more fatalistic than any essentially political or satirical poetry could permit. When Fearing says that fools and villains will have the glory "forever and ever," the hopelessness sounds less like his target than like his shelter, his home. Thus, in his attack on complacency, Fearing may be accused of complacency himself, as he cherishes the immutability of what he criticizes. Here are the last six lines of "Conclusion":

> And as you know, at last, that all of this will be,
> As you walk among millions, indifferent to them,
> Or stop and read the journals filled with studied alarm,
> Or pause and hear, with no concern, the statesman vending manufactured bliss,
>
> You will be grateful for an easy death,
> Your silence will praise them for killing you.

Fearing's sense of everyone's complicity in harmful social arrangements does not undo, though it does qualify, his awareness that some people egregiously enjoy and profit from those arrangements. "Dividends" is one of several poems in which he enters the psychology of a winner, a capitalist executive, to expose not only the moral vacuity but the dreary patterned banality of the winner's daily life. "Dividends" tempts us to read it as an interior monologue in the mind of one character (a good later poem, "Engagements for Tomorrow," fits this description better), but the poem is more original and stranger than that. The "speaker" of "Dividends" is better interpreted not as one man but as a state of mind, a worldview shared by many rich men; we might call it a class voice— but this voice is twice interrupted or invaded by a frightening prophetic voice that would seem foreign to the magnate mind.

Dividends

> This advantage to be seized; and here, an escape prepared against an evil day;
> So it is arranged, consummately, to meet the issues. Convenience and order.
>   Necessary murder and divorce. A decent repute.
>
> Such are the plans, in clear detail.
> She thought it was too soon but they said no, it was too late. They didn't trust

the other people.
Sell now.
He was a fool to ignore the market. It could be explained, he said. With the
woman, and after the theater she made a scene. None of them felt the
crash for a long time.

(But what is swifter than time?)

So it is resolved, upon awakening. This way it is devised, preparing for sleep.
So it is revealed, uneasily, in strange dreams.
A defense against gray, hungry, envious millions. A veiled watch to be kept
upon this friend.
Dread that handclasp. Seek this one. Smile.
They didn't trust the others. They were wary. It looked suspicious. They
preferred to wait, they said.

Gentlemen, here is a statement for the third month,
And here, Mildred, is the easiest way.
Such is the evidence, convertible to profit. These are the dividends, waiting
to be used.
Here are the demands again, considered again, and again the endless issues are
all secure.
Such are the facts. Such are the details. Such are the proofs.

Almighty God, these are the plans,
These are the plans until the last moment of the last hour of the last day,
And then the end. By error or accident.
Burke of cancer. Jackson out at the secret meeting of the board. Hendricks
through the window of the nineteenth floor.
Maggots and darkness will attend the alibi.

Peace on earth. And the finer things.
So it is all devised.
Thomas, the car.

The overall effect of "Dividends" strikes me as somewhat muddy, but it is impressive as one of Fearing's experiments in shifts of subjectivity. The point of view that can perceive the capitalist's routine as "A defense against gray, hungry, envious millions" is not the point of view that primly idealizes "Convenience and order" and says "here, Mildred, is the easiest way." The parenthetical intrusion "(But what is swifter than time?)" sounds like a sententious Sophoclean chorus, but it succeeds in complicating the question of whether ideas beyond the Machiavellian seizing of advantage may pass through the mind of a capitalist who does, after all, have "strange dreams." And then the very Eliot-influenced Burke-Johnson-Hendricks passage (echoing the Guiterriez-Boudin-Floret passage in "Animula," which appeared five years earlier, in 1929) injects startling fear into "Dividends," causing us to wonder if the rationalizing plutocrat has a secretly cancerous conscience, buried each day when he summons his chauffeur and carries on with his ostensibly unrevisable plans.

That plutocrat may be culpably complacent in his feeling that the patterns of his life are fixed, but in Fearing's world, *everyone* does less real choosing than he or she imagines and escapes the deterministic grip of economic-social-cultural forces only by means of illusions and delusions—terribly fragile myths proposing the specialness of the individual. Individuals haplessly invest themselves in dreams of wealth, fame, glamour, romantic love, heroism, escape to another world, transcendence via art (including poetry) . . . . When Fearing is sticking to what we might call his official program, all these dreams are debunked, deflated, mocked—exposed as corrupt or exposed as doomed, or both.

> Shall we meet at 8 o'clock and kiss and exclaim and arrange another meeting,
>   as though there were love,
> Pretend, even alone, we believe the things we say,
> Laugh along the boulevard as though there could be laughter,
> Make our plans and nourish hope, pretending, what is the truth, that we
>   ourselves are fooled?

That's a stanza from the third of Fearing's five poems entitled "American Rhapsody." Here is the whole of the fourth poem:

American Rhapsody (4)

Tomorrow, yes, tomorrow,
There will suddenly be new success, like Easter clothes, and a strange and
    different fate,
And bona-fide life will arrive at last, stepping from a non-stop monoplane
    with chromium doors and a silver wing and straight white staring
    lights.

There will be the sound of silvery thunder again to stifle the insane silence;
A new, tremendous sound will shatter the final unspoken question and
    drown the last, mute, terrible reply;
Rockets, rockets, Roman candles, flares, will burst in every corner of the night,
    to veil with snakes of silvery fire the nothingness that waits and waits;
There will be a bright, shimmering, silver veil stretched everywhere, tight,
    to hide the deep, black, empty, terrible bottom of the world where
    people fall who are alone, or dead,

Sick or alone,
Alone or poor,
Weak, or mad, or doomed, or alone;

Tomorrow, yes, tomorrow, surely we begin at last to live,
With lots and lots of laughter,
Solid silver laughter,
Laughter, with a few simple instructions, and a bona-fide guarantee.

Not a subtle poem, I realize. There is no ambiguity to ponder. Fearing knows
there is a magic in the word *silver* for all of us who keep harboring idiotic expectations of transcendence, and he tries to make us gag on the word. Is the poem
too simple to be good? I think it has power—it has a kind of deft purity, a knife-
like directness that reminds me of the best angry poems of D. H. Lawrence.
But the fatalism of Fearing, the sense that he, too, along with everyone else, is
permanently mired in folly, this is not shared by the defiant and disputatious
Lawrence.

"Laughter, with a few simple instructions, and a bona-fide guarantee"—we should note the obvious satire of advertising here, the suggestion that the culture, with its manipulative marketing, has sold us our dreams like quack nostrums or drugs. Satirical jabs at the teasing, hypnotizing, maddening dishonesty of what we now call the media—Hollywood films especially, and also radio, newspapers, magazines, popular fiction, billboards—come frequently in Fearing, and I'll give more examples, but again, I want to recall that Fearing's vision of what's wrong with human life—whether it's a fair vision or not—runs deeper than any one set of historical circumstances, as "X Minus X" suggested. This is my chance to present the amazing early poem "Angel Arms." It appeared in a journal in 1927 and became the title poem of Fearing's first book in 1929. Thus, it obviously can't be called a Depression-era poem, nor does it contain any charge that Hollywood or Madison Avenue or Calvin Coolidge are particularly to blame for the protagonist's being forever humiliated and tantalized.

Angel Arms

She is the little pink mouse, his far away star,
    The pure angel in his sleep,
    With skirts blowing back over stark, bright thighs,
     And knees that are ivory, or white, or pink,
Pink as the little pink mouse, his far away star,
    The pure angel in a deep dream, his lonely girl.
She is going to be Feldman's girl some day.
    No damn immoral scum will ever kiss her lips,
    No crazy black fiend will ever stain her thighs
    With a touch, or a glance,
    Or dare to think of them,
    Not even Feldman,
    Not anyone, she is so clean,
    She is so pure,
She is so strange, she is so clean,
She is a little pink mouse
    Squeaking among the rubbish and dried tobacco juice of black alleys,
    A blazing star among dirty electric lights in warehouse lofts,

A Bible angel smiling up at him from a starched bed,
　　Telling him to be a good, pure Feldman . . That's what he is . .
　　　　That's what he is . .
Do they think he is a woman-faced roach,
　　A walking sewer, with his girl a bottle-fly buzzing on the rim,
　　Do they think he is a hunch-backed yellow poodle
　　Screaming under the wheels of red engines that squawk through
　　　　streets?
Some day he is going to kill all the morons,
　　Be applauded by crowds,
　　Praised in the churches,
　　Cheered by the gang,
Be smiled upon by the little pink mouse, his faraway star,
　　His pure angel with her skirts torn away over blinding thighs,
　　She is going to be Feldman's girl some day.
Hand in hand, heart joined to heart,
　　A new day dawned,
　　Happy and sweet and sunny and pure.
Some hot summer night
　　When the city trembles like a forest after battle
　　And Feldman's brain is an iron claw
　　She will drop from an "L" train sliding through the sky like a
　　　　burning snake
　　And give him the wink, and he will come along . .
He will come along . .
She is the little pink mouse that whispers "Coo-coo, Feldman!"
　　A touch-me-not star,
　　His smiling angel with her soft angel arms
　　Jerking the barbed wire caught in his bones.

Sheesh! It's as if a whole Nathanael West novel were compressed into two pages. I wonder if we glimpse a streak of craziness in the young Kenneth Fearing here. (And occasionally throughout *Complete Poems,* there are jolts of hostility and paranoia that seem over the edge, too frantic or uncalled for to seem satirical or artful; examples are in "American Rhapsody (2)," "C Stands for Civilization," "Net," "Happy New Year," "Dirge.") The roach-sewer-poodle passage in "Angel Arms" comes from somewhere deeper and darker than a cartoon Everyman. Like Tennyson in the later sections of *Maud,* Fearing seems to know insane rage from the inside.

The grotesqueness of "pink mouse" to identify this working-class hero's idealized Daisy makes Feldman seem more deluded and more scary than Fitzgerald's half-heroic Gatsby. "Angel Arms" achieves a volatile bubbling mixture of sympathy with contempt and disgust. If it was influenced by the fascinated revulsion against sexual desire in Eliot's Sweeney poems, it manages to be more complicated than those poems (in one way) by including convincing sympathy for its creepy protagonist. At the same time, we can hardly wish for the ultimate union of the frustrated male with his touch-me-not dream girl. We are not invited to feel that this union, though impossible, is a marvelous beautiful goal that glorifies the quester, as in (for instance) Hart Crane's "For the Marriage of Faustus and Helen." Feldman is no worthy Faustus, and his pink mouse is no Helen.

Lawrence, Tennyson, West, Fitzgerald, Eliot, Crane—my impulse to pile on references to great writers reflects my wish to make you think that Kenneth Fearing should not be too easily consigned to a lower echelon.

His poems that satirize the products and messages of popular culture seem remarkably undated, as relevant to the mass media ethos of the early twenty-first century as they were to the decades when nationally circulated images and messages and products first unified the United States as a "mass culture" society. Consider "Jack Knuckles Falters," published in 1926, Fearing's first very good poem. Just four years after *The Waste Land* (and four years before *The 42nd Parallel* by John Dos Passos), Fearing has mastered the use of interruption to create a sense of the helplessness of the individual caught in the currents of a decadent culture. (Thinkers about postmodernism who want to claim discontinuity as big news in the last ten or twenty or thirty or forty years should be required to notice "Jack Knuckles Falters.") Here is the whole poem:

Jack Knuckles Falters

(*But Reads Own Statement at His Execution While Wardens Watch*)
HAS LITTLE TO SAY
Gentlemen, I
Feel there is little I

Care to say at this moment, but the reporters have urged that I
Express a few appropriate remarks.

THANKS WARDEN FOR KINDNESS

I am grateful to Warden E. J. Springer for the many kindnesses he has shown me
    in the last six months,
And I also wish to thank my friends who stuck by me to the last.
As one who entered his nation's defense

STAGGERS WHEN HE SEES ELECTRIC CHAIR

Five days after war was declared, I was hoping for a pardon from the governor,
But evidently the government has forgotten its veterans in their moment of need.
What brought me to the chair

WILL RUMANIAN PRINCE WED AGAIN?

Was keeping bad companions against the advice of my mother and companions.
How I

WISHES HE COULD HAVE ANOTHER CHANCE

Wish I could live my life over again. If I
Could only be given another chance I would show the world how to be a man,
    but I

"I AM AN INNOCENT MAN," DECLARES KNUCKLES

Declare before God gentlemen that I am an innocent man,
As innocent as any of you now standing before me, and the final sworn word I

POSITIVE IDENTIFICATION CLINCHED KNUCKLES VERDICT

Publish to the world is that I was framed. I
Never saw the dead man in all my life, did not know about the killing until

BODY PLUNGES AS CURRENT KILLS

My arrest, and I
Swear to you with my last breath that I
Was not on the corner of Lexington and Fifty-ninth Streets at eight o'clock.

SEE U.S. INVOLVED IN FISHERY DISPUTE

EARTHQUAKE REPORTED IN PERU

The poem is not interested in whether Jack Knuckles is guilty or innocent. His "appropriate remarks" have a canned quality, but this seems inevitable since they were produced at the behest of reporters whose objective is neatly packageable news, and indeed, Jack is understandably engaged in his own last attempt at spin control. What interests Fearing is the terribly shallow kind of interest felt by Jack's audience, not the prison wardens but the newspaper-reading public. That public is mildly diverted, perhaps momentarily titillated by the image of a war veteran stoutly maintaining his innocence at the moment of his execution, but mostly they just want to read that a bad man has been electrocuted, and in any case, the public's interest is extremely evanescent, ready in a microsecond to be distracted by another headline. "WILL RUMANIAN PRINCE WED AGAIN?"

The capitalized lines in the poem that refer to Jack Knuckles sound like sub-headlines in the newspaper article about his execution, an article jostled in the casual reader's consciousness by various other reports emphatically irrelevant to Jack, and the purpose of those sub-headlines is to guide the reader smoothly and comfortably through the event, including a dash of pathos ("WISHES HE COULD HAVE ANOTHER CHANCE") but not allowing any serious doubt as to whether justice has been done, and leading to the thrill of sanctioned murder. The title of the poem reflects journalism's power—so easily misused—to tilt a set of putative facts toward an appealing digestible inference. "He faltered," the news reader is invited to infer, "because he knew he was guilty, and also because he was a coward, as villains secretly are." There is no invitation to think twice about Jack's punishment or capital punishment in general; on the contrary, the reader's attention is immediately summoned to other stories, which are co-present with the execution story and appear to be just as important or unimportant. Fearing in 1926 (before television, before the internet) is not calling for some practical redesigning of news delivery; he is asking his reader to think about the psychological effect of the simultaneous availability of countless bits of information, all formatted for quick-snack consumption.

"How shall these accounts be balanced, otherwise than in personal flesh and blood?" Along with poor Mr. Knuckles, we need some divinely sensitive registration of our many fates, whereby each of us will be recognized as specially interesting, not infinitesimal like the fish in a fishery dispute or the unimaginably distant peasants of Peru. We need a "fiery comptometer"—it won't be Saint Peter, nor will it be the newspaper; could it be, to some degree, poetry?

Fearing refers very seldom to poetry in his poetry, and then only satirically. Several poems point to the absurd inadequacy of popular literature, its failure to address the realities of tedium and injustice and pain—or failure to do so in ways that will nourish any serious new hope. "Scheherazade" presents a catalog of rejection slips, a catalog of topics for books that we can't use. The first line of this catalog crystallizes Fearing's refusal to write personal lyric poetry, poetry based on an illusion of individual specialness. Notice also, though, that the last line of the catalog turns the attack against Fearing himself, who could sometimes see that cynicism, thickened by alcohol, threatened the value of his work. Here is all but the last three lines of "Scheherazade":

> Not the saga of your soul at grips with fate, bleedingheart, for we have
>   troubles of our own,
> Not the inside story of the campaign scandal, wise-guy, for we were there
>   ourselves, or else we have forgotten it years ago;
> Not all the answers, oracle, to politics and life and love; you have them,
>   but your book is out of date;
> No, nor why you are not a heel, smooth baby, for that is a lie, nor why you
>   had to become one, for that is much too true,
> Nor the neighborhood doings five years ago, rosebud, nor the ruined childhood,
>   nor the total story of friendship betrayed,
> Nor how cynical you are, rumpot, and why you became so.

The concluding three lines of "Scheherazade" call for literature that is useful or clear or deeply new, but Fearing doesn't sound hopeful or expectant like a William Carlos Williams demanding freshly immediate art, and the strange example Fearing gives of something deeply new is (assuming no reference to Babe Ruth, who was already a legend in 1938) an ancient story of exile and steadfast love:

> Give us, instead (if you must), something that we can use, like a telephone number,
> Or something we can understand, like a longshot tip on tomorrow's card,
> Or something that we have never heard before, like the legend of Ruth.

The implication is either that we have lost any connection to sacred texts or that we need new fictions as archetypally resonant as the Old Testament, or both.

Another poem about popular literature, "$2.50" (the price of a new book in 1934) bitterly mocks the kinds of fiction and drama and poetry produced to please an aristocratic "cracker" (slang for a charming playboy) or a liberal "clublady." The poem then declares that the ingredients for such entertainment have been wiped out or discredited by the Depression and (apparently) by imperialism, and finally, the poem undertakes—in a tone uncharacteristically uncynical— to evoke a sense of a possible new literature that would meet the demand of the present.

> But the faith is all gone,
> And all the courage is gone, used up, devoured on the first morning of a home
>   relief menu,
> You'll have to borrow it from the picket killed last Tuesday on the fancy
>   knitgoods line;
> And the glamor, the ice for the cocktails, the shy appeal, the favors for the subdeb
>   ball? O.K.,
> O.K.,
> But they smell of exports to the cannibals,
> Reek of something blown away from the muzzle of a twenty-inch gun;
>
> Lady, the demand is for a dream that lives and grows and does not fade when
>   the midnight theater special pulls out on track 15;
> Cracker, the demand is for a dream that stands and quickens and does not
>   crumble when a General Motors dividend is passed;
> Lady, the demand is for a dream that lives and grows and does not die when
>   the national guardsmen fix those cold, bright bayonets;
> Cracker, the demand is for a dream that stays, grows real, withstands the benign,
>   afternoon vision of the clublady, survives the cracker's evening fantasy
>   of honor, and profit, and grace.

This poem "$2.50" is one to read alongside Wallace Stevens's "Sad Strains of a Gay Waltz" (1935). Both poems powerfully lament the failure of established art forms (symbolized by music in Stevens) to deal with the turmoil of present history, and both hypothesize a new art that will rise to the occasion. But Stevens, in his austere way, is more hopeful than Fearing. Fearing's imaginative experience is much more thoroughly colored by the un-sublimatable realities of national guardsmen, picket lines, and what "$2.50" calls "the flophouse, workhouse, warehouse, whorehouse, bughouse life of man." We can hear Fearing's cynicism seeping back into the poem at the end, where the words *honor* and *grace*—which we'd like to associate with the good dream, the durable dream that would correspond to Stevens's "new music" or supreme fiction—are instead aligned with the word *profit* (a very suspect ideal in a Depression poem) and confined to "the cracker's evening fantasy."

Popular culture, meanwhile, never ceases to sell fantasies, pseudo-solutions to the spirit's yearning, momentary palliatives in the absence of meaning. The insidiously deferential voice in "Radio Blues" is all too familiar to all of us today, we who might have supposed that over eighty years ago, an American's consciousness was safe from the white noise of commercial propositions that we have constantly to filter. This 1938 poem is entirely relevant to the electronic culture of today.

Radio Blues

Try 5 on the dial, try 10, 15;
Just the ghost of an inch, did you know, divides Japan and Peru?
20, 25;
Is that what you want, static and a speech and the fragment of a waltz, is that
     just right?
Or what do you want at twelve o'clock, with the visitors gone, and the Scotch
     running low?

30, 35, 35 to 40 and 40 to 50;
Free samples of cocoa, and the Better Beer Trio, and hurricane effects for
     a shipwreck at sea,
But is that just right to match the feeling that you have?

From 60 to 70 the voice in your home may be a friend of yours,
From 70 to 80 the voice in your home may have a purpose of its own,

From 80 to 90 the voice in your home may bring you love, or war,
But is that what you want?

100, 200, 300, 400;
Would you like to tune in on the year before last?
500, 600,
Or the decade after this, with the final results of the final madness and the final
     killing?

600, 700, 800, 900;
What program do you want at midnight, or at noon, at three in the morning,
At 6 A.M. or at 6 P.M.,
With the wind still rattling the windows, and shaking the blinds?
Would you care to bring in the stations past the stars?
Would you care to tune in on your dead love's grave?

1000, 2000, 3000, 4000;
Is that just right to match the feeling that you want?
5000, 6000;
Is that just right?
7000, 8000;
Is that what you want to match the feeling that you have?
9000, 10,000;
Would you like to tune in upon your very own life, gone somewhere far away?

The insight in this poem is that media mediation of our thoughts eventually transforms them and floats them out of our possession. The time comes when we not only can't shape our own lives; we're not even sure what we'd want if we could. Relentless accommodation of our whims becomes debilitation of our spirits. Like "Jack Knuckles Falters," then, "Radio Blues" is a picture of a world in which the authentic individual voice can't be heard, can't even hear itself, and may indeed cease to exist except as a marketable myth.

How good a poem is "Radio Blues"? I remind myself of what critics often forget, that a poem's handiness for the making of points about cultural and social history is not identical with emotional power, psychological depth, artistic achievement. Is "Radio Blues" too obvious? Like many Fearing poems, it unfolds according to a simple pattern (the list of radio frequencies) and thus can be attacked as an example of "the gimmick poem"—but any wholesale dismissal of catalog devices would cost us lots of great poetry, Whitman being the outstanding example. When Fearing sets up, or gestures toward setting up, a comprehensive catalog, what comes across is the desperation for artifice in a mind seeking brief stays against confusion. What makes "Radio Blues" good is the itch in it. Its catalog of radio offerings is not cleverly predictable. It is audibly driven by the desperation than can underlie what we now call channel surfing, with a sense that "your very own life" has already sunk under the waves.

That same fear drives other good Fearing poems such as "Suburban Sunset, Pre-War, or What Are We Missing?" and "King Juke" (which aggressively presses the question "What have you got, a juke-box hasn't got?") and is anatomized most explicitly and discursively in "Reception Good." At bottom, all of Fearing's poems about cultural media are rooted in the fear that individual agency, individual will, individual creation of meaning—in a society broadcasting easy substitutes for those things and perhaps in *any* society—is impossible.

But surely poetry cannot come into being without some belief in individual creation of meaning? This may be called a Romantic view, but I think Chaucer and Dante and Virgil, while they thanked heaven for their talent, knew they were making something important that no other person could make. And they knew its importance depended on its transmission to others, to readers. Poetry requires a belief that it can be deeply heard, that one person *can* communicate profoundly with another. When his depression and cynicism gripped him too firmly, Fearing ran the risk we might call the Beckettian risk—it could as well be called the Swiftian risk—that dismay and disgust will strangle art. So far, in my anxiety to fend off reductive ways of categorizing and then ignoring Kenneth Fearing, I've touched on this problem only gingerly. But there's no denying that Fearing's work, read in bulk, invites summaries like this by Carl Rakosi: "To him America was already an all-enveloping nightmare in which he felt trapped like a rat and from which he could not awaken." That's too florid and melodramatic, but Fearing (so to speak) asked for it. In a poem called "Class Reunion," he catalogs the failures and defeats of old classmates and says: "White mice, running mazes in behavior tests, have never displayed more cunning than these, who arrived by such devious routes at such incredible ends." In context, *incredible* means all-too-credibly foolish and pathetic, and the failure or folly of any grand or Romantic or even merely earnest aspiration was too constantly credible to Fearing.

Artistic representation of despair can be bracing, even cathartically invigorating, in sudden shots and tours de force. But ongoing relentless despair becomes dreary, in art as in life. Tedium is thus one danger. An opposite danger is hysteria, when despair suddenly blossoms in brief ungoverned hyperbole. This came up in connection with a passage in "Angel Arms," and it comes to mind when "Radio Blues" refers to "the decade after this, with the final results of the final madness and the final killing" (but perhaps we should consider that line more prophetic than hysterical in a poem of 1938!), and when an interruptive all-caps voice in "Happy New Year" says, "BUT IF IT IS TRUE THAT THE NERVE AND BREATH AND PULSE ARE FOR SALE." In a way that would not seem odd to psychologists, the dreary coolness of depression gets intermittently punctuated by hot jolts of hysteria that the depressed person or poet is too depressed to evaluate critically.

Similar alternation between the d-feelings (dreariness, depression, dejection, dismay, despair) and hysteria afflicts the poetry of Weldon Kees, that talented and darkly narrow poet who was a blood brother to Fearing in interesting ways. Kees reviewed Fearing ambivalently in *Poetry* in 1941, complaining that "his repetitions and lists . . . become tiresome and mechanical, degenerating into a facile and overwrought shrillness." This is a case of the pot recognizing the kettle. Kees (1914–55) seems to have burned with an even more debilitating despair than Fearing, or so we are apt to infer from his apparent suicide at the age of forty-one. In satiric poems such as "The Clinic," Kees comes close to Fearing's style, but Kees's main style is grimly iambic and formal; he seems trapped in the style as he seems trapped in bitterness; both Kees and Fearing may be seen as hooked on the despair in early Eliot, but Fearing finds more ways to wriggle on the hook. An example of hysteria in Kees is the ending of "Crime Club"—it's an attractive deft poem about the unsolved murder of a conventional genteel citizen who was secretly lost in anomie, but Kees can't resist having the detective in the case become "incurably insane."

And sits alone in a white room in a white gown,
Screaming that all the world is mad, that clues

Lead nowhere, or to walls so high their tops cannot be seen;
Screaming all day of war, screaming that nothing can be solved.

Those three uses of the word *screaming* sound compulsive, a giving in to temptation.

Meanwhile, the tedium of sourness is more of a limitation for Kees, I think, than for Fearing. In "River Song," Kees's speaker tells of being crucified while life goes on around him.

The bands were playing when they cut me down
By the dirty river where the children cried,
And a man made a speech in a long black gown.

He called me a hero. I didn't care.
The river ran blood and the children died.
And I wanted to die, but they left me there.

In that ending, we hear Kees settling for his alienation. He seems too burned, too far gone, to entertain new thoughts. It's a problem in Fearing, too, as I've admitted. "Engagements for Tomorrow" is a pretty good Fearing poem in the form of an interior monologue by a corporate executive coaching himself to be tough. Here are the poem's last three lines:

Sometime. Soon. Before it's too late.
Because, after all.
And so on, and so on, and so on, and so on.

The poet who writes that last line is in danger—the danger of being too well acquainted with the night so that he cannot separate his voice from the blankness of life without meaning. "Dirge" presents a satiric eulogy for an executive less successful than the one in "Engagements for Tomorrow." Here is the last third of "Dirge":

And wow he died as wow he lived,
Going whop to the office and blooie home to sleep and biff got married and bam

had children and oof got fired,
Zowie did he live and zowie did he die,

With who the hell are you at the corner of his casket, and where the hell're we going
on the right-hand silver knob, and who the hell cares walking second from
the end with an American Beauty wreath from why the hell not,

Very much missed by the circulation staff of the New York Evening Post; deeply,
deeply mourned by the B.M.T.

Wham, Mr. Roosevelt; pow, Sears Roebuck; awk, big dipper; bop, summer rain;
Bong, Mr., bong, Mr., bong, Mr., bong.

That mindless bonging threatens to bong the poet himself, Mr. Fearing, into a kind of death, the numbed condition I called "alienated empty-heartedness" in discussing "Statistics."

Still, as I've suggested throughout, Fearing finds many ways to vary and color his observations of human failure and folly. The comparison with Kees helped me see this. Weldon Kees is an underrated poet, but Fearing is more versatile, more surprising, finally more original. The difference is somehow related to Kees's investment in the Romantic lyrical protagonist—most Kees poems involve a protagonist who, though blighted, is specially blighted, impressively sensitive, whereas Fearing keeps reminding us that each sufferer is like a thousand or million others.

But that comparative point makes me uneasy, since I'm not willing to imply that Fearing is *necessarily* the better poet because he refuses the self-steeped blues of the lyrical "I." Indeed, as I suggested in discussing "Memo," traces of an un-snuffable romanticism contribute crucially to Fearing's poetic power. Against what he purports to consider his better judgment, Fearing sometimes contrives not to quite destroy the possibility of meaningful life, imaginative transcendence, joy—recognizing that "no heart could beat if this were not so."

One instance waiting to be mentioned is the six-page poem "Denouement" (1935), which Robert M. Ryley calls Fearing's only "explicitly Marxist" poem because it imagines masses of people protesting oppression until "millions of voices become one voice." But "Denouement" as a whole is far from being an optimistic battle cry, and it ends with a picture of a world where there is "no light but the lamp that shines on a trooper's drawn and ready bayonet."

Deeper glimpses of hope are those that are more clearly emotional and unpolitical, irrational but necessary, in poems in which Fearing finds a way to avoid blacking the hope with pessimism or cynicism.

If Money

Why do you glance above you, for a moment, before you stop and go inside,
Why do you lay aside the book in the middle of the chapter to rise and walk
　　to the window and stare into the street,
What do you listen for, briefly, among the afternoon voices, that the others
　　do not,
Where are your thoughts, when the train whistles or the telephone rings,
　　that you turn your head,
Why do you look, so often, at the calendar, the clock?

What rainbow waits, especially, for you,
Who will call your number, that angel chorales will float across the wire,
What magic score do you hope to make,
What final sweeps do you expect to win that the sky will drop clusters of stars
　　in your hair and rain them at your feet,
What do you care whose voice, whose face, what hour, what day, what month,
　　what year?

Reading this poem, we expect Fearing to expose all the yearning as folly, but this time he doesn't quite do so; moreover, the poem's title works to imply an affirmation: money (practicality, greedy gain, power) must *not* be all that matters because look how we keep seeking transcendence. Far from being a Marxist poem, "If Money" is an anti-materialist poem. Anti-cynical too. We recall the line in "Scheherazade" rejecting the story of "how cynical you are, rumpot, and why you became so." Fearing occasionally (though not often enough) saw the dead-endedness of cynicism. An early poem "Minnie and Mrs. Hoyne" is a funny and eerie portrait of a cleaning woman named Minnie whose unreflective cynicism—pointedly not so different from the poet's—both disguises and reinforces her secret desperation.

At his best, Fearing knows we can't live without meaning and hope and knows, moreover, that for most of us—no matter how similar we may ultimately be to our neighbors, colleagues, and rivals—meaning and hope will require some sense of one's special individual worth. A poem called "Flophouse," grim but not nihilistic, pivots on the necessity of making meaning out of the meager ingredients in each person's life.

Flophouse

Out of the frailest texture, somehow, and by some means from the shabbiest
    odds and ends,
If that is all there is;
In some way, of even the shaken will,

If, now, there is nothing else left,
Now and here in the pulse and breath,
Locked, somewhere, in the faded eyes, careful voice, graying hair, impassive
face—

Out of the last remnants of skill and the last fragments of splendor,
If nothing else, now, remains,
Somehow there must be another day,
One more week, month, season to be pieced together,
Yet one more year must be raised, even from the ashes, and fanned to warmth
    and light,

Out of so much fantastic knowledge,
Surgeon, engineer, or clerk,
From the rags and scraps of dismembered life;
And if now there is nothing, nothing, nothing,
From even the fatigue sealed deep in the bones,
From even the chill in the oldest wound.

Fatigue and chill seem to have the last word there, until we realize that even they are to be enlisted as last-ditch energy sources in the campaign for renewal of life. Fearing's flophouse is Yeats's rag-and-bone shop.

As I hope to have shown, a key fascination of Kenneth Fearing's poetry is the tension in it between a grim collectivist vision—conveyed more importantly by his determination to eschew any romanticized protagonists than by his few skittish hints in favor of communism—and un-reconstructable romantic individualism. Dramatized in many ways in the *Complete Poems,* this tension is even more pervasive and basic than the tension between depression and anger. The constant presence of both these tensions may tend to make Fearing a narrow poet, yet he is full of surprises within his narrowness. Turning his pages, one feels the kind of excitement David Ferry has described as the pleasure of reading Horace: "How is he going to do it *this* time?"

Deluded egocentrism in other people can seem repulsive, absurd, and perhaps terrifying and did often seem so to Fearing. Besides his many satirical responses to this, he wrote good poems of drastic bleakness in which all hope is felt to be delusion; standouts I haven't mentioned include "4 A.M.," "Tomorrow," and "Lunch with the Sole Survivor." Meanwhile, though, deluded egocentrism in oneself is much harder to identify, to dig out. I love the moments when Fearing implicitly acknowledges that he can't scrape it from his own soul. One more example: "Requiem" is a beautiful poem about imagining the ordinary world after one's own death. The poem refuses to pretend that any immortality or even any specialness can be claimed for the individual who dies, but it honors our astonishment that oblivion is our fate.

Requiem

Will they stop,
Will they stand there for a moment, perhaps before some shop where you have
    gone so many times
(Stand with the same blue sky above them and the stones, so often walked,
    beneath)

Will it be a day like this—
As though there could be such a day again—

And will their own concerns still be about the same,
And will the feeling still be this that you have felt so many times,
Will they meet and stop and speak, one perplexed and one aloof,

Saying: Have you heard,
Have you heard,
Have you heard about the death?

Yes, choosing the words, tragic, yes, a shock,
One who had so much of this, they will say, a life so filled with that,
Then will one say that the days are growing crisp again, the other that the leaves
    are turning,
And will they say good-bye, good-bye, you must look me up sometime, good-bye,
Then turn and go, each of them thinking, and yet, and yet,

Each feeling, if it were I, instead, would that be all,
Each wondering, suddenly alone, if that is all, in fact—

And will that be all?
On a day like this, with motors streaming through the fresh parks, the streets
    alive with casual people,
And everywhere, on all of it, the brightness of the sun.

"Requiem" is simpler than Stevens's "A Postcard from the Volcano," another poem that imagines what our survivors will say of us, but "Requiem" has a candid plangency of its own and is not wiped out in the comparison. Both poems end with sunlight. Stevens often evoked sunlight as the paradox of a heartless benevolence, a blessing from no blesser, a generosity from no philanthropist except ourselves in our eagerness to feel loved. Fearing tried to resist even such equivocal praise of the universe, but when he imagines having lost the world, in "Requiem," his cityscape basks in the unrefusable sunshine of a day whose value ("As though there could be such a day again") becomes visible when it's out of reach. This doesn't mean Fearing's world is revealed to be good, but here Fearing is a long way from "Bong, Mr., bong, Mr., bong, Mr., bong." Here he knows that a lost life does deserve a requiem, as a lived life deserves poems.

KENNETH FEARING
AND HUMAN LIFETIMES

The poetry of Kenneth Fearing (1902–61) is embroiled in—and one is tempted to say devoted to—that range of human feelings that begin with *d*: depression, dejection, dismay, disgust, desperation, despair. Fearing's consistent tendency—across three decades of poetry—to express that limited range of feelings no doubt signals a limitation of his achievement, but it's a limitation much less damaging than has often been suggested. Ever since Robert M. Ryley's excellent edition of Fearing's *Complete Poems* (1994) made me aware of him, I've considered Fearing a drastically underrated poet deserving renewed attention for the intelligence in his bitterness, his irritable versatility within his thematic range, and his convincing unsentimental sympathy for persons beaten down and duped and used up by twentieth-century metropolitan capitalist culture.

In scores of poems, Fearing evokes the pain and confusion of individuals who expected lives of glory, triumph, even ecstasy, to result from their participation in the vast competitive arena of American hustle—in the 1920s, 1930s, 1940s—and who sank instead into frustration, fury, failure. Now more than twenty years after writing the preceding essay, I find myself wanting to write about Fearing again—not with a changed opinion about him but with (naturally) a changed sense of my own stage of life. There are so many good Fearing poems that it's easy to choose examples different from the good ones I wrote about in "Damned Good Poet" in 2001.

Fearing's protagonists are almost never at peace. Sometimes they are immersed in trouble that is felt as emergent and dramatic. Remarkably often, though, a poem's vantage point is looking-back-upon-the-life-that-went-wrong. Such a poem confronts the grim question of what a lifetime has come to—what has it amounted to? What has it all meant? What was it all for? This potentially terrifying question is apt to agitate the sleep and the reveries of individuals in their sixties, seventies, eighties, yet Fearing compulsively brings it into view in poems he wrote in his thirties and forties. He writes in the grip of a premature awareness of the regrets and indignities of old age. He seems irresistibly drawn toward a taking-stock-of-a-lifetime even while observation or intuition tells him that the story is overwhelmingly likely to be a story of depletion, bafflement, and eventual helplessness.

I realize that generalization may not portend a set of poems you especially want to read! Yet by noticing the choices Fearing makes in many of these poems of retrospect on a lifetime, I hope to interest readers in the force and reach of his sympathy with life's losers (arguably all of us sooner or later) down under the skin, in the fretful disappointed heart scarred by many years of thwarted desire. Thus, I write here in a spirit of advocacy as much as of analysis. But is Fearing as good as I will claim he is? As I seek passages to quote from his poems, I worry that the passages may strike a reasonable reader as too blunt, too flat, too predetermined by Fearing's assurance that a life story must be a tale of defeat. Perhaps what I should be worrying about is my own persistent attraction to this poet?

Do I feel that my own life story is a tale of hapless defeat? No! Not mostly—not mainly! Though the question immediately makes me remember certain boxes of papers in my attic . . . . In my five-plus decades of adulthood I have often used my time unwisely and ineffectually—as you have done also, haven't you? In my twenties (especially), I wrote hundreds and hundreds of pages (fiction, poetry, essays) that were under-pondered, jejune, pretentious, skewed by neurotic self-comforting . . . . Okay, that is true. And in some sense, my life ever since my twenties has been shadowed by those hundreds and hundreds of pages (some of them still in the attic), all that poorly used energy—but that is really rather normal for any writer, is it not? The hundreds of hours of misused intellect and half-serious imagining in your younger years or mine do not in themselves ineluctably constitute evidence of a wasted life, do they? "Wasted" compared to what? Compared to the life of monumental achievements we once anticipated, perhaps, or to some coherent goodness and rightness harder to define but seemingly possible.

"Don't have a wasted life / I love you too much"—this line in a 1982 song by Tom Petty has run through my mind a thousand times, as if spoken by me to myself. If that line connects with your own introspective shadows, your flarings of self-reviewing, then you are susceptible to the kind of unhappiness that Kenneth Fearing gave expression to in his retrospective poems.

What has your life amounted to, at the end of the day? Many of Fearing's poems are explicitly or implicitly evening songs, evoking the state of mind of a person worn out by the difficulties of a long day, someone who needs sleep but fears bad dreams or a sleep too deathlike. This crepuscular mood prevails in Fearing's last book of poems, *Stranger at Coney Island* (1948), published when he was not, say, sixty-six years old but only forty-six. "This Day" addresses a protagonist alive "in a numbered house on a street with a name" who has come across a letter he received long ago; he can't recapture the feelings associated with the letter; he is flooded with a sense of evanescence, of the sheer impermanence of his unique experience, a truth that applies pervasively not only to his deep past but to his present moment:

> As though this long but crowded day, itself, could sometime fade,
> Had in fact already slipped through the fingers and now were gone, gone,
> simply gone—
>
> Leaving no one, least of all yourself, to enact the unfinished drama that you,
>   alone, once knew so well,
> No one to complete the triumph, to understand or even believe in the disaster
>   that must be repaired,
> No one to glimpse this plan that seemed, at one time, must, must, must be
>   fulfilled.

That is the end of "This Day." We are left with the crushed realization that the brooder's great plan will not be fulfilled, the drama will not be enacted to its rightful conclusion, the disaster will not be repaired, the desired triumph will never be completed. The poem comes to rest in the finality of the feeling that *it has all come to nothing.* That is a simplifying feeling ("gone, simply gone"), and it offers the cold comfort of simplicity as escape from restlessness. This escaping from the complexities of struggle (struggle for achievement or triumph or love or belief) is the temptation that most endangers Fearing's poetry.

I would have to agree that the firmness of the dismissal of hope at the end of "This Day" renders the poem less interesting than a conceivable poem that would entertain some variety of possible outcomes for the protagonist's med-itation on his past and future. Nevertheless, I call "This Day" a good poem. My admiration for it involves the poem's emphasis on an individual's sense of being *not* merely one-example-among-millions but, rather, someone with an unusual fascinating identity; the poem resorts to four of the words we turn to when we want to assert individuality: *personal, special, particular, unique.* Like Thomas Hardy, Kenneth Fearing feels that the truth he should not dodge re-quires puncturing romantic illusions of the self's specialness. In Fearing, as in Hardy, no one is exempt from time's depredations. Yet both poets, I think, reach greatness by writing with such convincing knowledge of the pathos of the self's wishing. Hardy, in "Afterwards," wonders what people will remember of him after his death.

> If, when hearing that I have been stilled at last, they stand at the door,
>   Watching the full-starred heavens that winter sees,
> Will this thought rise on those who will meet my face no more,
>   "He was one who had an eye for such mysteries"?

Hardy allows that such remembering is possible, but it is not at all guaranteed, and it is a meager sort of immortality for a lifetime of thoughts and emotions. Fearing contemplates the same kind of terribly reductive commemoration in his poignant poem "Requiem." The comparison with Hardy helps me bear in mind the idea that a poet can be great notwithstanding a thematic range that may be considered narrow.

Poets are apt to be forgettable, eventually, like everyone else, but poets are apt to hope that their work attains unforgettable lastingness. Fearing never in his poetry lets himself appear with self-conscious explicitness as poet-writing-a-poem, but he does glance toward that traditional hope "That in black ink my love may still shine bright." Looking back at the long last line of "This Day," we notice that one of the unhappy upshots contemplated is that there will not only be a "plan" left unfulfilled but that there will be "No one to glimpse this plan"—calling to mind the fact that a person craves recognition (in the eyes of other persons) for wishes and strivings even if these wishes and strivings remain unfulfilled. One way to feel *glimpsed* in one's aspirations is to write and publish a poem evoking them. Kenneth Fearing is not only the brooder in "This Day" but the poet who depicted the brooder. The thought that Fearing's identity as poet distinguishes him implicitly from his most abjectly defeated speakers and characters does flare up sporadically in the *Complete Poems.*

But that thread of hope will have to remain tenuous in a poet so alert to the folly of comforting illusions. Fearing detests the prospect of being comfort's fool. This aversion—arising from fear—creates the danger that his attitude toward his thwarted protagonists will become flatly condescending and mocking when he imagines them trying to feel better about their lives. Succumbing to this danger is one version of escape from complexity.

Often the protagonists seem to be current or former business executives whose notions of glory were ravaged by the Great Depression, but Fearing was already attuned to day's-end dejection before 1929. In "Evening Song" (1927), a man named McKade needs to sleep, and the poem advises him on how to relax; the poem's attitude does tilt toward contempt, yet I think "Evening Song" is saved from flat contempt by Fearing's implicit awareness that we all—like the rabbit-self in Stevens's "A Rabbit as King of the Ghosts"—need mental strategies for relinquishing anxiety at the end of the day.

> Take apart your brain,
> Close the mouths in it that have been hungry, they are fed for a while,
> Go to sleep, you are a gentleman, McKade, alive and sane, a gentleman of position.
> Tip your hat to the lady;
> Speak to the mayor;
> You are a friend of the mayor's, are you not?
> True, a friend of the mayor's.
> And you met the Queen of Rumania? True.
>
> Then go to sleep;
> Be a dog sleeping in the old sun;
> Be an animal dreaming in the old sun, beside a Roman road.

You and I, we may not have accomplished what we hoped over the last several decades, but we did have some distinguished minutes, for instance when we chatted with someone famous like the Queen of Rumania . . .

That unexpectedly Roman road beside which the weary dog could sleep registers Fearing's sense that the new American empire burns up individual lives in ways comparable to the exploitations inflicted by ancient empires. *Stranger at Coney Island* includes a monologue entitled "Lanista," spoken by Arius, a trainer of Roman gladiators. Near the end of his long career, in which he has killed twenty-eight adversaries, Arius contemplates the news that on this day the gladiatorial games are to be shut down permanently. Instead of celebrating relief from grotesque violence, the veteran lanista is alarmed by the news—his alarm turns out to be ignited by something deeper than loss of personal glory.

> And knowing as well a certain midnight of the spirit that comes to all, when each,
>> in his cell, must be chained against self-destruction,
> Only to be scourged on the very next day, by whips and red-hot irons, to the
> dangerous fight—
>
> Yet now I hear, with wonder, that none of this has been of any avail,
> These combats have had no meaning and are in fact nothing less than nothing
> at all—
>
> As though the fight between the women and the dwarfs had been for nothing,
> And the combat between the crippled and the blind, had that no point?

Fearing's persona wants to feel that all the grisly lethal events had meaning. His deepest nightmare is not pain or death but sheer waste of lifetime. *All for nothing* is the specter that haunts Fearing's poetry. In the line immediately following this passage, the battered old teacher of gladiators implies a worthy purpose for the dramas of suffering he has organized: "Is it not good that the race shall ever behold itself with pride and disgust, horror and fright?" To help humanity see its human contradictions vividly—this is an educational value to which not only a professional fighter but a poet is likely to aspire. So "Lanista" is implicitly animated by Kenneth Fearing's worry as to the lasting merit of his hundreds of bitter poems written across more than twenty years.

Thus, "Lanista" has an ironic kinship with a career-retrospective poem by a poet who had spent those same decades usually urging humanity to embrace a sense of human meaning derived from imaginative health. Wallace Stevens, in "As You Leave the Room" (1954), worries, anticipating departure from the world, that he has "lived a skeleton's life" dwelling in the fleshless realm of representations. It is a worry that contradicts the confidence about human imagining famously crystallized in Stevens's praise (in 1936) for the singing of a woman on a Florida shore, in "The Idea of Order at Key West"—and the older Stevens is determined to recover promptly from his doubt by way of comfortingly hazy rhetoric, assuring himself that his present experience

> becomes . . . part of
> An appreciation of a reality
>
> And thus an elevation.

Stevens does not have Fearing's willingness to tolerate (or Stevens might say to wallow in) depression or despair; Stevens very seldom allows a poem to *remain* in those conditions; he desires centrally to be an encouraging poet. From his perspective, a poet of the d-feelings, like Fearing, is too limply willing to settle into hopelessness.

When that same complaint is leveled against Samuel Beckett, Beckett's admirers are apt to point to his passionate devotion to literary art as evidence that his vision is not simply nihilistic. Similarly, one narrow reply to the complaint that Kenneth Fearing's pessimism is too pervasively rigid (limply rigid or rigidly limp!) becomes available when we notice that Fearing does occasionally—as in the last line of "This Day"—glance at the hope that representation of empty or blighted lives can give meaning to the life of the representer. At the end of "Lanista," the old choreographer of murderous staged combats is heard reassuring himself that society will not be able to abjure his genre of entertainment. We can interpret his assurance—albeit via the poem's insistently grim metaphor—as a minimal assertion of the necessity and lastingness of art.

Having suggested that, I'm anxious to find other spots where Fearing permits hints of the idea that art (poetry, for instance) is a non-ridiculous generator of value for a person's life. Seeking such spots, I don't mean to suppress the fact that the default ending for a Fearing poem is to debouch upon the abyss of the d-feelings. True, yet the tension between the dominant default demolition of hope and the unkillable wishing for meaning is audible in scores of poems; one example is "A Pattern" (1938), in which the protagonist wakes in the morning with radical ontological misgiving—"The alarm that shatters sleep, at least, is real"—and wants to take stock of the essential pattern of his life. Unlike Stevens's morning hero in "The Latest Freed Man" (also 1938), Fearing's waking man finds that fundamental unknowing does not feel like liberation. Some of us, thank goodness, sometimes sense that new or renewed meaningfulness can be inscribed on the blank slate of a sunny morning, but in "A Pattern," Fearing makes room for such radiance only in parenthesis and only for a second: "(Briefly, here, the recollection of some old, imagined splendor, to be quickly dropped and crushed completely out.)" Within a few lines, Fearing is battering his man with aggressive questions:

> Or are you, in fact, a privileged ghost returned, as usual, to haunt yourself?
> A vigorous, smiling corpse come back to tour the morgues?
> To inspect the scene of the silent torture and the invisible death, and then to
>   report?
> And if to report, are there any different answers now, at last?

I realize that the bitter garish hyperbole of that passage may seem silly to a reader, rather than seriously troubled. My inclination to find poetic depth in the passage has to do with Fearing's nettled edgy taunting of the waking man (a version of himself, surely) whose vitality—privileged, vigorous, smiling—sets him up to be a sucker, deceived by mere animal health. The waking man apparently understands himself to have a task (like an unacknowledged legislator of the world), to inspect and to report, even if what he observes is a scene of misery and even if his findings are repetitive. We hear Fearing alluding to his own sense of poetic vocation—hoping it is not simply absurd but afraid of being suckered.

The naive version of that hope is Fearing's target in many poems. In an early poem called "Portrait," a drinker named William Lowell (no reference to Robert Lowell, who was only twelve years old in 1929, when the poem appeared) seeks refuge through alcohol from nightmarish fears and regrets. The relief the drinker dreams of would involve expression, reportage, representation:

> If the world knew,
> There is a reason for his thousand failures, vows, treacheries, lies, escapes,
> And if the world would hear him,
> William Lowell would be at peace with all mankind for one hour before the white

corridors and echoing streets and staring skulls knew him no more,
William Lowell, the child of blue skies.

Childhood and children almost never show up in Fearing's downtown land-scape. For him, William Lowell's helpless delusion of being still essentially "the child of blue skies" is what Wordsworth's elaborate mythifying of youth must eventually collapse into.

And yet I want to insist that Fearing's attitude toward even a pathetic character like William Lowell is not flatly contemptuous. The man may be weak, but Fearing does not reduce him to a cartoon; he is not driven by the stupid capitalist greed that infects some of Fearing's Manhattan denizens. In these lines from earlier in "Portrait," our poet knows he is portraying self-pity, but he is not mocking so much as identifying:

> If the world knew his life,
> Knew the hundred forces seeking to destroy him;
> If there were an eye of God to see him as he is, know his motives in spite of
> evasion and compromise,
> See him alone in desolate rooms, broken by remorse—

The implication is that if adequate recognition of the damaged person could come—whether from society or from the divine—there *would* be some essential worthiness recognizable.

That baseline human respect, together with sympathy, gives Fearing's poetry a crucial dimension saving it from embittered simplicity—so I've been contending—and there are many poems that offer to be adduced, when I imagine defending Fearing against a critic who would describe him as simply sour and snarky. Here I will look at just three more: "Flophouse," "Invitation," and "Class Reunion."

A man whose career has collapsed and/or a man who has sunk into alcoholism and ruined relationships, such a man in the metropolis may have to live in a cheap boardinghouse or "residential hotel"—a flophouse. Fearing saw many such steep declines around him during the 1930s. "Flophouse" (discussed also in the preceding essay) is among the many Fearing poems that might be cited as expressing dead-end despair, but a careful reading finds that it is, like "Portrait" and "This Day," one of the poems in which Fearing uses suspended syntax to prevent a hopeful possibility from being utterly erased.

Forever wary of the trap waiting in affirmation, the trap of being comfort's fool, Fearing finds ways to hedge and shadow and half-disguise any implication that human beings can be noble and heroic. A reader glancing at "Flophouse" sees that the poem of seventeen lines consists of one long sentence and that its vision is loaded with the broad-brush nihilism in this clause near the end: "And if now there is nothing, nothing, nothing." But truly the heart of the poem, though surrounded by darkness, is this affirmation of rock-bottom human perseverance:

> Somehow there must be another day,
> One more week, month, season to be pieced together,
> Yet one more year must be raised, even from the ashes, and fanned to warmth
>   and light.

The man in the cheap boardinghouse whose work has come to nothing may not be expected to defiantly exult in a place of stone, but Fearing imagines him rising in the morning to assemble *something* undestroyed "From the rags and scraps of dismembered life." Fearing's obsession is the dire tattered version of the daily test of mental health that Stevens contemplated in the opening lines of "The Well Dressed Man with a Beard" (1941):

> After the final no there comes a yes
> And on that yes the future world depends.
> No was the night. Yes is this present sun.

If Kenneth Fearing could have lived to the age of eighty, he could have heard Bruce Springsteen sing "Reason to Believe," a song entirely in tune with "Flophouse"—

> Struck me kinda funny
> Funny, yeah, indeed

How at the end of every hard-earned day
People find some reason to believe.

It makes sense that the critic Mark Halliday, a longtime Springsteen fan, wrote in 2001 that Fearing saw "the dead-endedness of cynicism" and that he was not finally willing to extinguish "un-reconstructable romantic individualism."

You and I like to think that our love relationships give our lives inextinguishable meaning. It is remarkable how seldom Fearing—whose life included two marriages that ended unhappily—turns toward the sustenance of love in his poetry. Romantic love calls for an intense (though preferably not obsessive) focus on the beloved, but Fearing seems to have always perceived love framed by a huge grim social context within which it must all but disappear. His early poem "Invitation" (1929) comes on as a come-on, as if to lay before the woman a panorama of pleasures to be anticipated in romance. Fearing's Passionate Shepherd, though, loses no time evoking the urban environment in his opening lines: "We will make love, when the hospitals are quiet and the blue police car stops to unload prisoners, / We will sleep, while the searchlights go across the sky." And soon the life he offers sounds like a life of crazing vicissitudes: "It will be night when pleasure turns to agony, agony to terror, terror to rage, rage to delight, / It will be morning when we forget."

Nevertheless (here is the *nevertheless* move I keep needing), I feel that I'm not merely foolishly seduced if I say that a hope for the sustenance of tender human relationships is sustained by the last of the three long last lines of "Invitation":

We will be urged by the hunger of the live, trapped by the relentless purposes
    of millions,
With the millions we will know this, and we will forget,
We will be aroused, we will make love, we will dream, we will travel through
    endless spaces, and we will smile across the room.

Those three lines could be felt to describe a marriage that might not fail.

A class reunion, where many a divorce is likely to be acknowledged, is a social ritual almost guaranteed to prompt painful retrospection. (I've avoided all my class reunions, over more than fifty years.) When in the preceding essay I mentioned "Class Reunion"—a poem Fearing published when he was thirty-eight—I quoted the long line that you would quote if you wanted a vivid illustration of his depressive doubt about the chances for individual dignity: "White mice, running mazes in behavior tests, have never displayed more cunning than these, who arrived by such devious routes at such incredible ends." But here what I want to emphasize is that in the poem's quick sketches of five classmates (Steve, Clark, Dale, Elvira, Henderson), we *don't* see that they have abysmally failed. Their lives have turned out to be different from what they once expected or hoped, but their lives have not come to nothing. We hear of classmate Clark that he was once a medical student "who played Chopin and quoted Keats"—and then we get this reflection: "Perhaps Clark did much better in drygoods, to tell the truth, than he would have with surgery or Keats." Is that line fueled by condescending nastiness? I think, instead, we can hear it as dryly realistic while respectful, even mildly affectionate.

And I prefer to hear the poem's treatment of Elvira in the same vein. The first of the two lines about her is lightly sarcastic, but what it recalls about the young woman is like what you remember about yourself or a good friend in long-ago sophomoric days—the poem asks what became of "Elvira, who dealt in nothing less than truths that were absolute?" Fearing could have made Elvira turn out to be criminal or crazy or cripplingly confused—we could call this the Weldon Kees tendency—but, instead, he writes: "It may be Elvira came as close to the thing, with her absolutes, as anyone else. She's the mother of five." Looking at this 1940 poem now, many decades later, we notice that while the male classmates are observed with regard to their careers, the only female classmate is simply seen to have matured into motherhood. Still, the poem does not dismiss but affirms that Elvira's choices may have brought her as close to a meaningful lifetime as anyone else.

Moreover, Fearing could have—in the manner of his often-quoted sarcastic 1934 poem "Dirge"—indicated that the reunited classmates are now forever locked into their limited mundane lives. Instead, he contrives to end "Class Reunion" on a note of eerie possibility, hypothesizing a future encounter for each classmate with "a figure on a dark street" who will represent "destiny moving in still another direction." Admittedly, this shadowy figure makes us think of the destiny that is death, but in the poem's final words, the figure's invitation sounds auspicious rather than murderous: "Tonight something new is coming up. Let's go."

Does a lifetime have to be wasted? Are we doomed to feel that we have wasted our lives? If you insist on comparing yourself with Jesus or Buddha or Plato or Shakespeare or George Eliot or Abraham Lincoln, you can set yourself up for disappointment, but your life will be better—for you and for people around you—if you can imaginatively seek ways to believe in the dignity and worth of your particular human struggle. (Cue Sinatra singing, "I did it my way.") Wallace Stevens knew that such belief can be hard to separate from illusion, but he also knew it is necessary; hence, in his phrase "supreme fiction," the adjective is filled with emotional force. Kenneth Fearing knew this, too, and despite his many dives into depression, disgust, desperation, even despair, he knew that poems can provide a place for rendering belief in a human life's value palpable.

Poems are more likely to achieve this by being movingly crystallized pictures of the struggle toward belief than by the kind of hortatory exclamations that Walt Whitman offered when he was writing at cruising speed, as in "Salut au Monde!"

> Each of us inevitable,
> Each of us limitless—each of us with his or her right upon the earth,
> Each of us allow'd the eternal purports of the earth,
> Each of us here as divinely as any is here.

Even if Whitman had only always written in that manner, we would still be grateful for his energy and nerve and indeed for his encouragement. But Whitman's greatness pulses more powerfully where he admits that depression and despair are not safely foreign to a human lifetime—as in the terrific "dark patches" section of "Crossing Brooklyn Ferry" or the "baffled, balk'd, bent" riff in "As I Ebb'd with the Ocean of Life." Those passages convince us that we are not alone when we wonder whether our lives have cohered into anything significant; we share our anxiety with one of the great spirits in the history of poetry. We need to believe—with Whitman and with Stevens—that we have not lived a skeleton's life; our story is not simply a story of missed opportunity and waste. As Fearing says in an uncharacteristic interjection in his wonderful poem "Memo," responding to the question whether in an intense human interaction there is any lasting importance: "There must be, there has to be, no heart could beat if this were not so." Kenneth Fearing, though we can't call him an American Romantic as positively as we say this about Whitman or Stevens, produced work in his unhappy lifetime that has helped me believe in poetic greatness after the Moderns and thus to go on believing—contrary to his own gravitation toward despair—in the value and importance of human lifetimes, at the end of the day.

KENNETH KOCH AND THE FUN
OF BEING A POET

To be a poet: it is a grave and austere responsibility, is it not? Well, yes and no. If you've been pondering Shelley, Arnold, Rilke, Eliot, Akhmatova, Hart Crane, Sylvia Plath, Paul Celan, Adrienne Rich, or Geoffrey Hill recently, you perhaps feel it is—but even those intensely dissatisfied and sometimes desperate poets must sometimes have felt shots of sheer joy in knowing themselves to be poets and participating in the great endless dialogue of poetry. Perhaps no important poet has more consistently acknowledged the manifold pleasures of the vocation than Kenneth Koch (1925–2002). Throughout his amazingly, indeed almost bizarrely, various poetry, we can always hear Koch's charismatic voice urging us not to deny the fun in poetry—the fun in writing it, reading it, arguing about it, daydreaming about it, knowing it is in the world.

This aliveness to the pleasure of being alive poetically was something Koch shared with his friend Frank O'Hara (1926–66). In a 1995 interview with Jordan Davis, Koch said, "I love the quality in Frank's work that makes its message always that life is so rich, so full of variety and excitement that one would be crazy to think that anything else was the theme and crazier not to participate in it as much as one could." O'Hara, though, died at the age of forty, having already written some poems in which melancholy yearning undermines the ebullience; Koch lived on through another three and a half decades of middle age and early old age, decades in which the splendidness of being young and brilliant naturally tends to give way to other truths of disappointment, regret, and loss. Thanks to Koch's honesty, that concession is a crucial part of the story presented by his work across the years. However, what never disappears from his poetry is the palpable and contagious feeling that to be a poet is great luck. The poet's vocation often induces anxiety, yes, but the anxiety is part of an adventure not to be missed.

To illustrate this vocational happiness in Koch's work, countless examples could be offered; I'll look mainly at passages from four poems representing different phases of Koch's long career. My hope is to evoke a profound healthiness that flows through his oeuvre and invites other poets to acknowledge their own vocational good fortune and take heart.

"A Time Zone," in *One Train* (1994), is a buoyantly nostalgic poem, in impetuously unmeasured rhyming couplets, about the early 1950s; here's a passage referring to his absurdly long poem "When the Sun Tries to Go On":

> I'm smoking it's a little too much I'm not sure I can get through it alone
> Frank and I read each other segments of these long works daily on the phone
> Janice finds it funny now that I've dropped this bunch of pages
> That I can't get them back in the right order well I do but it's by stages
> It is April I have a job at the Hunter College Library
> I come down to the Cedar on a bus hoping to see O'Hara and Ashbery
> Astonishingly on the bus I don't know why it's the only occasion
> I write a poem Where Am I Kenneth? It's on some torn-out notebook pages
> The Cedar and the Five Spot each is a usable place
> A celebrated comment Interviewer What do you think of space? De Kooning
> Fuck space!
> In any case Frank is there he says he likes Where Am I Kenneth?
> I carry this news home pleasantly and the poem it mentions her to Janice
> John's poem Europe is full of avant-garde ardor
> I am thinking it's making an order out of a great disorder
> I wonder at what stage in life does this get harder.

Obviously, that last line dares the reader to say, "It all should have been much harder then!" But Koch felt sure throughout his career that some kinds of difficulty were mere laboriousness or cultivated grimness. In an autobiographical talk in 1994, he said: "I also needed poets who could show me how to avoid dead seriousness, high seriousness. I grew up in a time when T. S. Eliot was, as Delmore Schwartz said, the literary dictator of the West, and not only were you supposed to be serious, you were supposed to be a little depressed. You could read through the quarterlies—the *Kenyon Review,* the *Partisan Review,* the *Sewanee Review*—all the big journals of those days, and nobody was seeing anything at the end of that tunnel. They were not even seeing the tunnel."

Koch's most famous response to that 1950s academic culture is the wonderful poem "Fresh Air" (1956). That is the quintessential poem for my subject, but it has so often been cited that I'll emphasize other examples of Koch's candid demonstration that excitement and humor and joy are involved in being a poet.

As a professor at Columbia in the late 1960s, Koch (like all his colleagues) found the protest movement against the Vietnam War dominating the daily atmosphere—everything was political, and every activity, including the writing of poetry, was called upon to oppose LBJ and then Nixon and the majority culture supporting them. Instead of hiding from this demand, Koch devised a way of responding to it vigorously without violating his central intuition that war only mattered because it interfered (horribly) with the infinite potential joys of living. He wrote a sixteen-page poem entitled "The Pleasures of Peace." Though he made sure it was goofy and unpredictable, he had a vivid sense of how the politically righteous people around him would strive to assimilate it into their culture of protest. Here is the second segment of the poem:

> "I love your work, *The Pleasures of Peace*," the Professor said to me next day;
> "I think it adequately encompasses the hysteria of our era
> And puts certain people in their rightful place. Chapeau! Bravo!"
> "You don't get it," I said. "I like all this. I called this poem
> *Pleasures of Peace* because I'm not sure they will be lasting!
> I wanted people to be able to see what these pleasures are
> That they may come back to them." "But they are all so hysterical, so—
>   so transitory,"
> The critic replied. "I mean, how can you—what kind of pleasures are these?
> They seem more like pains to me—if I may say what I mean."
> "Well, I don't know, Professor," I said; "permanent joys
> Have so far been denied this hysterical person. Though I confess
> Far other joys I've had and will describe in time.
> And then too there's the pleasure of *writing* these—perhaps to experience is
>   not the same."
> The Professor paused, lightly, upon the temple stair.
> "I will mention you among the immortals, Ken," he said,

"Because you have the courage of what you believe.
But there I will never mention those sniveling rats
Who only claim to like these things because they're fashionable."
"Professor!" I cried, "My darling! my dream!" And she stripped, and
　　I saw there
Creamy female marble, the waist and thighs of which I had always dreamed.
"Professor! Loved one! why the disguise?" "It was a test," she said,
"Of which you have now only passed the first portion.
You must write More, and More—"
"And be equally persuasive?" I questioned, but She
Had vanished through the Promontory door.

The dialogue in the first half of that passage is lightly satirical—while at the same time expressing Koch's refusal to be heavily satirical. The Professor assumes that the poet must intend to be some sort of social critic and must want to be defined in opposition to "sniveling rats" or some other "certain people." Having developed a satirical portrayal of this Professor's attitude, Koch then twists the poem quickly away from the comfortable clarity of that point. This is Koch's most characteristic impulse: to suddenly swerve, diverge from a path of meaning before its foam congeals. (Ashbery's trademark maneuver can be similarly described, yet the flavor is quite different; Ashbery's swerves are smoother, more oiled and at-first-invisible; Koch's are more itchy, noisy, jarring, impetuous.) "'Professor!' I cried, 'My darling! my dream!'" It seems the Professor's flattery—"I will mention you among the immortals, Ken"—has abruptly bypassed the poet's defenses, touching him at the quick, in his fantasy of sublime greatness. Koch's comic rendition of this sudden enthrallment is the revelation that the Professor is actually a goddess of beauty (since nothing is more beautiful or more sexy than the sudden intimation of immortality). The comedy here contains a self-insight that many a much-published poet might well own up to, or be embarrassed by.

The goddess instructs the poet in a way that is deliberately and self-satirically a burlesque diminishment of Moneta's instructions to Keats: "You must write More, and More—"; this is not intimidating advice for a jazzed-up young (or forty-four-year-old) poet interested in pleasure. In these lines, Koch seems aware of his deep-seated resistance to any somber requirement that he must register the sufferings of all mankind. Now, we do need poets who will attempt that, but we also need poets capable of registering the connection between ambition and egotism, capable of brashly cutting through sobriety lest it dry into piety.

Before Ken can receive more challenging guidance, the goddess conveniently disappears: "She / Had vanished through the Promontory door." Through the what? I don't think Koch cared about any specific meaning for *Promontory* here—he just wanted an elevated-sounding adjective with a nicely iambic rhythm. If so, then *Promontory* is a tiny flash of the zany impulsive nondiscursive Koch flaring up within a discursive or narrative passage.

And there are many more such flarings in "The Pleasures of Peace"—indeed, nonsensical high jinks dominate the poem. However, the bit that follows right after the *Promontory* passage is very discursive, a foretaste of the hyperdiscursive essay poems to come in *The Art of Love* (1975).

> So now I must devote my days to The Pleasures of Peace—
> To my contemporaries I'll leave the Horrors of War,
> They can do them better than I—each poet shares only a portion
> Of the vast Territory of Rhyme. Here in Peace shall I stake out
> My temporal and permanent claim. But such silver as I find
> I will give to the Universe—the gold I'll put in other poems.
> Thus in time there'll be a mountain range of gold
> Of considerable interest. Oh may you come back in time
> And in my lifetime to see it, most perfect and most delectable reader!
> We poets in our youth begin with fantasies,
> But then at least we think they may be realities—
> The poems we create in our age
> Require your hand upon our shoulder, your eye on our page.

This passage charmingly shows the balancing between modesty and ambition in the poet's view of his effort—his awareness that his claim is "temporal" versus his desire to believe it is "permanent." We notice that he intends to invest any "gold" his poem discovers in his own future poems, while the less sublime "silver" he will donate to the world. Arrogant self-involvement is consciously and nakedly expressed here—along with the feeling that art is more important than the temporal Universe. But by the end of this passage, pride has slid down-hill fast into a sense that the aging poet (forty-four in 1969) will be dependent on gently sympathetic readers. (The note struck here anticipates the elegiac tones of later discursive poems that I especially love.)

Ten pages later in "The Pleasures of Peace," Koch seems to have won a com-petition with a poet named Giorgio Finogle—both poets having tried to pro-duce the ultimate peace poem. We get a parodic montage of readers' responses.

> "A wonder!" "A rout!" "No need now for any further poems!" "A Banzai
>   for peace!" "He can speak to us all!"
> And "Great, man!" "Impressive!" "Something new for you, Ken!"
>   "Astounding!" "A real
> Epic!" "The worst poem I have ever read!" "Abominably tasteless!" "Too
>   funny!" "Dead, man!
> A cop out! a real white man's poem! a folderol of honky blank
>   spitzenburger smugglerout Caucasian gyp
> Of phony bourgeois peace poetry, a total shrig!" "Terrific!" "I will expect
>   you at six!"
> "A lovely starry catalogue for peace!" "Is it Shakespeare or Byron who
>   breathes
> In the lines of his poem?" "You have given us the Pleasures of Peace,
> Now where is the real thing?" "Koch has studied his history!" "Bold!"
>   "Stunning!" "It touches us like leaves
> Sparkling in April—but is that all there is
> To his peace plea?" Well, you be the one
> To conclude it, if you think it needs more—I want to end it,
> I want to see real Peace again! Oh peace barns!

I love the quick-footed moves of that catalog—they give a vivid taste of 1969, a year when everyone had a loud opinion.

That passage also sounds quite like some of the hilarious passages in Koch's "Fresh Air," which burns with comic exasperation at the stodginess of professor-poets trying to establish themselves as junior Eliots and Pounds. It's interesting to note, meanwhile, that though "Fresh Air" is zany and rebellious and satiri-cal, this 1956 poem as a whole is much more coherent and indeed disciplined

than the late-1960s "Pleasures of Peace." In 1956, Koch could feel unquestion-
ably brave and special as a radical sort of poet, along with a few others such as
O'Hara and Ashbery, and Allen Ginsberg. By 1969, *radical* suggested dozens of
stances in relation to America, and all sorts of people in art and politics claimed
noble outsider status; "The Pleasures of Peace" seems a poem written amid daz-
ing cacophony.

Koch was never embarrassed by the obvious reality that the most engaged
readers of one's poetry will be people who write poems or want to write poems;
thus, to write poetry about being a poet can be a choice fundamentally generous rather than narcissistic. The title poem of *Days and Nights* (1982) consists
frankly of an accumulation of notes and conversational pensées about the life
of poetry.

> You've got to sit down and write. Solved!
> But what I write isn't any good. Unsolved!
> Try harder. Solved! No results. Unsolved!
> Try taking a walk. Solved! An intelligent, pliable,
> Luminous, spurting, quiet, delicate, amiable, slender line
> Like someone who really loves me
> For one second. What a life! (Solved!) Temporarily.

What is the bright critic to say about that bit? It's another of Koch's countless
expressions of the nervous excitement of creation. Some stiffer poets have offered scores of pages of raptly self-observing prose that essentially say no more
than Koch says in those seven lines. Candidly, he acknowledges the similarity—
or indeed the siblinghood—between artistic energy and romantic-sexual energy. As, again, in these three lines from earlier in "Days and Nights":

> *Extase de mes vingt ans—*
> French girl with pure gold eyes
> In which shine internal rhyme and new kinds of stanzas.

The glory of being twentysomething—brimming over with unmeasured
undefined potentialities (creative, and sexual)—was the implicit subject in most
of Koch's early poetry and then became increasingly an explicit subject, haunt-

ing each of his later collections, starting with *The Art of Love* (1975) and *The Burning Mystery of Anna in 1951* (1979). The shift is audible if we juxtapose the following passage, from "Days and Nights" with the "Pleasures of Peace" passage quoted earlier, both of them concerning the fecklessness of public response to the poet.

> I said to so many people once, "I write poetry."
> They said, "Oh, so you are a poet." Or they said,
> "What kind of poetry do you write? modern poetry?"
> Or "My brother-in-law is a poet also."
> Now if I say, "I am the poet Kenneth Koch," they say "I think I've heard of you"
> Or "I'm sorry but that doesn't ring a bell" or
> "Would you please move out of the way? You're blocking my view
> Of that enormous piece of meat that they are lowering into the Bay
> Of Pigs." What? Or "What kind of poetry do you write?"

By 1982, Koch found himself remarkably unfamous (except as the author of *Wishes, Lies, and Dreams,* his book about teaching poetry to children), while his old friend John Ashbery was becoming strangely famous. The passage just quoted is part of an admirably humorous and graceful response to that fate, a response Koch sustained with both clarity and lightness in his later books, not succumbing to resentment or bitterness. (Long-delayed recognition did come in the last years of his life, including the Bollingen Prize in 1995.) It's true that the Bay of Pigs passage could be categorized under the heading of Nursing One's Ego, but many a poet does this covertly—or transparently pretends not to care. I find Koch's candor not only refreshing but invigorating—it gives that Koch sensation of a cutting through into new oxygen.

And a four-line bit lower on the same page of "Days and Nights" gives that sensation too, and if chalked on blackboards in poetry workshops could obviate many tedious hours of canned discourse:

> You must learn to write in forms first, said the dumb poet.
> After several years of that you can write in free verse.
> But of course no verse is really "free," said the dumb poet.
> Thank you, I said. It's been great talking to you!

New oxygen flows from the deflation of pomposity. Hundreds of Koch passages are apposite; let's turn to his early poem "The Artist," which appeared (along with "Fresh Air") in *Thank You* (1962). The speaker of this poem is some sort of avant-garde landscape artist and conceptual sculptor, a genius in his myth of himself. The fact that this persona is not a poet seems to help Koch convey a sweetness within the absurdity of the artist's egomania. The eight pages of "The Artist" present his diary entries recording vicissitudes in his career and illustrating his boundless self-absorption.

> I often think *Play* was my best work.
> It is an open field with a few boards in it.
>
> Children are allowed to come and play in *Play*
> By permission of the Cleveland Museum.
> I look up at the white clouds, I wonder what I shall do, and smile.
>
> Perhaps somebody will grow up having been influenced by *Play,*
> I think—but what good will that do?
> Meanwhile I am interested in steel cigarettes . . . .

The egotistical innocence of this speaker calls to mind the wonderful comic characters acted by Christopher Guest in the films *This Is Spinal Tap* and *Waiting for Guffman.*

A page later: "*Play* seems to me now like a juvenile experience!" The Artist is at work on a project called *Bee,* which is "a sixty-yards-long covering for the elevator shaft opening in the foundry sub-basement / Near my home." In the next passage, he frets about comments on his work.

> June 8th. *Bee* is still not finished. I have introduced a huge number of red balloons into it. How will it work?
> Yesterday X. said, "Are you still working on *Bee?* What's happened to your interest in steel cigarettes?"
> Y. said, "He hasn't been doing any work at all on them since he went to Cleveland." A shrewd guess! But how much can they possibly know?

Such passages, like those I've quoted from "Days and Nights" and "The Pleasures of Peace," don't cry out for professional analysis. Koch never had the Ashbery knack of tantalizing the reader with just enough traces of meaning so that the professional explicator senses a potential article and pops open his or her tool kit. Instead, Koch's oeuvre veers between abundant charming clarity, on the one hand, and obviously unprofound silliness, on the other hand. (There are lovely hybrid exceptions, such as "Hearing" and "Locks" and "At Extremes.")

The gentle satire and self-satire in Koch's many lucidly comic passages about poets and artists demonstrate that one can be obsessively—and sophisticatedly—devoted to poetry while at the same time alert to the pomposities and delusions of poets and very ready to expose those pomposities and delusions in one's own poetry—*not* in a spirit of crushing one's enemies but in a spirit of sharing in the susceptibilities being exposed.

The Artist worries about *Bee* for another page, and then we get the following two passages (apparently separated by considerable intervals of time):

I just found these notes written many years ago.
How seriously I always take myself! Let it be a lesson to me.
To bring things up to date: I have just finished *Campaign,* which is a tremendous
    piece of charcoal.
Its shape is difficult to describe; but it is extremely large and would reach to the
    sixth floor of the Empire State Building. I have been very successful in the
    past fourteen or fifteen years.

* * *

Summer Night, shall I never succeed in finishing you? Oh you are the absolute
    end of all my creation! The ethereal beauty of that practically infinite number of white stone slabs stretching into the blue secrecy of ink! O stabs in
    my heart!

. . . Why not a work *Stabs in My Heart?* But *Summer Night?*
January. . . . A troubled sleep. Can I make two things at once? What way is there
    to be sure that the impulse to work on *Stabs in My Heart* is serious? It seems
    occasioned only by my problem about finishing *Summer Night* . . . ?

A delicious moment of pure Koch—a touch that would not be easy to imitate, a touch that a lesser satirist would have overplayed—is in the flow from "Empire State Building" to "I have been very successful in the past fourteen or fifteen years." This Artist may suffer heart stabs and insomnia, but we feel sure he will be happy in his self-myth for a long time. His happiness involves his feeling of endless possibility, his feeling that there is nothing he cannot do in art, sooner or later. Throughout at least the first half of his career, Koch felt the same way.

But it would be wrong to imply that in his vocational pleasure, Koch was simply oblivious of suffering and the darkness of twentieth-century history. The emphasis on pleasure was a choice among possibilities, as Koch strikingly acknowledges at one point in the Jordan Davis interview: "In an Eliot-dominated poetic ambience, even the slightest sensations of happiness or pleasure seemed rare and revolutionary poetic occasions. If happy, positive, excited poetry were the 'scene,' I might have been looking for the nuances of the losses and sorrows in my life for the subjects of poems."

Ultimately, I think Koch's greatest power comes when optimism and brashness rub up against time, fatigue, defeat, and loss. I hear a delicate truth of this friction evoked in the last stanza of "Days and Nights."

> Z said It isn't poetry
> And R said It's the greatest thing I ever read
> And Y said I'm sick. I want to get up
> Out of bed. Then we can talk about poetry
> And L said There is some wine
> With lunch, if you want some
> And N (the bad poet) said
> Listen to this. And J said I'm tired and
> M said Why don't you go to sleep. We laughed
> And the afternoon-evening ended
> At the house in bella Firenze.

The longest day of enjoyable talk must dwindle at last. Sad, yet Koch's presenting of this realization in this confidently, suavely "unpoetic" passage affects me as both comforting and encouraging in the lightness and honesty with which it celebrates the *bella vita* of poetry.

Whatever the fluctuations in his sense of the size and importance of his own talent, Koch never lost his feeling that to be a true poet is fabulous good fortune. My impression is that this feeling is more rare, and more tenuous, among poets born since, say, 1960. Why? The all-too-obvious answers involve the emergence of new arenas where language can be dazzlingly employed and displayed for huge audiences: television, the internet, and pop music in its many flavors. When I wonder why my poet friends and I feel less gloriously lucky to be poets than Koch and O'Hara felt and why our students seem mostly even less sure that their calling is grand, I think particularly of the overwhelming charisma of rock 'n' roll. A young writer in the early to-mid-1950s might admire Frank Sinatra or Ella Fitzgerald or Elvis Presley or Little Richard but probably never felt these singers (who were not mainly songwriters) constituted powerful competition in brilliant use of language as such. The great rock music of the 1960s—which, I note with generational pride, is still enjoyed today by my thirty-something son and his friends—dished out terrifically engaging lyrics (along with, of course, stupid lyrics; every art always has its wannabes and hacks) so abundantly that the line between *song* and *poem* came to seem much less definite. Well, maybe this sense of overlap between song and poem was inspired in earlier decades by Cole Porter, Noel Coward, Ira Gershwin, Johnny Mercer—each generation has its brilliant songwriters; still, sixties rock is so loaded with lyrics that propose to show *a deep spirit speaking from the heart* that ever since, a young person writing poetry is likely to think, "But maybe I should learn guitar!" As a boomer rock fan, I can't regret this, but I do feel some envy for the cheerfully brash poet-pride of Koch and O'Hara. (It is so different from the anxious tense striving of Roethke, Berryman, Jarrell, Lowell, Schwartz.) Koch never tolerated the idea that Bob Dylan was great. I tried several times in the 1990s to interest Koch in some of Dylan's songs, and to point out a few similarities between the songs and his poems, but Koch couldn't even begin to take the comparison seriously. This sort of deafness was salubrious for Koch's ego, I suggest, in a way that is less possible for twenty-first-century poets writing amid a constant storm of pop songs *and* infinite internet hypertexty discourse, all saturated with postmodern awareness of our cacophony of wit: always already a dozen other voices wielding one's metaphor du jour. But Kenneth Koch's vocational pride and satisfaction should not be defined or dismissed as nothing but a dated flaring of 1950s-fostered male egotism. Emily Dickinson, though she was a poet of suffering more often than not, had no doubt that to be a poet was to be a wondrous source of happiness, of life.

> I reckon—when I count at all—
> First—Poets—Then the Sun—
> Then Summer—Then the Heaven of God—
> And then—the List is done—
>
> But, looking back—the First so seems
> To comprehend the Whole—
> The Others look a needless Show—
> So I write—Poets—All—

Surely Emily Dickinson felt joy as she wrote those lines, an unreasonable sort of joy not bothered by the claims of composers, painters, novelists, architects, or any other creative spirits who try to give humanity something sublime. One doesn't want to be unreasonable all the time, but in occasional doses, this joy—felt so abundantly by Kenneth Koch in the 1950s and often enough thereafter—is a lucky and invigorating thing for a poet to feel.

KENNETH KOCH AND ELEGY

Suddenly in 1975, when Kenneth Koch was fifty years old, a current of elegy emerged in his poetry, with "The Circus" (II), and this elegiac current flows in each of his later books and becomes the central force driving his best collection, *New Addresses* (2000), published not long before his death from leukemia in July 2002 at the age of seventy-seven. I think Koch's most lasting poetry, and one of his strongest claims to greatness, is his elegiac poetry. (In this discussion, *elegiac* has the broad meaning of concern with loss of what was good in the past, rather than the narrow meaning of lament for the dead.) This would not be an odd thing to say about some poets, but it's a remarkable thing to say about the poet who for so long—brashly throughout the first half of a long career and ambivalently throughout the second half as well—understood himself to be a poet of excitement and joy, celebrator of the pleasures, thrills, and comedy of romantic, sexual, aesthetic, and intellectual adventure.

Many commentators have noted the new dimension brought into Koch's poetry by "The Circus" (II); Koch particularly called attention to the poem's self-questioning, self-revisioning quality by naming it after his earlier poem ("The Circus," in the 1962 collection *Thank You*) and by placing the new poem first in his unexpectedly discursive and lucid 1975 collection, *The Art of Love*. Still, the significance of "The Circus" (II) as a breakthrough in Koch's oeuvre is made dramatically visible in a new way by *The Collected Poems of Kenneth Koch* (2005). Such thick *Collected* volumes can be awkward and cumbersome, but they do serve a purpose, and not only for scholars; in Koch's case, to see the poems printed chronologically, book after book within one big volume, is not only to see the restless experimental variety of his work but to see a poet growing into maturity and depth almost "against his will"—that is, against the powerful magnetism of his devotion to his youthful iconoclastic brilliance.

Most of us look back on our twenties and thirties with some nostalgia, and no doubt there is a similarity among everyone's memories of those years: we were so foolish, so confused, so amusingly volatile, but also so energetic, so bright, so *full of life!* We were discovering ourselves! These common denominators, of course, must tend to make our poems of nostalgia for youth turn out to be trite. All right, but triteness threatens the expression of *any* deep current of human feeling; there must be a way for nostalgic poetry to be good, even great. Koch wades boldly into this problem in his elegiac poems, beginning with "The Circus" (II)—so boldly, indeed, that at times he seems not to notice the danger that his own nostalgia might be too much like anyone else's. In order for anyone to keep writing poems, it is necessary to develop and cherish a myth of one's own uniqueness: "*My* response to all this loss or sorrow or doubt or danger or joy is *not* the same as anyone else's!" To sense such myth building in a poet's work across many decades is only to notice something normal and indispensable; it becomes embarrassing or repellent only when we realize the myth has ballooned too far from reality. In Koch's elegiac poems, we sense the nursing of the myth, but this comes mixed with remarkably clear quavers of worry: *Am I still the man who was so marvelous then?* And even more disturbing: *Was that man so entirely marvelous as I've thought?*

In the second "Circus," Koch is trying to recall the full reality of his life at the time when he wrote the first "Circus"—in Paris, in 1954. Some twenty-one years have passed between that excitable time and the publication of "The Circus" (II) in 1975; a man in his late forties, puzzled to be no longer young, is remembering the life of a twenty-nine-year-old man. The younger man was newly married to a woman named Janice, and the older man addresses the elegiac poem to her, after they have separated. Here is how the poem begins:

I remember when I wrote The Circus
I was living in Paris, or rather we were living in Paris
Janice, Frank was alive, the Whitney Museum
Was still on 8th Street, or was it still something else?
Fernand Léger lived in our building
Well it wasn't really our building it was the building we lived in
Next to a Grand Guignol troupe who made a lot of noise
So that one day I yelled through a hole in the wall
Of our apartment I don't know why there was a hole there
Shut up! And the voice came back to me saying something

I don't know what. Once I saw Léger walk out of the building
I think. Stanley Kunitz came to dinner.

There are some readers who could never be convinced that those are lines of good poetry, lines that could constitute the first eighth of an extremely good poem. Readers whose crucial values for poetry are compression of phrasing, elevation of language, and density of metaphor can't be won over to such talky discursive poetry. In response to those readers, I say that other values can sometimes be crucial for me and that I find the opening of "The Circus" (II) to be compelling.

Why? My impulsive answer is to say that in those lines we hear the voice of a real person. But the point needs to be made more carefully. It's not that talky discursiveness and a sense of personal presence necessarily go together. Would I want to imply that in Shakespeare's sonnet "That time of year thou mayst in me behold" we hear the voice of an "unreal" person or that we don't "hear" a "voice" at all? Those two propositions immediately collapse. Shakespeare certainly creates a voice; we feel we can hear its human tones. At the same time, we are conscious of the artful elevation and compression of the sonnet's language. Shall I say that in those opening lines of "The Circus" (II), Koch has jettisoned artfulness, so as to give the poem over entirely to imitation of real-life talk? Well, clearly he is experimenting with shifting the poetry farther along the spectrum toward sheer echo of real-life talk—farther in that direction than, say, Frost, who went farther in that direction than Wordsworth, who went farther than Pope, who went farther than Shakespeare (in the sonnets), who went farther than Spenser . . . . But when I look carefully at Koch's lines, to understand why I like them so much, they don't seem artless; instead, they seem artfully to imitate artlessness for the sake of creating the complexly believable character who is the poem's speaker and subject.

Like a person thinking aloud in real life, Koch is already correcting himself in the second line of the poem, realizing that the pronoun *I* is misleading and unfair:

I remember when I wrote The Circus
I was living in Paris, or rather we were living in Paris
Janice . . .

The point of leaving the self-correction visible is to help us hear the voice; we get a sense of a man speaking extemporaneously, and we get a hint that this man has a tendency to forget the claims of other people when he's thinking about his own achievements and adventures. In the next moment, his mind jumps from Paris to New York—the city he and Janice left for their Paris sojourn and the city in which he now tries to remember that period: "Frank was alive, the Whitney Museum / Was still on 8th Street, or was it still something else?"

The location and previous name of the Whitney Museum are not logically needed for the poem's evocation of the Paris life in which Koch wrote "The Circus" (I), but there is a psychological truth in the associative flow that links Paris, Janice, Frank, and the museum—all aspects of the good life that was; all connections that Koch was and is proud of as components of his marvelous story: he lived and wrote for a while in Paris, he had an interesting marriage, he was well informed about the visual arts, and he had a brilliant close friend— Frank O'Hara—whose death in 1966 has contributed (by the time of writing "The Circus" [II]) to a sense of the irretrievability of the good life long ago. Paris, Janice, Frank, the Whitney—glowing panels in a collage of long-ago happiness.

Writing "The Circus" (II) in 1975, does Koch take for granted that the reader will understand "Frank" to be "Frank O'Hara" and will agree that Frank was important? Yes, he probably does; unless it's truer to say that Koch isn't really interested in readers who wouldn't know about O'Hara. For him, the name Frank is radiant with significance. I wonder if Koch would argue that someone else's poem about having lived an exciting year in, say, Kalamazoo or Dublin and having lost a friend named Herb or Gerry *could* be very good and could appealingly include in passing the phrase "Gerry was alive"? I suspect he would so argue, if the question arose, but it would seem to be a question that did not especially arise for him. His own past seemed special. The egotism is there, but it makes possible the poem.

If he weren't aswim in his sense of having lost a fabulously interesting world, he might not have the courage to set forth (and keep) scraps of memory such as the shouts exchanged with a French actor through a broken wall—the anecdote goes nowhere (though I could argue, if pressed, that it symbolizes the young American's comically limited access to a baffling foreign culture); it's like most of our memories of a happy phase of life: it seems to matter simply because of the larger texture it was part of. And that is analogous to what I claim about many further casual or repetitive or self-indulgent remarks and moves in the poem: they are valuable because the truth of the poem's meditation—Self Portrait of the Poet as a Puzzled Nostalgic Middle-Aged Man—depends on them. Preparing now to quote the next portion of "The Circus" (II), I again feel how impossible it will be to win over readers for whom a poetic poem could never contain the line "You were back in the apartment what a dump actually we liked it." Also, I fear that I could spend so many pages commenting on this poem that the reader's patience will be exhausted before I turn to other elegiac poems by Koch, such as "Fate" and "Seasons on Earth" and "A Time Zone" and "Passing Time in Skansen" and "Currency" and numerous poems in *New Addresses*. I'm writing an essay, not a book, on Koch. Even in a book, though, it would take a kind of nerve to write a thorough appreciation of such a poem as "The Circus" (II) because its one hundred lines are transparently readable, and readers of such discursive poems can resent being coaxed to find more value than they've already noticed. Yet I persist!

Since you and I are—to some extent—egotistical self-mythologizers, as writers and as persons, we shouldn't pretend that the self-concern in these next lines is essentially irrelevant to us.

> I wrote The Circus
> In two tries, the first getting most of the first stanza;
> That fall I also wrote an opera libretto called Louisa or Matilda.
> Jean-Claude came to dinner. He said (about "cocktail sauce")
> It should be good on something but not on these (oysters).
> By that time I think I had already written The Circus.
> Part of the inspiration came while walking to the post office one night
> And I wrote a big segment of The Circus
> When I came back, having been annoyed to have to go
> I forget what I went there about
> You were back in the apartment what a dump actually we liked it
> I think with your hair and your writing and the pans
> Moving strummingly about the kitchen and I wrote The Circus
> It was a summer night no it was an autumn one summer when
> I remember it but actually no autumn that black dusk toward the post office
> And I wrote many other poems then but The Circus was the best

> Maybe not by far the best Geography was also wonderful
> And the Airplane Betty poems (inspired by you) but The Circus was the best.

The man is savoring memories; he is like someone showing us an old photo album and providing more detail than we would have asked for. He loves the memories, though at the same time he loves his uncertainties—"an opera libretto called Louisa or Matilda"—there is a pleasure for him in such uncertainty, for several reasons: first, it's delightful to feel that one could rather easily write a libretto entitled either "Louisa" or "Matilda" or indeed both (or is it that the libretto was entitled "Louisa or Matilda"?); meanwhile, the uncertainty reinforces the impression that he is trying to be scrupulously truthful; but also, the uncertainty suggests that he is not fanatically insisting on total recall ("I forget what I went there about") and is therefore not absurdly enamored with every fact; yet also the uncertainty stimulates a sense that what matters is his effort to construct a story from the jumble of memories. The writing of "The Circus" preceded the dinner with Jean-Claude, but Jean-Claude and his remark about cocktail sauce somehow epitomized the spirit (iconoclastic, experimental—"It should be good on something but not on these") of the period in which the writing was done. Now, admittedly, when someone shows you old photos and verbosely can't decide whether they date from July or October of a certain year, it's boring. But I find Koch's passage very unboring.

Momentum is part of the reason. The passage flows through the uncertainties of memory with a momentum arising from an urgency in the motivating questions: *What did I have? What really mattered in it? Have I lost it all?* Lineation and lack of punctuation are crucial to the effect. "You were back in the apartment what a dump actually we liked it / I think." The young couple's happiness in that apartment included their awareness that by some objective standard it was a dump; there is a kind of pleasure that comes from seeing oneself thriving in nonideal circumstances. The line with its unpunctuated momentum evokes this feeling both precisely and unpretentiously, unpuffily.

Janice was there in the apartment "with your hair and your writing and the pans / Moving strummingly about the kitchen." The phrasing here is a short inch from bad writing—as a middle-minded workshopper would be quick to point out—but such an inch is as good as a glorious mile, in Dickinson, Wordsworth, and many another great poet who takes chances. As Koch summons up a vision of Janice in that apartment, he sees first her hair; there is a helplessness in the unadorned phrase—"with your hair"—that I find touching: the absence of adjectives creates a sense of the woman's hair having been beautiful to the young husband in a way not rationally explainable. (I think it's possible Koch was remembering phrases at the end of Browning's "A Toccata of Galuppi's": "Dear dead women, with such hair, too . . . I feel chilly and grown old.") Janice was there with her hair and her writing and the cooking pans. Three words acknowledge something not mentioned elsewhere in the poem, that while young Kenneth was busily writing heaps of experimental poetry, his wife was also a writer. Looking back from the end of "The Circus" (II), we detect in the phrase "and your writing" a rueful acknowledgment of something perhaps inadequately respected at the time, Janice's intellectual life. The reference to her writing is there in the line but only as a flash in the montage of images, and we get a sharp sense that while Kenneth was scribbling "The Circus," Janice was not writing—she was cooking. The sounds of her cooking made a music to the ears of the inspired poet in the next room: Janice was "Moving strummingly about the kitchen" in a scene so animated it was as if the pots and pans were clanging cheerfully of their own accord. All these implications are made possible by Koch's bold fidelity to the momentum and imperfect organization of his memories: "It was a summer night no it was an autumn one summer when / I remember it but actually no autumn that black dusk toward the post office."

Another poet might decide to omit the uncertainty here. Or, still another poet might choose to make an elegant, elaborated point about the treacherousness of memory. Koch honestly includes his uncertainty—summer or autumn?—in a manner that conveys anxiety while also pressing on toward the mystery of what was and wasn't achieved that night. Moreover, there is the lightest hint of symbolic meaning in the idea that his mythmaking memory has located that night in summer, whereas realistic recollection places it in autumn, in a time when loss has begun. (The last line of "The Circus" [I] is "The soft wind of summer blew in the light green trees.")

> And I wrote many other poems then but The Circus was the best
> Maybe not by far the best Geography was also wonderful
> And the Airplane Betty poems (inspired by you) but The Circus was the best.

Every poet writes letters that contain sentences rather like that, I believe. One's poems of long ago shine in the dimness of the lost years, signaling that not everything was wasted and that some beauties are indestructible. What Koch does here could be obnoxious in a bad or mediocre poet, I realize—it's dreary enough to see such a poet caressing his own old poems in a letter, but in a new poem! Yet there is a human truth in the egotism of such self-accounting that can be poignantly revealed. Wallace Stevens achieves this in "As You Leave the Room" and "The Planet on the Table," and there must be other cases, but not many; I think Koch's candor in "The Circus" (II) is brave and beautiful, as I've been arguing. His assertion that "The Circus" was his best poem (though with close competitors!) in the early 1950s prepares for a more troubling assertion that will come at the end of "The Circus" (II): "And this is not as good a poem as The Circus / And I wonder if any good will come of either of them all the same."

What then was so great about the first Circus poem? A dreamlike cartoon-like narrative about a traveling circus, in twelve numbered sections, it runs four and a quarter pages in *The Collected Poems*. The circus goes from town to town, we glimpse the performers—Orville the Midget, Paul the Separated Man, the elephant man, the circus master, "The sky-blue lion tamer comes in, and the red giraffe manager" (throughout his career Koch felt that vivacity could efficiently be injected into a poem simply by declaring things to be unexpectedly red, blue, yellow, green, orange, purple, pink)—and especially the pretty circus girls in tight costumes. In section 8, trouble invades this cartoon world when Aileen the trapeze artist falls to the ground and nearly dies. How much can her injury matter in such a world? A speaker in section 9 offers an answer that conveys the spirit of fervent heedless vitalism that underlies the whole poem.

> "What is death in the circus? That depends on if it is spring.
> Then, if elephants are there, *mon père*, we are not completely lost.
> Oh the sweet strong odor of beasts which laughs at decay!
> Decay! Decay! We are like the elements in a kaleidoscope,
> But such passions we feel! bigger than beaches and
> Rustier than harpoons."

I think the clash between Aileen's suffering and the circus hurly-burly is fairly interesting and gives potential weight to a largely feckless poem. But I'm afraid this chance is frittered away. "The Circus" (I) doesn't bear rereading, unless you're content merely to admire the swaggering impulsiveness of the writing. Everywhere the poem cheerfully flaunts the overconfidence of its composing. Why should those passions be described as "bigger than beaches and / Rustier than harpoons"? Why not "wilder than peaches and / Deeper than lagoons"? Or "more tenacious than leeches and / Ruder than buffoons"? Or "swingier than birches and / More radical than hot prunes"? It's impossible to feel that Koch pondered many possible phrases and then chose the one about beaches and harpoons, and I find it impossible to feel that his phrases are deeply right, inspired; instead, the unavoidable impression is that Koch wrote fast and never looked back, enthralled by an enthusiasm that felt like inspiration. "The Circus" (I) is dazzling on first encounter, but it wants that initial bedazzlement to be a permanent response, which is not possible. The poem—like many of Koch's early poems—is an orgy of self-belief, in which a talent for charming phrases roams around unchecked by reflection.

Meanwhile, Janice was cooking.

Returning to "The Circus" (II) where we left it, we find Koch expressing a pervasive bemusement about life's complications.

> There are so many factors engaging our attention!
> At every moment the happiness of others, the health of those we know
>   and our own!
> And the millions upon millions of people we don't know and their
>   well-being to think about
> So it seems strange I found time to write The Circus
> And even spent two evenings on it, and that I have also the time
> To remember that I did it, and remember you and me then, and
>   write this poem about it
> At the beginning of The Circus
> The Circus girls are rushing through the night
> In the circus wagons and tulips and other flowers will be picked
> A long time from now this poem wants to get off on its own
> Someplace like a painting not held to a depiction of composing
>   The Circus.

In the first six lines of this passage, Koch is pushing the experiment of anti-poeticality (an experiment tried somehow by interesting writers in each generation) pretty far—not so much by imitating real-life talk as by allowing a seemingly naive, helpless banality devoid of images, staking everything on the value of disarmed, candid wonder. For me, that value does sustain those six lines, but something needs to change soon; sensing this, Koch slides momentarily into the style of the first Circus poem—for him, there is still (and there would be throughout his life) a strong magnetism in fizzy juxtapositions like "circus wagons and tulips." By including the flash of temptation—in which the colorful circus suggests an infinite world of colorful blooms—and then refusing to permit the elegiac poem to devolve into an imitation of "The Circus" (I), Koch makes more palpable the tension in his elegiac honesty.

"The Circus" (II) wanders in bemusement for a while until Koch realizes that love—not self-love, not love of one's own imagination, but love for others—is the urgency that midlife meditation is insisting upon. He remembers being nervously competitive with friends in the exciting younger days; now he finds himself more focused on *keeping* than on winning:

> Like Noel Lee I was interested in my career
> And still am but now it is like a town I don't want to leave
> Not a tower I am climbing opposed by ferocious enemies

That realization is followed by a further one, about the importance of friendship, in lines that acknowledge time's painful trick whereby we appreciate what we've lost more than when we had it:

> I never mentioned my friends in my poems at the time I wrote The Circus
> Although they meant almost more than anything to me
> Of this now for some time I've felt an attenuation
> So I'm mentioning them maybe this will bring them back to me
> Not them perhaps but what I felt about them
> John Ashbery Jane Freilicher Larry Rivers Frank O'Hara
> Their names alone bring tears to my eyes.

There is an unexpected flintiness to the word *attenuation* that does something to protect these lines from sappiness; Koch is admitting that the intensity of the friendships has diminished, while he can now focus on that diminished value more clearly than he could when it was full and taken for granted. In this passage, we see elegy blossoming as a theme Koch's poetry will from now on not be able to dodge for many pages at a stretch. "It is beautiful at any time but the paradox is leaving it / In order to feel it"—here is an epitome of much of Thomas Hardy's poetry of belated appreciations.

"John Ashbery Jane Freilicher Larry Rivers Frank O'Hara"—famous poets and artists. Again, we may pause to ask: Isn't he bragging here? Isn't he arrogantly presuming that some poetic magic inheres in "Their names alone" that would not be present in a list of your old friends or mine—"David Cashman Laird Holby Jessica Murray Rich Rosen"? Well, yes. But again, I say there is a nakedness to Koch's lament, including its ingredient of arrogance, that makes it touching, and again, I would argue that this passage, with its shifts of thought and its momentum, is less common and less imitable than it might appear.

After those roaring twenties and thirties have gone, one finds oneself alone—or more aware of one's ongoing aloneness—in midlife.

> And you are left alone well you put up with that your sureness is like
>   the sun
> While you have it but when you don't its lack's a black and icy night.
>   I came home
> And wrote The Circus that night, Janice. I didn't come and speak to you
> And put my arm around you and ask you if you'd like to take a walk
> Or go to the Cirque Medrano though that's what I wrote poems about
> And am writing about that now, and now I'm alone
>
> And this is not as good a poem as The Circus
> And I wonder if any good will come of either of them all the same.

As I've said, I think Koch is mistaken there, at the end of "The Circus" (II), to rate the earlier Circus poem as superior; but what matters for the poetic power of "The Circus" (II) is to feel how that judgment arises from the bleakly remorseful mood that shadows the final passage. Melancholy nostalgia has given way to a frightened lack of "sureness." Koch seldom allowed the "black and icy night" of existential doubt and fear to darken his exuberant pages, which is why in the context of his *Collected Poems,* this last passage of "The Circus" (II) strikes with extra force. Now the latent theme of excessive self-absorption emerges inescapably, and we sense that much of the story of a marriage may be distilled in the lines about what he did and didn't do that evening in 1954. We can feel how, in this bleak mood, Koch not only doubts the value of his present discursive autobiographical style but also *needs* to believe that the first Circus poem—created at the expense of warm connection with Janice—was something good.

I hope to have shown why I consider the second Circus poem something good and why its apparent drifting and inefficiency are deeply involved in the poignancy of a meditation felt to be unfolding in the present of utterance. Convincing examples of this latter quality—which we may call "dramatic emergence"—are not very common in poetry, especially if we ask for clarity and vigorous intelligence along with the dramatic presentness of meditation. Soliloquies by Hamlet and monologues by Browning and Jarrell come to mind—but what about poems with an autobiographical speaker like Koch's speaker? (Eliot's Prufrock is a problematic case, mainly a persona albeit with a whiff of the autobiographical.) Wordsworth's "Tintern Abbey" and Coleridge's "Dejection: An Ode" are much honored, but how often convincingly imitated? I hold to my view that Koch's achievement in "The Circus" (II) was remarkably original in 1975 and has few rivals still.

Koch's next book, *The Burning Mystery of Anna in 1951*, published in 1979, contained an elegiac poem less emotionally complex than "The Circus" (II) but even more daring in its attempt to convey presentness of thought through formal experiment. "Fate" is a nakedly vulnerable poem, deliberately opening itself to the suspicion of artistic laziness, tempting any hostile reader to think, "Koch just jotted this down in a notebook and couldn't be bothered to revise it." The poem tries to recapture what it was like to return to New York in 1951 after his first trip to Europe (a few years before the Paris time of "The Circus"). Here are the first eleven lines of "Fate":

> In a room on West Tenth Street in June
> Of nineteen fifty-one, Frank O'Hara and I
> And Larry Rivers (I actually do not remember
> If Larry was there, but he would be there

Later, some winter night, on the stairway
Sitting waiting, "a demented telephone"
As Frank said in an article about him but then
On the stairs unhappy in a youthful manner, much
Happened later), Frank, John Ashbery,
Jane Freilicher and I, and I
Had just come back from Europe for the first time.

I'm going to argue that this poem is wonderful, though it lacks the gravity and shading of the ruefulness that develops in "The Circus" (II). Koch himself came to worry that "Fate" might be too vulnerable—he omitted it from his *Selected Poems* in 1985 and from the second *Selected, On the Great Atlantic Rainway* (1994)—but it is an experiment boldly fulfilled, and in *The Collected Poems,* it stands out as a link in the elegiac chain that continues (among so many other elements in the work of this outstandingly restless poet) to the end of Koch's career.

Like the hesitations and self-corrections we noticed in "The Circus" (II), the six-line parenthesis that starts in line 3 of "Fate" creates a sense of unpremeditated thinking-right-now. I can imagine readers who would be immediately exasperated by

I actually do not remember
If Larry was there, but he would be there
Later, some winter night, on the stairway.

Get it straight and then tell the story, such readers would cry. But the subject of "Fate" is not what happened one evening in June 1951 but, rather, what happens in remembering—the way the mind tries to assemble a story or pattern out of images that may derive from a handful of related experiences long ago. Larry Rivers has apparently been transposed by Koch's memory from later gatherings (perhaps in 1952) to the evening in 1951 when Koch enthusiastically reported to his friends about his European travels. And by the time the poem's long first sentence has ended, the dramatis personae have changed. Now, such transposings in memory could be pondered in poems more elegant or "poetic" than "Fate," but here the mental activity is *enacted* as it is in great passages of

Leopold Bloom's reveries in *Ulysses*. To my ear, it is delightfully disarming; it is a relief from poetical elevation; it is a breath of fresh air to encounter the phrase "I actually do not remember / If Larry was there." I realize—I never stop needing to realize—that this kind of freshness could become stale with overexposure. "The Circus" (II) prompted me earlier to note this: we can imagine a deadly series of poems in which the poet keeps fretting about little accuracies and inaccuracies of memory. Kenneth Koch was a person, and a reader, more quickly and suddenly bored than most, as is reflected in the carnivalesque variety of his oeuvre (variety that interfered with his pursuit of acclaim), and he would have spurned such a repetitious series of autobiographical poems sooner than I or even you would. He worried that "Fate" was too much like "The Circus" (II). But his writing in "Fate" shows confident fidelity to the poem's purpose.

If all one's undergraduate students wrote imitations of the next passage in "Fate," most of the results would indeed be dreary—but maybe not all! The challenge is to be faithful to the flow of elegiac reverie. I won't make big claims for all of Koch's moves in the passage; as in the case of "The Circus" (II), there is an element of complacency in the assurance that his own friends were "brilliant" and that "we had met at Harvard" counts in a way that "we had met at NC State" wouldn't count; still, I love the convincingness of the voice; and as the passage progresses, we hear Koch reaching several insights *through* the flow of recollection.

> I had a bottle of Irish whiskey I had
> Bought in Shannon, where the plane stopped
> And we drank it and I told
> My friends about Europe, they'd never
> Been there, how much I'd loved it, I
> Was so happy to be there with them, and my
> Europe, too, which I had, Greece, Italy, France,
> Scandinavia, and England—imagine
> Having all that the first time. The walls
> Were white in that little apartment, so tiny
> The rooms are so small but we all fitted into one
> And talked, Frank so sure of his
> Talent but didn't say it that way, I

Didn't know it till after he was
Dead just how sure he had been, and John
Unhappy and brilliant and silly and of them all my
First friend, we had met at Harvard they
Tended except Frank to pooh-pooh
What I said about Europe and even
Frank was more interested but ever polite
When sober I couldn't tell it but
Barely tended they tended to be much more
Interested in gossip such as
Who had been sleeping with whom and what
Was selling and going on whereat I
Was a little hurt but used to it my
Expectations from my friendships were
Absurd but that way I got so
Much out of them in fact it wasn't
Causal but the two ways at once I was
Never so happy with anyone
As I was with those friends
At that particular time on that day with
That bottle of Irish whiskey the time
Four in the afternoon or two or five
I don't know what and why do I think
That my being so happy is so urgent
And important? it seems some kind
Of evidence of the truth as if
I could go back and take it? or do
I just want to hold what
There is of it now? thinking says hold
Something now which is why
Despite me and liking me that
Afternoon who was sleeping with
Whom was best and
My happiness picking up
A glass Frank What was it like Kenny.

As in "The Circus" (II), the self-absorption becomes touching by way of its nakedness—"I / Was so happy to be there with them"—this is an experimental line (written by a professor versed in Ariosto, Dante, Byron, Shelley) in the sense that it experiments with unadorned, innocent declaration. When Koch exclaims on the joy of *having* Europe, the innocence of his American voice swells beyond conscious experiment, I suspect—because he was an enthusiastic tourist all his life and very susceptible to the impression that in visiting a country he had come into possession of its cultural essence:

> Greece, Italy, France,
> Scandinavia, and England—imagine
> Having all that the first time.

The effectiveness of "Fate" as a narrative flows partly from its allowing us to sympathize with the friends whose attention to Koch's travel report was amiable but also skeptical, not enthralled:

> they
> Tended except Frank to pooh-pooh
> What I said about Europe . . .

(The straightforward use of the verb *pooh-pooh* epitomizes this poem's commitment to a non-elevated, non-lyrical voice.) The exception of Frank leads into a qualifying admission—"and even / Frank was more interested"—that becomes syntactically garbled:

> even
> Frank was more interested but ever polite
> When sober I couldn't tell it but
> Barely tended they tended to be much more
> Interested in gossip.

I won't deny there is a wobble of bad writing in these lines, yet I accept them as an expression of the mental traffic congestion that occurs when we try to sustain a narrative momentum while also permitting digressive qualifications. The acknowledgment that all his friends including Frank

> tended to be much more
> Interested in gossip such as
> Who had been sleeping with whom

pulls the poem into a series of thoughts more complicated than the poem's first twenty-eight lines seemed to expect. Koch realizes that he unreasonably sought an ideal communion of enthusiasm with his friends, then quickly he considers and resists the idea that the joy of friendship depended on that unreasonableness—he seems not to want to claim too much credit for the successes of friendship:

> my
> Expectations from my friendships were
> Absurd but that way I got so
> Much out of them in fact it wasn't
> Causal but the two ways at once I was
> Never so happy with anyone
> As I was with those friends.

A few lines later, the silliness of the impulse to pin down the exact time when he was happy—

> Four in the afternoon or
> Three in the afternoon or two or five
> I don't know what

—triggers the worry that the whole obsession with this memory might be a foolish inflation, unworthy of a poem. Facing this question, Koch asks what he wants to do with the truth that is the essence of the memory, and two answers occur to him; the first answer suggests the romantic illusion of reentry and recapture of *le temps perdu* in some totalizing spiritual way; the second answer suggests a more realistic refreshing of appreciation of what can be presently enjoyed.

> and why do I think
> That my being so happy is so urgent

And important? it seems some kind
Of evidence of the truth as if
I could go back and take it? or do
I just want to hold what
There is of it now? thinking says hold
Something now.

Those lines crystallize a tension between romantic nostalgia for youth and mature acceptance of a less thrilled, less kaleidoscopic middle age, a tension that will underlie all of Koch's later elegiac poems and will especially haunt *New Addresses*. In their non-elevated, non-lyrical way, these lines carry "Fate" into a kinship with Wordsworth's Immortality Ode, wondering how devastating it is to feel "that there hath past away a glory from the earth."

In the momentum of his meditation, Koch identifies his second hypothesis as the key motive for his plunge into a memory of 1951: "thinking says hold / Something now"—this is an acknowledgment of the imperiously vital claim of the present (the desire to experience adventure and pleasure now, to hold something now, to embrace someone now) as against the past (even a grand and/or very recent past, like a tour of Europe), and it leads immediately to a newly empathetic understanding of his friends' strong interest in topics hotter than Kenny's recent travels:

> thinking says hold
Something now which is why
Despite me and liking me that
Afternoon who was sleeping with
Whom was best and
My happiness picking up
A glass Frank What was it like Kenny.

The emergent forgiving acceptance of his friends' fascination with sexual gossip as a form of the yearning to "hold / Something now" beautifully opens a Proustian door into the poem's most intense moment of presentness-of-the-past: "My happiness picking up / A glass Frank What was it like Kenny"—for an instant O'Hara, dead thirteen years when "Fate" appeared in *The Burning Mystery of Anna in 1951*, returns to life in the current of Koch's meditation.

But the present is always leaving, always leaving; "Fate" inevitably down-shifts from the moment of "What was it like Kenny" into anxious efforts to summarize and reflect and frustrated expressions of the elusiveness of the past. The present is always leaving, which is why "hold / Something now" can't be a sufficient motto for most of us; the day is as unseizable as water—and why we need to write and read elegies. Kenneth Koch found this harder to admit than, say, Tennyson or Arnold or Hardy or Eliot, and therefore Koch's elegies have a particular quality of breakthrough that comes when a poet resists his or her own comfortable tendencies. In order to allow lamentation into his work, Koch had to resist his temperamental tilt toward celebration of an effulgent present. On most days and most pages, he was a fervent affirmer.

William Wordsworth can also be called an affirmer, though in a different way. Probably no one ever referred to Wordsworth as "Doctor Fun"—a nick-name for the young Koch. Wordsworth, in *The Prelude,* is impelled by a deep desire to affirm that all his past experience has served a purpose in fostering the growth of his soul and is thus in an essential way not lost. In *The Prelude,* the flavor, the quiddity, the emergent strangeness of experience, is not ignored, but it is constantly dissolving into the abstractions whereby Wordsworth affirms the spiritual value of experience; Koch's phrase

> it seems some kind
> Of evidence of the truth as if
> I could go back and take it

—though I've interpreted it (with emphasis on "go back") as imagining a magical return into the past—may also be interpreted (with emphasis on "evidence" and "the truth") as sharing in Wordsworth's impulse to declare a perma-nent time-transcending usefulness in the adventures of long ago. In any case, what I want to note is the unpretentious modesty of Koch's attitude in "Fate." Unlike Wordsworth, Koch is not trying to establish dominance over memory, not trying to prove that everything in memory makes purposeful sense. Instead, though he does inevitably meditate on the remembered scene (in Jane's apart-ment in 1951), Koch keeps trying to inhabit the memory in all its comically un-controlled freshness, to "hold / Something now" even while the remembered scene itself highlights the already-gone-ness of his European escapades.

The comparison with Wordsworth can be sharpened if we look at a passage in book 7 of *The Prelude,* in which Wordsworth writes about the impact of the London theater on his young mind. We see Wordsworth trying to pull himself away from the intrinsic charms of the past scene, toward his theme of "progress" in "meditations holy and sublime."

> Through the night,
> Between the show, and many-headed mass
> Of the spectators, and each several nook
> Filled with its fray or brawl, how eagerly
> And with what flashes, as it were, the mind
> Turned this way—that way! sportive and alert
> And watchful, as a kitten when at play,
> While winds are eddying round her, among straws
> And rustling leaves. Enchanting age and sweet!
> Romantic almost, looked at through a space,
> How small, of intervening years! For then,
> Though surely no mean progress had been made
> In meditations holy and sublime,
> Yet something of a girlish child-like gloss
> Of novelty survived for scenes like these.

(7.433–47)

Though Wordsworth writes well, elsewhere in book 7, about the social tumult of London, still we can say that Koch's effort in "Fate"—modest in one way yet also artistically brash—is to stay more faithfully *within* the kittenish or boyish or girlish sensation of "gloss / of novelty" that imbued the remembered scene and to resist Wordsworthian sublimation of all that.

Yes, but the present is always leaving, and "Fate" is too honest a poem to pretend it isn't. Koch ruefully makes fun of his own effort to visit the afternoon in 1951 by showing that he can't recapture the dialogue of that day:

> And John said Um hum and hum and hum I
> Don't remember the words Frank said Un hun
> Jane said An han and Larry if he

Was there said Boobledyboop so always
Said Larry or almost and I said
Aix-en-Provence.

A few lines later, as if feeling he must recover the poem from the dribbly incon-
sequence of "Um hum" and "Boobledyboop," Koch does allow himself to swell
toward a Wordsworthy generality, triggered by the word *birthday,* in which he
wants to affirm that sorrow is secondary while happiness is primary as he contemplates his friendships. For the originality and poignancy of "Fate," it is crucial that the poem's final passage falls back from would-be wisdom into unset-
tled, un-abstractable fidelity to the movement of memory as it gropes among
recollections that can never be fully recollected.

I remember I was in
A special position as if it
Were my birthday but
They were in fact as if my
Birthday or that is to say Who
Cares if he grows older if
He has friends like
These I mean who does not
Care? the celebration is the cause
Of the sorrow and not
The other way around. I also went
To Venice and to Vienna there were
Some people I drove there
With new sunshine Frank says
Let's go out Jane John Frank
And I (Larry was not there, I now
Remember) then mysteriously
Left

The one-word last line of "Fate," with its absence of a period, seems to me a
beautiful choice, aware that the poem's project is not about reaching a firm
conclusion from a sadder-but-wiser perspective. The poem's title gestures to-

ward a distanced overview that the body of the poem cannot attain because it is so attuned to the way the new sunshine of a moment (in Vienna perhaps) vanishes into the newer sunshine of a new moment (in Manhattan) that must imminently vanish.

Koch's next important experiment in elegy does attempt a distanced overview of a period of his past, without the mood and mode of immersion in reverie that we've examined in "The Circus" (II) and "Fate." "Seasons on Earth" was written as an introductory poem for a book, also entitled *Seasons on Earth* (1987), that reprinted his two comic epic poems in ottava rima, *Ko, or a Season on Earth* (1960) and *The Duplications* (1977). (Because of this link to the book-length poems, "Seasons on Earth" is not included in *The Collected Poems*.) Like the second Circus poem, "Seasons on Earth" gazes back through the years asking, *How did I come to write what I wrote then? And how do I feel about it now?*

Because of its service as an introduction to other works and because it was composed, like them, in ottava rima, "Seasons on Earth" is an uneven, jumbly performance, and I don't nominate it as one of Koch's best poems, but I think some of its stanzas climb to poignant meditation and self-revelation, candidly bringing into focus the powerful tug of elegy that has by 1987 become a central force in Koch's spirit, despite his habitual idea of himself as a man "nuts for exhilaration." "Seasons on Earth" is haunted by the suspicion that the comic epics, *Ko* and *The Duplications,* are very far from being the great works Koch felt they were when he wrote them. Whereas in "The Circus" (II) he still believes, or says he believes, that the first Circus poem was wonderful, now the possibility that his younger effervescent self was self-deluded looms large.

As in "The Circus" (II), Koch addresses Janice, still yearning to justify to her— or to win again (six years after her death in 1981) her approval of—his exultant absorption in his writing throughout his late twenties and his thirties. His particular autobiographical focus is a period in 1956–57 when they lived in Florence and he wrote *Ko.* (As usual for Koch, life in Europe is felt to be inevitably inspiring.)

> Each midday found me
> Ecstatically in the present tense,
> Writing. And you would have to come and pound me

Quite hard to drag me from my innocence.
That sense that now seems almost unbelievable—
I love it, loved it—is it irretrievable?

Those lines, nervously balanced between ruefulness (implicit in "my innocence") and defiant pride ("Ecstatically," "I love it") reprise the essence of "The
Circus" (II). Two losses are in the air: loss of the day-to-day happiness of long
ago (as in "Fate"); and loss of belief in his own happy genius, the presumed
genius that could sustain a book-length poem about a Japanese pitching ace
named Ko and countless other characters whose adventures are blatantly influenced by the poem's commitment to a rhyme scheme more feasible in Ariosto's
Italian than in English.

I was at that time thirty-one or thirty-
Two, even then glad I had lived so long,
Long enough to influence history's verdict
(I still believed in that) by my big song
Of baseball, youth, and love. No way the Arctic
Of death, disease, or pain had bent the strong
Support floor of my being: happiness,
I thought, was what life came to, more or less.

Whitman had moods in which he excitedly implied that happiness is what
life comes to, more or less, but the inadequacy of the statement as an artistic
credo is so naked that we can feel some courage in Koch's being willing to present it as shorthand for his vision in young adulthood. This courage is what I
would stress in trying to convince a skeptical reader—someone inclined to see
the playful rhyming as merely goofy doggerelitis and the long-windedness as
narcissism—that "Seasons on Earth" is worthwhile. Though still in love with
his "innocence," Koch at the same time—often in the same stanza—can gaze
steadily and seriously upon his life's pattern, cast a cold eye; when he does this,
he attains a sad dignity like that which gives weight to Robert Lowell's line, in
"Dolphin," "My eyes have seen what my hand did."

It's in that light that I read a stanza of "Seasons" in which Koch (at age sixty)
improvises an imitation of his style at age thirty-one.

You can call me on Saturday she said.
The hippopotamus walked in the room
And then, with a blue towel around its head,
Ran straight to the sky-mirroring lagoon,
Sank to its knees, rolled over, and played dead.
Meanwhile, Ceylon experienced a monsoon—
Such sequences, perhaps, if gotten right,
Might find the truth, as flowers find the light.

I find that stanza frighteningly sad. The Saturday-hippo-lagoon-Ceylon stuff is so obviously useless—child's play merely gilded with sophistication—that we know Koch all but knows it, and he all but says so. A poet writing a poem is not a flower unconsciously irresponsibly growing toward sunshine, and "the truth" of human life is not simple biological vitality. Or if biological vitality is one element of our human truth, the Saturday hippopotamus style is likely to evoke *only* that element, leaving everything else to be done by the kind of poets whom Koch tended to consider dreary, stiff, grim, glum, unhealthy, or pretentious.

Koch cannot bear to make "Seasons on Earth" an out-and-out repudiation of his old playfulness. The poem is, after all, presented as an introduction to his two republished Ariosto-Byronic monsters. It cannot try for the stark palinodial declaration of a break with past self that we find in Stevens's "Farewell to Florida" or Yeats's "The Circus Animals' Desertion." But Koch boldly makes the issue unignorable by including in "Seasons" a memory of serious misfortune: Janice suffered a dangerous miscarriage during the Florence year.

You, six months pregnant, lost the baby: it was
The saddest thing that ever happened to us.

You almost died. They tried to give you oxygen
In the wrong way, in the bare-beamed Municipal
Hospital. I helped save you. They were lax again
With blood. Good God! All life became peripheral,
A mess, a nightmare, until you were back again.
My poem had not a trace of these things medical;
But it was full of dyings and revivings
And strange events, that went past plain connivings—

The mismatch of subject matter and style in that stanza is simultaneously excruciating and touching—touching in its effort to show that Byronic ottava rima is not utterly incapable of dealing with horror and misery; and touching in its need for a vague rhymey escape ("revivings," "connivings") from horror and misery.

Shifting ahead "some years," "Seasons on Earth" briefly refers to the period when Koch wrote *The Duplications.* His marriage to Janice was in trouble; the writing was an escape:

> Sensation
> Was what it rode on, action its theology—
> Away from all that troubled you and me so,
> In a sort of poetic paradiso.

A severe critique of the comic epics themselves—and, by extension, of all the "carnival combustion" in his early work—hovers just beyond the passages I've quoted. "Seasons on Earth" avoids any frontal judgment of the poetry's value by shifting the focus from that to the gap between the author of the earlier poems and Koch's present self.

> Now fifteen more years later, looking at them,
> These poems, of different times and different systems
> Of using life as if one had a patent
> On its effects without regard to wisdom,
> I feel sometimes delight—and sometimes flattened.
> What is there, that I am at sixty, in them?
> How can I ever hope to get in synch with
> What they're about? What do I have to think with?

(The oppressiveness of clever rhyming is noticeable in the way that last phrase, "What do I have to think with?" is blurry, off target.) The nervous dance of misgiving-without-repudiation goes on for another sixteen stanzas. All in all, "Seasons on Earth" is a poem skewed by its occasion and its form but useful in relation to Koch's other elegiac poems, showing so clearly the anxiety in his looking back. An ambivalence in the word *regret* applies: he "regrets" his past life-and-work in the old sense of missing what is lost, of course, but he also, to some vacillating degree, regrets his past life-and-work in the more colloquial sense, suspecting he should have behaved differently and at moments wishing he could have done so.

The thread of elegy in Koch runs through "To Marina," in *The Burning Mystery of Anna in 1951* (1979), and "The World" and "With Janice" and the title poem in *Days and Nights* (1982), and several poems in *One Train* (1994), including "A Time Zone," which ranges among happy memories of the late 1940s and early 1950s and contains these lines about his first year with Janice:

> She's a little deflating and tells me that to be a great poet
> I have to do something she tells me but I forget exactly what
> I think have for all my poems some sort of system
> I am shaken but still feel secure in my avant-garde wisdom.

Again, he brings up what could be a disturbing issue about the value of his oeuvre but folds it back into the texture of elegiac reverie. When the task he gives himself is to evoke the flow-of-life-across-months-or-years (a "zone" of time), Koch has many successes—"Currency" in *Straits* (1998) is one—yet this way of shaping his subject helps him escape the knife-edge of any one question. The power of "The Circus" (II), as we saw, is in the way it manages not to escape.

I will turn to a few later poems in which Koch's elegiac feeling sustains its focus long enough for the poetry to move down beneath a colorful surface.

"Passing Time in Skansen," in *One Train,* is a lovely poem whose tone— relaxed, humorous, un-grandiose—might almost keep us from realizing how the poem gives us a narrative epitome of the entire story told by all of Koch's elegiac poetry: a story of youthful exultation and seemingly magical potentiality displaced and dissolved in a world that strangely neglects to make these feelings central and permanent.

Passing Time in Skansen

> I went dancing in Stockholm at a public dancing place
> Out-of-doors. It was a beautiful summer evening,
> Summer as it could only come in Sweden in nineteen-fifty.
> You had to be young to go there.

Or maybe you could be old. But I didn't even see old people then.
Humanity was divided into male and female, American and other,
    students and nonstudents, etcetera.
The only thing that I could say in Swedish
Was "Yog talar endast svenska"
Which meant I speak only Swedish, whereas I thought it meant
I DON'T speak Swedish.
So the young ladies, delighted, talked to me very fast
At which I smiled and understood nothing,
Though sometimes I would repeat
Yog talar endast svenska.
The evening ended, my part of it did, when they started to do folk dances.
I didn't even know how to look at them, though I tried for a while.
It was still light out though it was after eleven p.m.
I got on some kind of streetcar that eventually stopped near my hotel.

To dance with fascinatingly foreign young ladies on a beautiful summer evening—that's the life! Koch's poetry before 1975 usually wanted to affirm that such exhilaration is *the* life, the life that matters, the life worth talking about. Remembering "Fate," it is touching to realize that the adventure of dancing one night in Stockholm in 1950 must have been among the many dazzling European experiences that young Kenneth yearned to describe to his New York friends in 1951. If they had given him the chance to describe his Skansen evening, the spirit of his report would have been different from the wry, distanced wisdom we hear in "Passing Time in Skansen." In this poem, published when he was sixty-nine, Koch writes, "I didn't even see old people then." This simple honest admission has behind it the quiet realization that the poet himself has become one of those old folks invisible at the dance of youthful desire.

Trying to communicate with the Swedish beauties, young Kenneth was saying the opposite of what he meant to say and presumably appeared more foolish and lost than he realized. It would be overly academic to make too much of this charming anecdote, but it does show us a young poet (Kenneth in 1950, age twenty-five) using language much less effectively than he imagines. The difficulty of language is greater than the clever young Harvard graduate realizes. And the young Swedes share pleasures that exclude him not only as participant but as appreciator. Their evening of fun goes on in new forms—like the archetypal fun evening of energetic young people in each generation—leaving others outside the dance due to cultural background or due to age. The beautifully understated last four lines of "Passing Time in Skansen" metaphorically express the strange experience of aging more than half a lifetime and finding oneself to be far from the center of glory.

> The evening ended, my part of it did, when they started to do folk dances.
> I didn't even know how to look at them, though I tried for a while.
> It was still light out though it was after eleven p.m.
> I got on some kind of streetcar that eventually stopped near my hotel.

The world roars on, oblivious of the wishful self: this truth is caught in the deceptively casual phrase "The evening ended, my part of it did"—the self wants to believe there is no marvelous evening without him, but this illusion is not sustainable. Koch achieves an un-strident, quietly lucid expression of what time does to romance, connectable with what Thomas Hardy achieves in many poems, such as "The Missed Train," in which he remembers a long-ago night when he lay awake thinking of his beloved "after days of allure"—here are that poem's last two stanzas:

> Thus onetime to me . . .
> Dim wastes of dead years bar away
> Then from now. But such happenings to-day
>   Fall to lovers, may be!
>
>
> Years, years as shoaled seas,
> Truly, stretch now between! Less and less
> Shrink the visions then vast in me.—Yes,
>   Then in me: Now in these.

If Koch's books are compared in terms of evenness, *New Addresses* (2000) is the standout. Whereas Koch's other books are so fervently various, so devoted to unpredictability, that it is nearly impossible to imagine the thoughtful reader who could like *all* of any one book, *New Addresses* sticks with one mode (apostrophe) and one tone (relaxed, questioning, tender, forgiving) throughout. Even though my favorite dozen Koch poems are scattered among other books, I call *New Addresses* his best book because it is so reliably engaging. In *New Addresses,* Koch's concern with his vanished past is so pervasive and mostly so un-agonized that "elegiac" (even in the broad sense in which I've used the term) might be said to dissolve into the larger category of "autobiographical." Coming to *New Addresses* in *The Collected Poems,* we see the elegiac impulse—traceable heretofore in scattered poems—now fully indulged. The poet who often derided what he saw as the complacencies of autobiographical poets such as Lowell and Berryman now goes more nakedly autobiographical than any of his peers. A thorough accounting of the elegiac strain in Koch would have to deal with most of *New Addresses;* everywhere there is the mixture of appreciation and puzzlement that we've seen in poems discussed already: appreciation for his many kinds of good luck, and puzzlement at time's power to dismantle so much lucky glory. Also, there are a few flickers of the ruefulness we saw in "The Circus" (II) and "Seasons on Earth," but the mood of *New Addresses* is mainly grateful and wondering.

Ambivalence about his early circus poetry does show up in an apostrophe poem Koch published in *Poetry* in 2000 and decided (rightly, I think) to omit from *New Addresses.* In "To My Old Poems," he recalls the feeling of inspiration out of the blue that propelled the early poems and says he'd like to know

> if the ability to make you is a gift that comes back—
> One of you arriving, or being finished,
> Like an ace or a king or a queen
> In the hand of my otherwise foolish life. In any case
> You're friendlier than you have been for a long while—
> Things seem to be all right between us now.

Those last two lines confess that rueful misgivings about his early brilliance have indeed plagued him "for a long while."

Since *New Addresses* is a big subject in itself, and since I've written about it elsewhere (*Poetry Review* [London], spring 2002), I will comment on some even later poems. But first I will quote the last lines of "To My Fifties," published when Koch was seventy-five. He addresses a decade of his life:

What should it mean, exactly, that I am fifty-seven? I wanted to be
　　always feeling desire.
Now you're a young age to me. And, in you, as at every other time
I thought that one year would last forever.
"I did the best possible. I lasted my full ten years. Now I'm responsible
For someone else's decade and haven't time to talk to you,
　　which is a shame
Since I can never come back." My Fifties! Answer me one question!
Were you the culmination or a phase? "Neither and both." Explain!
　　"No time. Farewell!"

Those lines are certainly not rich in metaphor, nor do they have what gets called
"music," nor do they provide much business for the interpreter of obscurities.
But I find them un-banal in their characterization of a piece of one's past as benign but unable to impart wisdom to the rememberer because no longer in service to the rememberer. It's up to the rememberer to create whatever meaning
can be derived from the departed decade; one's younger self is not available for
cross-examination. That seems true to me; is it also obvious? Maybe, but I find
a sweetness in the clarity and frankness of those last lines of "To My Fifties."

Koch published one more collection of new poems, *A Possible World* (2002),
shortly before his death. If readers expected a thoroughly nostalgic follow-up
to the widely praised *New Addresses,* they were forgetting that unpredictability
was the lifeblood of Koch's originality as he understood it. Variety was his poetic
signature. *A Possible World* includes odd funny meditations, experiments, travel
poems, but the elegiac impulse is there too. I think Koch was determined not
to let it take over; repetition always seemed to him a denial of life's fecundity.
Frank O'Hara wrote, in "Day and Night in 1952," "Kenneth continually goes away
and by this device is able to remain intensely friendly if not actually intimate."

A Possible World ends with an eighteen-page poem entitled "A Memoir,"
which is mostly incoherent because it tries so hard to escape the reductiveness
of coherent memoir. One of the comparatively coherent passages in "A Memoir" goes like this:

　　When Janice felt lost
It was easy but I had to find her

> She was also a supreme self
As was Katherine
> Who was in my arms
I felt Let us no longer take up arms
> One against the other
I thought for at least ten years afterwards
> I've wasted my life I didn't stay in Paris
In fact my life went ho ho ho
> And flattened itself out in New York
I could have made a memoir that was all loss
> Lost Marina lost marriage lost Paris lost inspiration
I would live in this Memoir for days
> But a birthday was obvious
Became all too clear
> I hadn't wasted my life because it wasn't wasted.

I'm sorry to say that here, and throughout "A Memoir," the busily "fresh" non-linear style is preventing the development of interesting thoughts. But clearly the impulse toward elegiac meditation is in the picture.

The first poem in *A Possible World* is "Bel Canto," a four-page meditation in ottava rima on the relation between his life and his poetry, thus a kind of sequel to "Seasons on Earth." It contains sweetly ingenuous exclamations:

> How my desire, when young to be a poet
> Made me attentive and oblivious every moment!
> . . .
> How much I'd like to live the whole thing over,
> But making some corrections as I go!
> To be a better husband and a father,
> Be with my babies on a sled in snow.

"Bel Canto" has its charm, though for me the ottava rima becomes, as in "Seasons on Earth," more of a bother than a delight. (That happens in Byron's *Don Juan* sometimes too, but Byron is more suavely at home in the form than Koch is.) If we see "Bel Canto" as a fond farewell to life written by a man dying of leukemia, we can't be unmoved. But the poem I want to offer as one last example of the elegiac spirit in Koch's work is one of the shortest in *A Possible World,* "A Big Clown-Face-Shaped Cloud."

Like "Passing Time in Skansen," this poem about a not-much-noticed, vigorous, but short-lived cloud obsessed with a possibly illusory sublimity floating just beyond its reach can be read as a metaphor for the life story of a poet.

A Big Clown-Face-Shaped Cloud

You just went by
With no one to see you, practically.
You were in good shape, for a cloud,
With perhaps several minutes more to exist
You were speaking, or seemed to be,
Mouth open wide, talking, to a
Belted angel-shaped cloud that was riding ahead.

Our cloud protagonist might look foolish (shaped like a clown's face); it is a dreamer and is itself made of the misty stuff of dreams. But it is not solipsistic; it is trying to communicate with one of its own kind—another cloud—even if the angel-shaped cloud has a magical quality not possessed by our protagonist. The yearning for intimacy between clouds is expressed in the shift from "speaking" to the less formal "talking." In its quixotic dedication, the "big clown-face-shaped cloud" shows one kind of heroism, and the poem honors this. I find it deeply touching as a poem written by a man who knows he is dying and who has sought many times to meet the fundamental human need for elegy without being heavy-handed.

It's true that Koch's elegiac poems may be called self-elegies, focused mainly on his loss of his own past. There are flashes of elegiac reference to Janice and to many friends but no full-scale elegies for others. Let's recall, though, that in great elegies like "Lycidas" and "Adonais," the poet's own possible defeat and death are very much at issue, along with grief for the person who has died. I would contend that in writing the poems I've discussed, Koch offers elegiac responses not only to his own mortality but to the mortality of all of us whose spirits seemed brilliantly excitable when young and then puzzlingly diminished yet still excitable in midlife and after. As a reader, I have not felt excluded by the egocentrism in Koch's accounts of his past; I can feel that they offer an image of my own egocentrism—and yours. Are we not sweetly yearning clouds?

Though I suggest that the elegiac current in Koch's oeuvre brings some of his best achievements, it's impossible to wish that he had committed himself more thoroughly to elegy or autobiography. He knew that to give himself over to any one kind of poetry would be to betray his heart's core love of variety. Koch is the king of the unexpected. Poets whose strangeness becomes formulaic in book after book give him no competition in this respect.

Elegies are certainly not what a reader of *Thank You* in 1962 would have anticipated in Koch's later work. As a poet grows older, however, he or she has to realize that a sense of loss is a crucial part of identity. Indeed, is it possible to be a serious poet in one's fifties, sixties, seventies, *without* writing elegiac poems? Yes, the example of Robert Frost shows it is possible. You have to be very alert to hear any elegiac notes in Frost's poetry, and when you do, he is apt to imply that your ears are sentimental, that the elegiac impulse is an error due to failure to be "versed in country things." Frost's oeuvre may be viewed as a lifelong fending off of elegy. That's why "Directive" is so maddeningly ambiguous and fascinatingly ambivalent. It seems as though for Frost, regret was a room too cavernous and dark for him to enter safely. Elegy ran against his grain because his deepest need was to feel untrapped, independent, balanced, ready for any future.

In a different way, elegy ran against Kenneth Koch's grain, too, as we've seen—emphatically so in the first half of the career, oscillatingly so after that; even *New Addresses* seeks to offset elegy's looming sorrow via the playfulness of apostrophizing. There is something particularly affecting in the way Koch's *Collected Poems* shows the elegiac impulse arising irresistibly in a mind so strongly inclined toward celebration of the present. The present keeps on being dazzling, but as we live on, the past keeps getting deeper, its claims more charismatic with their own radiance.

ROBERT PINSKY AND

FORGETTING

Like you and me, Robert Pinsky is scared by the destructions of time. Everything we've cared about is dissolving—and we let it happen! No, wait, it has to happen—time equals change equals loss—but we still seem guilty because we forget, we let go . . . . Yet also many of us (including most poets, arguably all poets) scheme to counteract the passage of time or at least to hang on heroically to traces, traces . . . . But the keepable traces are not the original realities, and anyway, they amount to one percent of one percent of one percent of what you cared about.

Pinsky's poem "The Garden," in *History of My Heart* (1984), is one of his efforts to acknowledge the inescapability of letting go. Persons known long ago—and even not so long ago—are led into a shady garden in the mind:

And like statuary of dark metal

Or pale stone around the pond, the living and the dead,
Young and old, gather where they are brought: some nameless;
Some victims and some brazen conquerors; the shamed and the haunters;

The harrowed; the cherished; the banished—or mere background figures,
Old men from a bench, girl with glasses from school—all brought beyond
Even memory's noises and rages, here in the quiet garden.

Although "the cherished" comprise only one of the many categories cited there, the whole poem is shadowed by the sense that as you live your life, you cherish the perceiving self who notices various other persons, and to lose so many individuals who once focused your attention is to lose some of your life, some of your self. This losing is involuntary—and necessary for sanity (since your mind can't function if it tries to retain every impression in accessible files). If so, then obsessing about this losing tilts toward neurosis, perhaps. Robert Pinsky's poetry has helped me think about this, again and again, in poems that I've wanted never to forget.

Memory and forgetting are adversaries in an endless contest that forgetting is always winning, by monstrous margins, though memory keeps achieving tiny brief local victories.

Throughout his career, Pinsky has wanted to be a poet of heroic unsurrendering memory—not just memory of one's own personal life, which is the terrain of innumerable good and bad autobiographical poets, but memory of the story of a community, a society, a culture, and even of our entire species. The ambition is consciously superhuman, pressing beyond the capacity of any individual mind—as Walt Whitman had to forget and realize and re-forget and re-realize throughout his decades of adding to *Leaves of Grass,* that giant work that ultimately could not escape being finite. Like Whitman, though with more ironic coolness than Whitman could tolerate, Pinsky has felt that the effort to see *everything,* to register everything insightfully, while guaranteed (from a rational vantage point) to fail, is nevertheless a beneficial and needful effort, an effort that may bring to readers some kinds of understanding and relief not provided by poetry that stays within one individual's experience.

Sustaining this godlike synoptic project through many poems requires (though it need not mushroom into Pound-like madness) a brazen, brash confidence; this spirit is floridly charming in Whitman (for those of us who love him) and is charming in a cooler, less ingratiating way in Pinsky. Whitman, when he was "afoot with his vision," felt beamingly sure of his huge power to see and appreciate. Pinsky may often have felt something like that sense of power, but in him, it is always shadowed by awareness of the foolish hubris into which any visionary is apt to slide. In Pinsky, there is a deep and central desire to be nobody's fool, including a desire not to be duped by the seeming authority of his own connective evocations of patterns in human experience. So the crucial energy in many—maybe most—of Pinsky's poems flows from the tension between the craving for transpersonal or suprapersonal *seeing* and the awareness of ways in which that seeing may be mistaken and will not remain intact.

The synoptic perception of countless phenomena that Pinsky temperamentally finds so desirable may be synchronic (wider horizontal seeing of the diverse present) or diachronic (deeper vertical seeing of the striated past)—or, ideally, both. The need for synchronic registering of one's contemporary social environment is evoked in one of my favorite Pinsky poems, "The Questions," in *History of My Heart.* He remembers working in his father's optician business as a boy and presents a brief catalog of the customers:

> The tall overloud old man with a tilted, ironic smirk
>
> To cover the gaps in his hearing; a woman who hummed one
> Prolonged note constantly, we called her "the hummer"—how
>
> Could her white fat husband (he looked like Rev. Peale)
> Bear hearing it day and night? And others: a coquettish old lady
>
> In a bandeau, a European. She worked for refugees who ran
> Gift shops or booths on the boardwalk in the summer;
>
> She must have lived in winter on Social Security. One man
> Always greeted my father in Masonic gestures and codes.

We recognize the extremely limited and distanced quality of these momentary sketches; we, too, remember hundreds of individuals from our past only in such tiny scraps of detail—until eventually most of them are conducted into the Garden of Forgottenness. Pinsky wonders explicitly why his mind worries at remembering his father's customers and why, decades later, he finds himself wishing for them "to be treated tenderly by the world."

> Why this new superfluous caring?
>
> I want for them not to have died in awful pain, friendless.
> Though many of the living are starving, I still pray for these,
>
> Dead, mostly anonymous (but Mr. Monk, Mrs. Rose Vogel)
> And barely remembered: that they had a little extra, something
>
> For pleasure, a good meal, a book or a decent television set.

The reason for such "superfluous caring" is not simply an all-inclusive Whitmanic benevolence. The caring is rooted in the mind's need for a coherent world. Pinsky doesn't answer his question ("Why this new superfluous caring?") directly but happens upon an implicit answer in the last part of "The Questions," where he says that "today" he saw a nun at the Post Office. We take the hint that this tiny encounter today may be what jostled his mind toward wondering about his father's customers long ago. Today the nun's bland cheerfulness about doing errands annoyed him, but it also reminded him of the way children have to form an orderly picture of their social environment—as in elementary school:

> as a name
> And person there, a Mary or John who learns that the janitor
>
> Is Mr. Woodhouse; the principal is Mr. Ringleven; the secretary
> In the office is Mrs. Apostolacos; the bus driver is Ray.

A person necessarily develops a constellation of significant presences around the self, and the self attains identity and meaning by its being located and perceptible within that constellation. Of course, for most of us (who are not nuns), the crucial social structure conferring meaning is the family, but the mind craves a larger, wider picture, an internet of relations whereby one's world makes sense. To care about those relations being understandable, worthwhile, even sweet in some way, is to care about oneself.

So "The Questions" is about that world-building activity in the life of an elementary school student and in the life of a teenager working in his father's shop. But it is also about being an adult with a long past who has had to realize the drastic tendency of innumerable world-constitutive minutiae to slide toward oblivion. Pinsky's question at the start of the poem—"What about the people who came to my father's office / For hearing aids and glasses"—arises from a suspicion that their reality—and therefore part of *his* reality—is quietly en route to being pulverized by forgetting. The mind hangs on to whatever bits it can retrieve: Mr. Monk, Mrs. Rose Vogel.

In the following pages, I want to discuss a handful of poems exemplifying Pinsky's twin obsessions with memory and forgetting. Doing this, I'm doing what I (or you) always do in writing about favorite poems or provocative poems: I'm trying to sharpen their contours in my memory, to keep them alive as stimuli in my lifelong inclination to be instructed, comforted, challenged, and encouraged by particularly effective poems.

The examples I've gathered may be sorted into two sets: poems that emphasize the inevitability of forgetting (like "The Garden"); and poems that emphasize, or at least guard a tenderness toward, the emotional craving to remember (like "The Questions"). The sorting, though, is artificial and will not allow me to forget that Pinsky never forgets forgetting: the characteristic stringency of his poetry centers in his refusal to be duped by the romance of clinging; thus, any sweet elegiac retentiveness in his poems is bound to be shadowed by a dry hint (or more than hint) that it is delusory. Nevertheless, I detect in myself (with my inveterately romantic personality) a wish to let this essay arrive finally at the idea that, for Pinsky and for any of us, strenuous efforts of memory and commemoration are not mere folly.

Pinsky's main action in many poems is to point out to us, or remind us of, a vast web of connections stretching from any present phenomenon outward across the present and backward through history. Each phenomenon—including any physical object on your desk (as in his sequence "First Things to Hand," in *Gulf Music* [2007])—is a momentary node or particle in an ever-changing pattern or wave.

The sentence I've just written echoes sentences earlier in this essay and will be echoed by later sentences. The abstraction of such a sweeping statement may feel dry, but Pinsky's poetry inspires a desire to form such a sweeping statement because we tune in to his effort to register a myriad things all at once—or the pattern implied by the myriad things. What makes his effort succeed *as poetry* (rather than meta-historical philosophy) is the restless yearning of his obsession. When he contemplates, for instance, the maddening intensity of romantic love, in "Antique," in *Gulf Music,* his need to affirm that this emotion has a crazily glorious history across many centuries is itself a palpably emotional need, itself a replay of, or latest instance of, passionate acknowledging performed by innumerable lovestruck artists. The lover who speaks "Antique" speaks for all lovers who have desperately loved.

> I drowned in the fire of having you, I burned
> In the river of not having you, we lived
> Together for hours in a house of a thousand rooms

And we were parted for a thousand years.
Ten minutes ago we raised our children who cover
The earth and have forgotten that we existed.

Notwithstanding the overwhelming ephemerality of individual passion acknowledged in those lines, the lover cherishes a representation of the beloved's face, and he feels the pull of the idea that the representation (photo or painting) will withstand Time's fell hand. Unlike Shakespeare in sonnets such as "Devouring Time, blunt thou the lion's paws" and "Shall I compare thee to a summer's day," Pinsky's speaker resists the illusory consolation of the permanence of art.

Someday far down that corridor of horror the future
Someone who buys this picture of you for the frame
At a stall in a dwindled city will study your face
And decide to harbor it for a little while longer
From the waters of anonymity, the acids of breath.

The only consolation for this lover is the sternly limited sense of kinship with some future admirer of human beauty who will guard the decontextualized image "for a little while." By ending at "the acids of breath," "Antique" may be said to rebuke the fantasy that a particular instance of human beauty can be remembered forever. And yet the poem as a whole comes across as a proud affirmation, a credo, crystallizing the heroism in Orpheus and Mark Antony and all other stubborn tortured lovers.

In another mood, though, Pinsky's awareness of "the waters of anonymity, the acids of breath" expands and smothers romanticism, crushing all sweetly particular examples of human identity like the Figured Wheel of fate that

rolls unrelentingly over

A cow plodding through car-traffic on a street in Iasi,
And over the haunts of Robert Pinsky's mother and father
And wife and children and his sweet self
Which he hereby unwillingly and inexpertly gives up, because it is

There, figured and pre-figured in the nothing-transfiguring wheel.

The extreme expression of this fatalistic mood is "Louie Louie," in *Gulf Music*. This strange poem, not readily recognizable as Pinskyesque, has an air of having insisted on existing against all odds—that is, it seems like something fiercely scribbled in a notebook and not yet tamed into poeticality. (Occasionally, we encounter such a poem in a book by a poet who normally seems calmly in control of his or her effects and mindful of the reader's expectations. Such a poem—call it the surprisingly uncensored or indecorous poem—may not be "a good poem," but it is exciting to come across and can shine a sudden penetrating beam into the poet's psyche. Think, for example, of Whitman's "Respondez!" or Eliot's "Hysteria" or Stevie Smith's "Thoughts about the Person from Porlock" or Fearing's "X Minus X" or Jarrell's "90 North.")

What fuels "Louie Louie" is helpless dismay at everyone's infinite tendency to ignore and to forget.

> I have heard of Black Irish but I never
> Heard of White Catholic or White Jew.
> I have heard of "Is Poetry Popular?" but I
> Never heard of Lawrence Welk Drove
> Sid Caesar Off Television.

Our ordinary question "Who is the speaker of this poem?" is even less appropriate for "Louie Louie" than for the collective-voiced "Antique." "Louie Louie" can be thought of as spoken—or murmured—by a chorus of citizens bemused by the randomness of their knowledge and the constant tidal wave of information they've barely even focused on, let alone possessed. Published in 2007, "Louie Louie" thus presents, in essence, a state of mind we mostly can't escape in the age of Google. Each sentence of the poem juxtaposes something the I has "heard of" with something he or she has "never heard of." We naturally try to discern a meaningful pattern in these juxtapositions—for instance, "I have heard of [an ultimately trivial pop culture phenomenon] but I have never heard of [something historically and morally important]." If that pattern were maintained, the poem would neatly shape up as a critique of the pathetic or frightening shallowness of knowledge in capitalist mass culture. This would indeed be a meaning not foreign to Pinsky's thinking, as we'll soon see in "The Forgetting"— but "Louie Louie" only gestures toward such an organized pattern of meaning, choosing instead a disorienting unaccountability in its juxtapositions.

After all, who has never heard of the demographic groups of Caucasian Catholics and Caucasian Jews? A speaker who asserts this ignorance would have to be either disingenuous or absurdly mixed up about demographic categories, and such a speaker might suppose that "Black Irish" refers to Irish people with black skin (rather than white skin and black hair). In its strange casualness, the first sentence of "Louie Louie" immediately undermines our impulse to infer a speaker who is a real individual. Moreover, the sentence wants to undermine our confidence that the sociological labels we deploy have reliable significance.

What about a speaker who has heard of "Is Poetry Popular?" We might expect such a speaker to be exposed as a philistine who has never heard of numerous important poets who are less famous than Robert Frost. Instead, this speaker is ignorant of the end of Sid Caesar's career as a star of TV comedy in the late 1950s. "Lawrence Welk Drove Sid Caesar Off Television" is actually an insight about American cultural history, which Pinsky cares about. (He has testified elsewhere to his love of Caesar's comedy.) But someone *could* feel serious respect for poetry without caring about and even without encountering an idea about Sid Caesar's career.

So the juxtapositions in that opening stanza of "Louie Louie" are deliberately askew. In the second stanza, the list of persons utterly unknown to the speaker is a list generated not by pointed ironies but by a game of empty jumping from name to name, like a list offered all-too-promptly by an internet search engine.

> I have heard of Kwanzaa but I have
> Never heard of Bert Williams.
> I have never heard of Will
> Rogers or Roger Williams
> Or Buck Rogers or Pearl Buck
> Or Frank Buck or Frank
> Merriwell At Yale.

What emerges is a sense of a mind helplessly engulfed in a flood of unseizable allusions, where *all* facts and allegedly significant signifiers seem equally atomistic and unimportant. Floundering in that flood, someone might be dimly aware of Kwanzaa (as a well-meaning but unrealistic attempt to import African culture into African American culture) while remaining oblivious of Bert Williams (a great Black American vaudeville entertainer who died in 1922; Pinsky in a note at the end of *Gulf Music* calls him "an angel of comic song"). In a world of apprehensions so incoherent and unrooted in history, there may be a thin consolation in the thought that evil actions and evil persons will turn out to be as forgettable as whatever you admire. Here's the third stanza of "Louie Louie":

> I have heard of Yale but I never
> Heard of George W. Bush.
> I have heard of Harvard but I
> Never heard of Numerus Clausus
> Which sounds to me like
> Some kind of Pig Latin.

In his note at the end of *Gulf Music*, Pinsky acknowledges the absurdity of someone claiming in 2007 to have never heard of George W. Bush and considers what justifications come to mind: "That there was a time not long ago when we had not heard of him—a failed oilman rich-boy son fronting for a baseball team? That someday someone, indeed many people, will not have heard of him?" Irritation here has bitterness behind it, and behind the bitterness is helpless dismay at social injustice *and* at the cluelessness of decent people who don't pay enough attention to prevent or impede injustice. What is "Numerus Clausus"? In his note, Pinsky specifies that it refers to the quota system whereby universities like Yale and Harvard guarded themselves against admitting too many Jewish students. To have never heard of Numerus Clausus is symptomatic of not having cared enough about bigotry. But who among us cares enough?

Relegating such information to an endnote, Pinsky manages to express his sense of the moral costs of obliviousness and forgetfulness without letting the poem itself escape being an epitome of that obliviousness and forgetfulness. "Louie Louie" wants to *be* that epitome without alleviating its depressing picture through wisdom or insight. We mostly live distracted, dazed, bedazzled, unable to organize a million impressions. Emerson, in his troubled essay "Experience," tries to find a healthy attitude toward our endless unknowing: "Dream delivers us to dream, and there is no end to illusion. Life is a train of moods like a string of beads, and as we pass through them they prove to be many-colored lenses which paint the world their own hue, and each shows only what lies in its focus. . . . Gladly we would anchor, but the anchorage is quicksand. . . . We live amid surfaces, and the true art of life is to skate well on them." A lot of our experience is like listening to the 1963 pop hit "Louie Louie" by the Kingsmen, a song whose lyrics famously *seem* to mean something but we can't decipher the words.

However, the obliquity of Pinsky's "Louie Louie" is, I should admit, mitigated for a reader reading along in *Gulf Music* by the poem that precedes it. "The Forgetting" is a Pinskyesque teacherly essayistic poem, saved from being flatly essayistic by deft shifts of tone and jumps from example to example. He muses on the way one's memory (especially if one is over fifty, say) is always a chaotic junkshop where meanings and non-meanings seem randomly heaped together: "Memory of so much crap, jumbled with so much that seems to matter." In the three two-line stanzas I'm about to quote, we hear Pinsky shift from an American boy's version of Horace's lament for unsung ancient heroes to an aging man's justifiably cantankerous smack at younger generations who neglect monuments of unaging intellect without sensing the weightlessness of their own preferences:

> I used to wonder, what if the Baseball Hall of Fame overflowed
> With too many thousands of greats all in time unremembered?
>
> Hardly anybody can name all eight of their great-grandparents.
> Can you? Will your children's grandchildren remember your name?
>
> You'll see, you little young jerks: your favorite music and your political
> Furors, too, will need to get sorted in dusty electronic corridors.

That last phrase forces us to notice the particular twist on the question of memory invoked by digital technology over the past thirty years: we are more and more willing to trust electronic devices to do our remembering for us, while we float in the haze between clicks.

Our collective forgetfulness can be disgusting when the moral cost of it comes into focus (Michael Brown, Philando Castile, Eric Garner, Tamir Rice, Walter Scott, Alton Sterling, names we try not to forget), and Pinsky ends "The Forgetting" with an account of the desolating collective unseriousness of an audience at the Dodge Poetry Festival hearing Amiri Baraka read "Somebody Blew Up America" in 2002.

> I was in the big tent when the guy read his poem about how the Jews
> Were warned to get out of the Twin Towers before the planes hit.
>
> The crowd was applauding and screaming, they were happy—it isn't
> That they were anti-Semitic, or anything. They just weren't listening.

The not-listening described here could be seen as trivial, perhaps, if it were not a banal epitome of nonthinking pervasive in our culture—a nonthinking that endorses, and becomes indistinguishable from, forgetting. Pinsky reaches this point by qualifying his assertion that the people in the festival crowd "just weren't listening." He says, "No, they were listening, but that certain way. In it comes, you hear it, and / That selfsame second you swallow it or expel it: an ecstasy of forgetting."

An "ecstasy of forgetting"—the phrase recognizes the attraction of surrender to the sort of cheery blather dished up by the song "Louie Louie." Thus, to turn the page in *Gulf Music* from "The Forgetting" to "Louie Louie" is to hear a poet experimenting (like Yeats in "Lines Written in Dejection" or Stevens in "Gubbinal") with a temporary surrender to a state of mind he actually finds repulsive.

The victories of obliviousness are so ubiquitous that some experiments with surrender—or call it acceptance—must be necessary for sanity; you can't be constantly raging against the tide of erasures. We heard in "The Garden" an acceptance that felt calm, not only calm but even awed and grateful. But such calm acceptance can only be rare and brief for a person, like Pinsky, so fascinated by the claims of memory and the tracing of the past in the present. A poem in *At the Foundling Hospital* (2016) called "The Orphan Quadrille" wants to be another expression of acceptance, but it manages this in an uneasy, edgy way, mixing tones ambivalently, with a quality of compression different from the discursiveness of "The Forgetting." "The Orphan Quadrille" offers dance as a metaphor for our survival on the infinite dance floor of culture littered with the discarded achievements and dissolved understandings of previous generations. Each of the poem's six stanzas has a fourth line in parentheses and italics, reminding us that we have to participate in the dance—"*(Step and turn, step to me darling)*" is the first of these. The poem's tension involves the way these dance instructions counterpoint lines that exemplify Pinsky's deep temperamental impulse to refuse forgetting. Here I will quote nine and a half lines omitting the dance instruction refrains, so as to focus on the very Pinskyesque montage of examples whose near-randomness—as in Whitman's catalogs—tries to imply a panoptic awareness that *could* notice everything and miss nothing.

> Lost arts of cochineal enamel and earthen bell foundry.
> Shelling of the Parthenon, flooding of Sioux burials.
> Let's caper in memory of our mothers and fathers.
>
> Faith-based razing of Buddhas, Torahs, Ikons
> To obey Clerics, Committees, Scholars, Inquisitions.
> Lost art of snake-handling, of speaking in tongues.
>
> Lost arts of the poor, the Barrio Gotico overwhelmed
> By galleries and bars. Let's rattle castanets to celebrate
> A Thai restaurant and jazz club—we are not purists,
>
> Our ancient glittering eyes grieve gaily.

The voice that says "Let's caper" and "Let's rattle castanets" actually does not sound cheerful or festive, and the allusion to the famous ending of Yeats's "Lapis Lazuli" actually has the effect of making us notice that the mind behind "The Orphan Quadrille" has *not* arrived at the Taoist wisdom Yeats attributed to his elderly Chinese sages who gaze out across a landscape of ceaseless change. We have to dance on, up to our knees in the detritus of "lost arts," but the dancing can't be blissful if we notice the losses.

Pushed to an extreme, such a vision of irresistible loss of the past inspires passivity, whether melancholic or gay; Yeats's Chinese sages don't do anything except watch the world and listen to music. Yet on most days, Pinsky (and I, and you if you've bothered to read an essay about poems about memory) can't help feeling that strenuous efforts to remember and commemorate are not mere folly. Mr. Monk, Mrs. Rose Vogel . . .

Unable to sleep, the mind forages through the past:

> in the ordinary plight
> Of insomnia reciting memorized
> Avenues through the expanses
> Of loss.

Those lines in "The Foundling Tokens," in *At the Foundling Hospital,* recall the long prose poem in *Jersey Rain* (2000) "An Alphabet of My Dead," in which Pinsky copes with insomnia by alphabetically listing persons who have vanished from his life: "I tell them over not as a memorial comfort, and not for the souls of the dead, but as evidence that I may be real." The poem—like our lives—is moving because of its details, its vagaries, digressions, surprising flashes of poignancy, its not being just an orderly list. We glimpse the humanness of obscure persons such as Harry Antonucci, Henry Dumas, Army Ippolito, Sir Arthur Quiller-Couch, Butch Voorhies, Yetta of Yetta's Market on Rockwell Avenue, along with several of Pinsky's relatives and friends. The inventory, of course, must always be colossally incomplete, and the weary mind, exhausted by quiddities, will sometimes drift from details to generalities—as in the J-K-L section of Pinsky's "Alphabet": "A drowsy spell: it is working. Plural dead in categories like counting sheep, the exterminated Jews of Europe, the obliviated Kallikaks of New Jersey, the dead Laborers who framed and plastered these bedroom walls threaded by other dead hands with snaking electrical wires and the dendritic systems of pipes and ducts, audible." Like Whitman, who resorted to generalities when his zest for particulars flagged, Pinsky conveys the difficulty of elegy not only when he strives to inscribe a figure but also when he relinquishes that striving and admits the supremacy of the Figured Wheel and of sleep.

We all seek rituals and ceremonies and institutional forms of honoring that will preserve the lineaments of persons we love or admire beyond the fleeting present, beyond "the dazzle / Where all things shift, glitter or swim" (the phrase is from "The Living," in *History of My Heart*). Baseball's Hall of Fame is one such attempt. In the short poem "Glory," in *At the Foundling Hospital,* Pinsky contemplates the athletic renown not of Sandy Koufax or Jackie Robinson (ballplayers he has honored elsewhere) but of an ancient Olympic discus thrower named Nikeus, known to us now only through an ode by Pindar. "Glory is greater than success." This opening line of "Glory" gestures toward a poem that will affirm the worth of public honoring. But the poem turns out to be bleakly equivocal about the solidity of glory, and it finds this same doubt in Pindar himself:

> And when Nikeus grunting whirled the stone
> Into the air, it flew past the marks of
> All competitors and Nikeus's countrymen
> Yelled his name, *Nikeus* after the stone.
> *What is someone?* the chorus chants
> In Pindar's victory ode, *What is a nobody?*—
> *Both creatures of a day.* At the Games,
> *Nikeus* his friends yelled, *Nikeus,*
> And the syllables, say the lines Pindar
> Composed for the chorus, echoed
> From the cold mirror of the moon.

The chilliness of that ending might suggest that "Glory" should be sorted with Pinsky's bleakest poems about the inevitability of oblivion, like "Louie Louie" and "The Forgetting." Is glory a sheer chimera? Nikeus is dust, or scattered atoms, and we can't really say we honor him. Nevertheless—and here I realize I am grasping for comfort as I did when I called "Antique" a proud affirmation and a credo—there is a lastingness of art that is *somewhat* stronger than the acclaim of crowds; Pinsky's "Glory" reminds us that Pindar's ode (along with "Glory" itself) has, at least till today, survived the waters of anonymity and the acids of breath.

Nice to think so! But most remembering will fail and dissolve, as all the poems I've discussed acknowledge in one mood or another, angrily or mournfully or resignedly or despairingly. Despair looms as a possibility in "In the Coma," in *At the Foundling Hospital,* when Pinsky describes visiting a friend who is in a coma and trying to use the language of shared memories to stir consciousness in his friend. The effort, probably doomed in any case, becomes troubling in a further way when Pinsky finds that he cannot summon various particulars in language—song lyrics, lines of verse, pop culture facts—that he assumed himself to possess. The thought arises that we, too, we the functional and conscious, exist in a condition not entirely unlike a coma, adrift amid un-connections. The most startling stanza in this eerie poem is this:

I struggled to tell things back from decades gone.
The mournful American soldier testifying
About My Lai: *I shot the older lady.*

What is that soldier doing in the poem? He figures as a person desperately out of his depth, or rather *immersed* in depths he has not been able (at least not in a crisis, at My Lai) to plumb, to see through. He helplessly followed a course of action that seemed inescapable. But when he reports on committing murder, the word *lady* comes to his lips as his mother tongue tries to remind him of civilized values that were too lightly inscribed in his mind to govern his behavior.

Helpless, helpless . . . The next line of "In the Coma" is this: "Viola Liuzzo, Spiro Agnew, Jim Jones." Is there any ordering here? Someone, and a corrupt politician, and a maniacal cult leader. Who is Viola Liuzzo, is she a villain less famous than Agnew or Jones? No, Wikipedia says she was a white civil rights activist shot dead by the Ku Klux Klan in 1965 in Alabama. She doesn't belong in a line with Spiro Agnew and Jim Jones—unless the point of the line is to evoke in microcosm the chaos of human remembering, where tidbits bob up into focus in unchosen and all-but-useless sequence. Helpless are we, conscious but not in control of consciousness—and so "In the Coma" ends thus: "Quiet of the deep, / Our mouths are open but we cannot sing."

Viola Liuzzo, Spiro Agnew, Jim Jones. The line is a brief instance of a signature move in Pinsky's poetry: presenting a series or montage of nouns or nominal phrases without verbs. This move, though almost entirely absent from the poems I've discussed, happens often enough in Pinsky's other poems to prompt reflection. One suspicion that comes to mind is that Pinsky's impulse to omit verbs comes from wariness about statement—he senses that his panoptic impersonal long-view visions of culture and history risk coalescing too obviously and too abstractly into august bardic declarations; handfuls of nominal phrases invite the reader to infer a linking statement, without nailing it down for us, thus partially concealing, or qualifying, the fact that the poems do approach us essentially as wisdom statements, saying in effect, "Here is a large truth for all of us."

(The living, the unfallen lords of life,
Move heavily through the dazzle
Where all things shift, glitter or swim.

. . .

Our mouths are open but we cannot sing.)

However, this essay's focus on remembering versus forgetting has led me to detect a deeper cause behind Pinsky's verbless passages, namely his wish honestly to acknowledge and depict the way our minds constantly generate a flotsam of tidbits (facts, factoids, names, memories, perceptions) that we will never coordinate into ideas. Wisdom is endlessly undermined by forgetfulness, which is sped by disconnection. And yet, at least to glance caringly at many kinds of things is better, Pinsky feels, than *only* seeing the life in one's own little autobiographical groove—even if the multiple diverse glimpses may fail to add up.

Disconnection from the past, from unifying meanings, from a sense of being at home in life, is metaphorically a kind of orphanhood (as in "The Orphan Quadrille")—this metaphor shadows the quasi-title poem of *At the Foundling Hospital,* "The Foundling Tokens." The poem explains that desperate indigent mothers who abandoned their babies at the Foundling Hospital (in eighteenth-century London) tended to leave the infant with some item betokening unique individuality.

> At the Foundling Hospital
> For each abandoned
> Baby a duly recorded token:
> Bit of lace or a pewter brooch,
> Identifying coin, button
> Or bangle. One crushed thimble,
> Noted at admission.

The mothers' tiny efforts to mitigate their babies' sheer lostness include bits of verse.

> *If Fortune should her favours give*
> *That I in better plight may Live*
> *I'd try to have my Boy again*
> *And train him up the best of Men.*

We glimpse a mother wishing that the time-defying, mutability-defying powers of rhyme and meter will somehow forge a lasting link (however slight!) between herself and her child—or at least, a lasting proof of her own unique caring. In her pathetic and stubborn hope, she is a sister to the lover in "Antique"—and to you and me as we cherish our slim volumes of poetry. And as Pinsky's poem explicitly says, she is like slaves and prisoners in innumerable awful lives who have sought some inscription, some betokening, of their individuality and their meaningful origin.

"The Foundling Tokens" is a heartrending poem. It achieves this effect without appeasing our wish to be comforted. Whitman in "To Think of Time" can't bear his awareness of time's ravages, so he resorts to cloudy reassurance:

It is not to diffuse you that you were born of your mother and father,
  it is to identify you,
It is not that you should be undecided, but that you should be decided,
Something long preparing and formless is arrived and form'd in you,
You are henceforth secure, whatever comes or goes.

Pinsky, though, does not end "The Foundling Tokens" with an unlikely-but-possible reunion of mother and child, reunion made possible by a cherished bit of lace or scrap of verse, as if in a Dickens novel. The last sentence of the poem comes abruptly, without softening: "Although almost never was / A foundling reclaimed, ever." A high priority for Pinsky, here and throughout his poetry, is his refusal to deceive and to be deceived. He is determined not to be a sucker or to make suckers of us. This determination fuels his insistence on seeing each human experience in a context of a thousand comparable experiences across continents and epochs. At the same time, it prompts his many rueful or grim acknowledgments of confusion, dazedness ("Louie Louie"), and forgetting. Moreover, this determination is deeply involved in the distance between Pinsky's style and the chummy verbose discursiveness of elegiac poets such as Albert Goldbarth or David Kirby. Each pervasive pattern of truth Pinsky perceives tends to be a bitter pill, and he provides little of the sugar of affability. Pinsky's core style, next to that of Goldbarth or Kirby (or Philip Levine or Robert Hass), seems uncomforting, cool, stark, even thorny. (This has, one suspects, alarmed many high school teachers who wanted to teach poems by a poet laureate.) The effect of a clean sharp edge, in Pinsky's style, is a choice with a cost (like all choices); it is one aesthetic value among many possible values. It is valuable to me, in something like the way I value Thomas Hardy, another poet who never stopped brooding on what is *not* retrievable. Like Hardy, Pinsky never forgets forgetting—an obsession causing them both to write poems I find unforgettable.

ART AGAINST LONELINESS

On Rachel Wetzsteon's *Sakura Park*

When I happened to read Rachel Wetzsteon's *Sakura Park* (2006) in 2008, I was impressed by the candor and courage of its obsessive meditations on loneliness and by its pursuit of wittiness wanted not only for wit's self-armoring power but for wit's more interesting power to reveal the self in need of armor. I wrote to Wetzsteon in June 2008, praising eight of the *Sakura Park* poems in particular. In her gracious reply, she said, "On the one hand I feel it's my best book by far so far" (it was her third), but that she was now absorbed in a newer manuscript. That manuscript would become her posthumous collection *Silver Roses,* published at the end of 2010—a year after Wetzsteon took her own life on Christmas Day 2009, at the age of forty-two. A poet's suicide always throws a new light on the poetry—a light sometimes lurid, sometimes in an awful way glamorous. For that reason, I'm glad to know that I saw the merit of *Sakura Park* before its author's death.

In most of this essay I focus on poems in *Sakura Park.* Like other readers, I've felt uneasy about responding to *Silver Roses.* The temptation is to honor Wetzsteon elegiacally by praising the posthumous book as a triumph, an advance beyond her previous work. On the whole, though, *Silver Roses* is not as strong as *Sakura Park*—a comparison pointedly difficult to avoid because the later book maintains the previous book's preoccupation with romantic love. We can feel *Silver Roses* trying to be different from *Sakura Park* in two ways: there is even more flourishing of verbal cleverness; and there is in some of the poems an anxious optimism about a new love relationship—we see Wetzsteon entertaining the notion that her long search has found its happy ending. That notion perhaps inclined her to display her talent as poet of witty cheer rather than as poet of smart misery.

Yet she was very conscious of the possibility that her poetic achievement *depended* on unhappiness. In one of the optimistic poems (so spooky in the light thrown by her suicide), she wonders: "When I hauled my bags from Frostbite Falls to Harmony Hall, did the decline of menace mean the advent of bland gladness?" Elsewhere in *Silver Roses,* she is self-aware enough to know that bland gladness is an extremely unlikely fate for someone with her depths of anxiety and hunger. The book certainly does not show her moving into regions of concern separate from romantic love and the threat of loneliness. To read it after *Sakura Park* is to feel wary chagrin at the persistence of those themes.

All important poets have obsessions. The poet of *Sakura Park* is obsessed with heartbreak and loneliness and the wearying courage needed by someone—in particular, an intellectual single woman in New York—who struggles against heartbreak and loneliness through many years. Wetzsteon's style is consciously artful, sometimes (for my taste) a shade too archly witty, too ostentatiously artificial; what is remarkable is the extent to which the artifice doesn't disguise the emotion but, instead, gives it edge. Indeed, it would be hard to find a good book whose poems are more open and alarmingly clear in feeling. The pain of loneliness and of romantic disappointment is so vivid, so naked, in *Sakura Park* as to make you glance away from the page in embarrassment—even in fear. Yet the effect is far from that of artless poems by citizens so unhappy that they seem, as Randall Jarrell put it, to have "sent you their ripped-out arms and legs, with 'This is a poem' scrawled on them in lipstick." Nor is it like Anne Sexton, whose poems often seem to luxuriate in misery, whereas Wetzsteon is constantly fighting—intelligently, imaginatively, with daredevil poise—*not* to give in. Again and again, she offers herself advice, and since she knows, and lets us know, how briefly she has been able to follow her own advice, she hopes the advice itself can be strengthened by the flair of its expression.

Banish clichés only
to reinstate them as polished jewels:
love hurts, but you must not say it like that.
Cry "scarlet canyon."
Yell "wound supreme."
And in so doing, sew the wound up, count the jewels.

The force of that stanza from "Rosalind in Manhattan" comes from the fragility of the resolution. Wetzsteon is too alert not to realize that the reinstating of clichés, whether bejeweled or not, is a dubious goal for a poet, even if it could be a useful self-therapeutic maneuver. And she is grimly aware that great comfort is not promised in the image of being a scarred survivor weighing a wealth very different from the wished-for wealth of love. She wants to imagine herself as the heroine of a Shakespearean comedy but fears she may be stuck in a tragedy—or in some painful drama less cathartic than a tragedy.

The reality of her unhappiness is borne in on us by her candid willingness to consider that it might be thought of as biochemical rather than psychological. In "Listening to the Ocean," she expresses her gratitude for antidepressant medication.

> The waves were bad. And if
> this false wall hides their horrors from my eyes
> I'll swallow very gladly, and feel it rise.

The lines are weighted with the emotional exhaustion that can make a drug desirable. But the metaphor warns that a false wall is doomed to be temporary and that an ocean will never evaporate. Pain will return. In "Evening News," our protagonist has coffee with her ex-lover. She goes into the occasion assuming that they can be "sweetly melancholy" together, calmly sharing the unspoken memory of former passion. But then the man says, "I'm seeing someone"—and the revelation shatters her illusion of being beyond caring.

> Before this wholly unexpected blast
>   from the past
> I thought I'd fallen into seas so deep
> that nothing else could ever make me weep;
> I thought I'd buried my dead love for good
> in an abandoned, dusty neighborhood.
> But I soon learned that corpses can survive,
>   half alive.

Jealousy forces her back into wretched aliveness.

That stanza—is it a tissue of clichés and melodramatic hyperboles? I can imagine a reader saying so; I can imagine myself saying so. Wetzsteon can imagine it too; the next and last stanza of "Evening News" anticipates the smirk of a sophisticated reader and drives on past it, determined to declare her misery in a way that is blatantly stark yet also fiercely formal.

> So bluster, wind, and smile, sophisticate;
>   I've been hit
> with tons and tons of strangely heavy bricks,
> I feel the brute force of a million kicks
> but I have never felt less well or wise.
> Perhaps some unborn demon will devise
> a hotter fury or a crueler one;
>   hell has none.

No fury like a woman scorned. The target and victim of this woman's fury, though, is herself. She does not resist claiming that her pain is huge. Of course, for a poet to say, "I hurt more than anyone else," is to invite mockery, the kind of mockery that Shelley defies (or fails to anticipate?) in the last two stanzas of "Ode to the West Wind." Somehow, though, the effect of "Evening News" is not to make me say, "Oh, come off it." Rather, I feel a flash of the anguish from which the poem springs. In a paradox crucial to Wetzsteon's poetry, the artifice of her versification has a naked, ingenuous quality: "I've been hit / with tons and tons of strangely heavy bricks"—the phrase is clumsy, yes, but I want to say it's the clumsiness of someone staggering under a barrage of suddenly wounding thoughts, and when the bricks rhyme with "the brute force of a million kicks," there's a sense that the victim is too stunned to produce a more clever metaphor. She clings to rhyme and structure as last-ditch defenses against the chaos of fury.

What I've said may not amount to a convincing case for the brutal flatness of phrasing in the stanzas I've quoted (*deep/weep, bricks/kicks*). Still I testify that "Evening News" as a whole moves me, through the consciously chosen openness of the speaker's vulnerability. You or I might have been less willing to reveal the insecurity implied by jealousy of one's former lover's new romance. It's not a condition one ordinarily feels proud of, and yet Wetzsteon's candor arises partly from pride. In "But for the Grace," she contemplates the loquacious distress of a "crazy friend" who can't get over a breakup, noting that she herself knows how "to wrap my secrets in veils of frilly / banter, thick webs of gauzy bravado." She realizes that another kind of bravado is finally what she needs:

> But lately I'm struck by
>
> the dignity of full disclosure, the glory of loud,
> mad lovers who lay their lives on the line
> and carry their hearts through the scandalized crowd
> crying, Like it or not, this mangled thing is mine.

In "At the Zen Mountain Monastery," she tries for serene detachment, but "it's hopeless"—Zen calm is not desirable to a New York romantic like her:

> though the tortures of the damned
> make waking difficult, they are my tortures;
> I want them raucous and I want them near,
> like howling pets I nonetheless adore
> and holler adamant instructions to—
> sprint, mad ambition! scavenge, hopeless love
> that begs requital!—on our evening stroll
> down Broadway and up West End Avenue.

I like the bloody defiance at the end of "But for the Grace," but I am even more touched by the sound of proud acceptance of one's own (Western, Wetzsteon) identity at the end of "At the Zen Mountain Monastery"—audible in the unstressed rhyme of *instructions to* with *West End Avenue.*

Wetzsteon's pride is not so stubborn as to keep her from trying to diagnose her misery and ameliorate it. Many of the most affecting moments in *Sakura Park* show her considering a cause for her unhappiness and a possible strategic response. She likes imagining herself as a female flaneur, sardonic and elusive and chic, but then fears she has overplayed the role. Here are two of her "Flaneur Haiku":

> Robed in mystery
> I sweep through parks, through parades.
> But cast no shadow!

* * *

Never to be known:
charming as a beginning,
chilly at the end.

In "Love and Work," she worries that her intellectual life prevents romantic adventures:

A chilling vision of the years ahead
invades my thoughts, and widens like a stain:
a barren dance card and a teeming brain,
a crowded bookcase and an empty bed . . . .

But then she argues that her reading and writing make her *more* ready for the right lover:

I'm burning all these candles not to shirk

a night of passion, but to give that night
a richly textured backdrop when it comes.

These lines have an ominous ring of wishful thinking, yet we realize that we have sometimes justified our own long hours of reading and writing in the same way.

There's an amazing dream poem called "Lawyers on the Left Bank" in which Wetzsteon's dream interpretation does not manage to come up with strategic optimism. The lawyers find themselves in a Parisian café that becomes a wild nightclub full of sexual play. Wetzsteon supposes that the lawyers represent "me at thirty-two," and she imagines three responses they might have to the bawdy scene:

Perhaps they harbor fantasies of trading in their suits
for clingy leather bodices and sleek stiletto boots;
perhaps they scan the revelry and contemplate a fate
where working hard is not the solemn foe of playing late;

or maybe they just tease the air with legions of small sighs
and burn holes in the carpet with averted bedroom eyes.

These three possible responses distill moods explored in many poems in *Sakura Park*. The idea of being a tough adventuress gives way to the idea (as in "Love and Work") of a life in which erotic adventure and intellectual labor are mutually enhancing, but the last word goes to her fear of lingering in helpless lonely passivity. Explicitly working as her own psychiatrist, Wetzsteon achieves a vivid, strangely cinematic epitome of her enduring quandary. By giving her diagnosis such artful structure—"Lawyers on the Left Bank" is a sonnet in rhymed heptameter couplets—she has given it a firm and appealing shape outside the hurly-burly of her dreaming mind, so it can be contemplated with cool humor.

If Rachel Wetzsteon were alive and happily married today, *Sakura Park* would still be a powerful book, a book about unhappiness that turned out to be escapable. Since her suicide, though, we can't escape the sharpened poignancy of passages in which she strives to coach herself toward optimism and resilience. In "Gusts," for example, she sees spring blossoms blown from trees and wonders if her tendency to interpret every experience metaphorically may be a mistake:

> And all night a low voice chides me
> for never giving my all to the moment;
> a question forms and grows urgent
> and won't take no answer for an answer:
> if I gave up stories, what would become
> of the gust, and the scatter, and the stillness after?
> Would the trees be robbed of what made them priceless
> or let their riches loose as never before?

Those lines express the intellectual's fear that she overthinks her life and thereby misses pleasure but also the stronger suspicion that without imagination's narrating, experiences would lose "what made them priceless." Intensely and sometimes agonizingly mindful, Wetzsteon is apt to feel revulsion as well as envy for people who seem happily mindless, like the travelers weaving their paths through New York's gigantic bus station, so she counsels herself (in "Skater's Waltz," a section of "Manhattan Triptych") to forgive and accept:

This was the challenge: not to succumb,
that late gray afternoon in Port Authority,
to easy fury at the piped-in music—
such carefree, glittering sound must surround

much happier commutes than mine—
but to let the lushness pierce the grayness,
discover myself gliding in
an indoor rink with all the other skaters.

Poetry is matched against depression, proposing to convert a throng of commuters into blithe skaters and to give the scene a deftly formal air via rhythm and the partial rhyme whereby *grayness* gives way to *skaters.*

Wetzsteon keeps hypothesizing cheerful and dauntless responses to betrayal and solitude, promising herself that with enough imagination, such responses can be hers. Reading *Sakura Park,* one finds the adjective *plucky* coming to mind, with an inevitable dark edge since Wetzsteon's death. She reveres the heroines of Hollywood screwball comedies, like Irene Dunne, who win their access to renewed happiness through wit, without needing drugs. A stanza from "Short Ode to Screwball Women":

Gaudy but sober: when your wayward husband
courted the heiress, you stormed her gates
disguised as a floozy—and asked the butler
to serve you gingerale. It was life
you'd rather be drunk on, roaring life
that told you there is no time for spirits
of dark staircases, only lightning ruses
that not only leave no bruises but give
all parties their wish: rinsed vision and second chances.

But "lightning ruses" are so much more feasible in movies than in our daily lives. And so in the last poem of *Sakura Park,* which is also the title poem, Wetzsteon is still counseling herself, still watching for a metaphor that will help her live. The park she walks in becomes her life: when the wind scatters blossoms,

I still can't tell
whether this dispersal resembles

a fist unclenching or waving goodbye.

The park tells her that changes have to be tolerated, and the book ends with lines in which our heroine has a dignity after long suffering that hauntingly reminds me both of Hopkins's "My own heart let me more have pity on" and the weary hope of Tennyson's Ulysses.

Give up on rooted happiness

(the stolid trees on fire!) and sweet reprieve
(a poor park but my own) will follow.

There is still a chance the empty gazebo
will draw crowds from the greater world.

And meanwhile, meanwhile's far from nothing:
the humming moment, the rustle of cherry trees.

The person who has to remind herself that "meanwhile's far from nothing" is clearly familiar with the fear that the mere beauty of the physical world is empty. A reader may want to call out to her: Rachel, don't walk alone in the park, have lunch with a friend! But it's easy for an undepressed person to condescend to depression.

True; still, for an undepressed reader, a possible complaint about *Sakura Park* (and *Silver Roses* too, alas) would be that it is myopically riveted on the self, so devoted to the protagonist's emotional drama as to be oblivious of all the other dramas—some involving physical misery—happening around her in New York City. In one poem, "Apologies to an Ambulance," Wetzsteon faces the idea that hers is not the only suffering in town. Seeing an ambulance pass, she at first performs her habitual figuration:

The red light was my racing heart,
the siren my pain made public,

and the body inside, a study in scarlet,
was battered yet somehow grotesquely pretty.

But then (without showing how the shift comes about) she decides she owes an apology to the ambulance's patient, "the wretch in the back"—

>   you come from a place
> where pulp's not fiction, you know a world
> where bullets are more than metaphors
> for lovely eyes, and though I roped you
> into my story I'll let you go now, wish you
> safe passage through a lifetime of green lights.

That realization may be too rare in *Sakura Park,* but to ask for much more of such empathy would be to ask for a different book. *Sakura Park* has the integrity of a book that knows what it *needs* to be about. "Like it or not, this mangled thing is mine." There are many books of poems that come across essentially as efforts at self-therapy without appearing to know—or to want us to know—how fully that is what's going on. Wetzsteon's book, by comparison, is admirably unpretentious.

Another striking and even brave (not just plucky) thing about *Sakura Park* is its commitment—not only in its formalities of structure and rhyme but also in its diction and idioms—to effects that are proudly not au courant. Wetzsteon's being a fan of screwball comedy heroines is suggestive; though she functioned as a high-achieving intellectual in the twenty-first-century metropolis (she had become poetry editor of *The New Republic* not long before her death), her visions of plausible joy and romantic success hark back to the 1930s, to an era when insincere men could unjokingly be called "heels." In some ways, Wetzsteon is the urbane, witty, vulnerable daughter of Edna St. Vincent Millay, a poet now underrated (though less interesting than Wetzsteon, I'd say). There are sentences and stanzas in *Sakura Park* that you could believe to be Millay's, and Wetzsteon must have recognized a mood of her own in Millay's famous lines:

> Life in itself
> Is nothing,
> An empty cup, a flight of uncarpeted stairs.

It is not enough that yearly, down this hill,
April
Comes like an idiot, babbling and strewing flowers.

Vitality without reliable romantic love was not enough for Rachel Wetz-steon. She knew she was no cherry tree, the way Whitman knew he was no Louisiana live oak. When she pretended, sometimes, to have found contentment, soon she was honest and brave enough to call her own bluff. In "A Bluff," she stands on an elevated spot, after having been rejected by a lover.

Looking down at the city below,
I am almost grateful that when I said
I have met my soul, my soul said no;
it was a verdict that nearly bled
the hope from my veins, but it got me thinking.

Hard for her to be grateful that the relationship failed, though she goes on to speculate that it might eventually have decayed into the bourgeois tedium of marital compromise.

I cry all the time; I hate the ghosts snoring
next to the people they love. But at least
I won't be someone who, smiling too often,
gives too much away; your shipwrecked
wandering stare won't cruelly soften
into the landlocked glare of wan respect.

In those lines, we see Wetzsteon doing something she often does, setting up an either-or opposition (either desperate adventuress or stultified spouse) as if no complicated in-between options were possible. Zen calm, on the one hand, mad ambition and hopeless love, on the other—binary oppositions like this are tempting because they avoid the confusion of hybrid conditions and also perhaps because they are convenient for the neat balances of a rhyme scheme. The binary tendency is there in a line quoted earlier, from "Lawyers on the Left Bank," wistfully trying to imagine "a fate / where working hard is not the solemn foe of playing late." It's there in many poems in *Silver Roses,* despite the emerging hope in that book that the latest love relationship will prove *both* reliable *and* lastingly interesting. In "A Dream Vision," Wetzsteon tells of being visited in sleep by two phantom versions of herself: one is an operatically un-happy victim whose injunction is "Complain"; the other is an innocent girl who whispers "Praise." The poem does not consider ways of allowing both selves to coexist. Instead,

> Half-awake in the predawn
> I tossed and turned,
> raged and burned,
> blearily staggered from bed to window
> and wondered which fled ghost
> would sign her name to the phrases I was forming.

I call "A Dream Vision" a good poem—its drama is simple but deftly and lucidly presented, and the feeling in those last lines is convincing. Still, the tendency to set up stark dichotomies (praise versus complaint, work versus play, peace versus thrill, safe boredom versus passionate misery) prompts a suspicion that this poet is drawn toward, almost addicted to, the frustration that such binaries make inevitable. We saw her chiding herself, in "Gusts," "for never giving my all to the moment"—a "giving" that would require her to give up "stories." Most of us most of the time, though, get along by sometimes giving a lot to the mo-ment (not our "all") *while* almost always forming our experience into narratives so that the wild jazz of life will feel meaningful and purposeful. In *Silver Roses,* a poem called "Midsummer Night's Swing" revisits the issue of immersion in the moment. Again, she laments her absorption in memory and hope at the expense of being-here-now.

> *One must live in the present tense,*
> observed Bette Davis, but I have
> always lived in the present
> tensely. Tell me
> about it: two absent-minded sisters,
> backward-peering and future-ogling,

took turns obscuring my vision,
and if managed a brief repose
I did it awkwardly:
my senses somehow took their pleasures
smoke and mirrorishly.

I admire the way that stanza combines wit with sad self-insight and does this so clearly. The effort to communicate clearly, throughout Wetzsteon's poetry, reflects her sense of poetry's importance. Life is too short for modish murk; obscurity is the minor amusement of poets who haven't come to care enough about poetry's power to help people live.

In the second (and last) stanza of "Midsummer Night's Swing," Wetzsteon addresses someone—perhaps her new partner?—who seems able to live entirely in the present pleasure of listening to the Dirty Dozen Brass Band at Lincoln Center Plaza. In keeping with her wish to write hopefully in *Silver Roses*, Wetzsteon resolves to imitate his immersion:

I'll try to do the same,
for I scribbled vainly all afternoon
and later will be lovely,
but so are these current presents
that make this, for now, the only concert—
trumpet, sky, fountain, dancing eyes.

This resolution—more being-a-good-sport than convinced—is touching; we sense how uncertain she feels about locating a tolerable life *between* the work of writing and the romance expected "later."

Wetzsteon's attraction to simplifying dichotomies animates one of the best poems in *Silver Roses*, "Year Zero." Hopeful in a new relationship, she is drawn to the idea of her life starting anew, a pure break between past suffering and new love. The impulse to absolutely separate the two seems brave but then seems also fanatical and delusory.

Raze the chamber where the Brahms piano music,
yearning and yearning outside the window,

nearly drove you mad that summer,
the railroad flat where the roommates took turns
questioning life's joy and purpose;
stand beside the space you've cleared,
say, "On this rock I build a lasting structure."

Pile high the letters sent and received,
then strike a match and cackle wildly
as pleas and feints and imprecations
melt into what you'd have known they were
if you'd only kept your head on: laughable ash.

Then she realizes that painful memories can't be wiped away by an act of will;
"Year Zero" ends with these nine lines:

But the very sad Intermezzo,
the ill-judged apple martini,
the plunges fueled by false trust
and misted mirrors are destroy-proof;
they hover at the edges of freshness
as relieved comparisons or, sometimes, bad dreams—
sign perhaps that a truly blank slate's
for amnesiacs and empty classrooms,
a purge that cannot prove how far you've come.

I suppose a therapist would welcome the wisdom there, but a therapist might also detect something worrisome in the word *prove* in that last line—Wetzsteon's longing for an unmistakable assurance that her life has changed. The hypothetical therapist might prefer an emphasis on self-understanding to be carried *from* the past into the future—and a flash of the pride that declared, in "At the Zen Mountain Monastery," "they are my tortures; / I want them raucous and I want them near."

Undoubtedly, anyone presuming to offer therapeutic advice to an emotionally troubled person is liable to be guilty of arrogant complacency. But I think no reader of *Sakura Park* and *Silver Roses* can escape trying to imagine wise counsel for the suffering heroine—because she so openly and so unrelentingly presents herself as a case, making her emotional well-being the central subject, almost the *only* subject of her poetry. Innumerable poets lead us through their vicissitudes of emotion, of course, but few make their misery-joy index so explicitly the topic directly engaged, and in Wetzsteon's outlook, notwithstanding many lines about the pleasures of reading and writing, joy is inseparable from having a lover. If I find myself wanting to say, "Rachel, think about something else!" my conscience reminds me how rivetingly interesting my own loneliness seemed to me during the phases of my life when I had no lover. Even in those phases, though, I tried to write *sometimes* about something else. For Rachel Wetzsteon, there was one subject, and in her treatment of it, courageous candor and neurotic obsession can't be disentangled. Because she examined her entanglement with so much intelligence and talent, her poetry lives on after her departure from the city of maddening romance and tough reality.

COURAGEOUS CLARITY

On Tony Hoagland's *Unincorporated Persons*
in the Late Honda Dynasty

To come right out in the open: I think *Unincorporated Persons in the Late Honda Dynasty* (2010) is an outstanding book, among the best poetry books in many years. It may be even better than Hoagland's strong previous book *What Narcissism Means to Me,* though I'm wary of the way reviewers and blurbers feel summoned to say that someone's latest book is his or her best. Hoagland made himself an important poet in our cacophonous American scene, by developing his nervy brash lucid style that jars the reader into embarrassed wakefulness. Hoagland barges right into issues—social class, racism, sexism, complicity in capitalism, many kinds of dishonesty—that most poets prefer merely to graze fleetingly as if nothing but cliché were possible any more in relation to those issues. Hoagland takes risks that are more significant than the kind of daring that consists only in sliding from very odd metaphor to even odder metaphor. Hoagland's daring does lead him into some moves that aren't subtle or insightful enough, I think (my friends know that I can't praise everything in *anyone's* book). But of the forty-six poems in *Unincorporated Persons,* there are at least a dozen that I'd rank alongside poems by Wisława Szymborska (to name a great poet outside the American whirl), and all but a few of the poems seem to me wonderfully engaging.

My desire to praise Hoagland's poetry runs deep and is not purely disinterested. (Perhaps the purely disinterested review is a chimera?) For one thing, he and I were friends—not close friends but friends—from 1994 till his death in 2018, and with many friends in common. Moreover, Hoagland's poetry resembles my own in some basic ways. Naturally, I'm invested in my belief that there are important differences between Hoagland and Halliday. (We all want to be special.) And I'd love to live in a world where smart persons would care enough to explore the comparison. Meanwhile, though, I have to realize that if Hoagland's poetry isn't admirable in some key ways, mine can't be either.

What strikes you first about Tony Hoagland's poems is their clarity. They come straight at you. They walk up and start talking to you, in a voice whose rueful wryness does not sound tricky but doesn't sound casual either. It's the sound of someone who has been bothered by something in life—something he will try to specify for you—and he is not interested in disguising it or teasing you with hints about it. The directness of his approach is not only bold but edgy, slightly aggressive even; there's a sense of a speaker who has grown impatient with artfully elliptical poetry (and speech) and wants to cut through the fog to a place where speaker and listener might live more healthily on a basis of candor. When Hoagland uses metaphors—whether in passing or as extended conceits—they have a clean, unornamented availability; if some are more telling and insightful than others, the reader is invited to discriminate among them without impediment. To write this way takes nerve.

Some poets lure the reader into syntactical and metaphorical mazes; there may be a lot going on in those mazes (intensity, complexity of thought, depth, finding of truth)—or not! Some difficult poets are great (Dickinson, Eliot, Stevens); many are bad. The same is true for poets who are easy or highly readable: many are bad, but some (Whitman, Hardy, Frost) attain a greatness inseparable from the openness and directness of their speech. We like to point out that Frost's meanings are more mysterious than they seemed to us (or our teachers) in high school, but there's still a serious reason why Frost *can* be successfully taught in high school. Of course, openness and directness are dangerous qualities for an artist because if the work is banal, the banality is not shrouded, not swathed in gauzy figuration and arcane references. American poetry is overpopulated with poets who seem to sense that they don't possess a strikingly fresh perspective on human problems, so they'd better weave bundles of oddities and feints and ironic gestures. Tony Hoagland, instead, accepted the risks of clarity.

The riskiness is most noticeable in the poems that address pervasive social conditions, the poems that get called "political" and are often quoted in reviews of Hoagland. (Actually, some of his best poems involve the inner life and are more personal than political, insofar as this dichotomy is tenable; a key impulse in Hoagland is to show how illusory the dichotomy is.) Consider a passage from "Dialectical Materialism," in which the speaker is strolling around a supermarket, feeling hyperaware of political and economic forces behind the tempting merchandise. Is the passage imaginatively engaging, or do you feel its import is embarrassingly overfamiliar?

> There was cornbread rising in the bakery department
> and in its warm aroma I believed that I could smell
>   the exhaled breath of vanished Iroquois,
> their journey west and
>   delicate withdrawal into the forests,
>
> whereas by comparison
> the coarse-grained wheat baguettes
> seemed to irrepressibly exude
> the sturdy sweat and labor of eighteenth-century Europe.
>
> My god there is so much sorrow in the grocery store!
> You would have to be high
> on the fumes of the piped-in pan flutes
>   of commodified Peruvian folk music
>
> not to be driven practically crazy
> with awe and shame,
> not to weep at the scale of subjugated matter:
>
> the ripped-up etymologies of kiwi fruit and bratwurst,
> the roads paved with dead languages,
> the jungles digested by foreign money.

For my (American) money, the passage *is* imaginatively engaging, both funny and troubling—while at the same time, we may say its meaning is embarrassingly familiar. That familiarity is a central subject for Hoagland, and the embarrassment is an objective. Hoagland knows perfectly well that anyone likely to read his book already "knows" that global capitalism is built on enormous destructions and oppressions that we can, on most days, avoid facing. The irksome task he often sets himself is to cut through our jaded knowingness to

reach fresh sensation. Watching his strategies for cutting through is a key pleasure in reading Hoagland. Writing "Dialectical Materialism," Hoagland takes
for granted that his reader remembers Ginsberg's "A Supermarket in California"
and "All Lost in the Supermarket" by The Clash and other artistic evocations of
the repressions behind capitalist abundance. Should the idea be simply avoided
because it's so Yesterday? Hoagland refuses that option, and he also declines the
possibilities of farcical satire or desperate phantasmagoria. He chooses a tensely
reflexive irony in broad daylight. The choice limits his style and tone and tacti-
cal moves (as all choices bring limits) while giving him chances to explore variations within the ironic mode. In Hoagland, unlike lots of poets, irony is not an
excuse for murkiness; on the contrary, his irony is like a machete clearing the
underbrush of distractions to make room for patches of earnestness.

Thus, he can make fun of his own hyped-up political consciousness in the
supermarket—

> I was seeing the whole produce section
> > as a system of cross-referenced signifiers
> in a textbook of historical economics

—without denying the serious moral perceptions that accompany his (and
our) liberal intellectual admiration-of-one's-own-consciousness. We know he
doesn't literally weep over the "subjugated matter" displayed in, and reflected
by, the supermarket, but we also realize he isn't kidding when he says that an
undrugged response to all this would be "to be driven practically crazy / with
awe and shame." The sorrow and anger are real—even if we fail to live up to
their moral implications. Unlike some proud hortatory poets who model admirable attitudes toward war, racism, pollution, and other evils, Hoagland keeps
remembering his own comfort within our social system. So he admits that as he
leaves the supermarket, he's feeling rather cheerful—

> the bossa nova muzak charmed me like a hypnotist
> and the pretty cashier with the shaved head and nose ring
> > said, *Have a nice day*

—and then, in the parking lot, he finds that a minor traffic accident has
occurred. Like many of us educated thoughtful comfortable Americans, Hoag-

land is very ready to see minor misfortune as a metaphor for national and global misfortune. Hence, the unhappy drivers are "these personified portions of my heart," and Hoagland imagines them thinking

> how at any minute,
> convenience can turn
>> into a kind of trouble you never wanted.

The point is that the convenience—the supermarket, the food industry, the auto industry—*contains* the causes of trouble that will nevertheless be surprising, even shocking, when it comes.

Having just written a sentence about "the point" of the ending of "Dialectical Materialism," I'll speak again about the transparent readability and thematic clarity of Hoagland's poetry. It has a nakedness. You can imagine a critique of "Dialectical Materialism" that would smirk at the word *muzak* in the poem's inventory of the supermarket's disturbing comforts, since to complain about muzak as a symptom of cultural decadence was already a cliché forty years ago. But the reply would be that muzak—along with all sorts of narcotic commodification epitomized by it—continues to affect us in our real lives. How is a poet to face the lives we really live? Rae Armantrout, Charles Bernstein, Carolyn Forché, Jorie Graham, Kent Johnson, Ron Silliman, Charles Simic, and any dozen Ashbery acolytes will all be shopping in a supermarket in the next few days.

We're all complicit. Yeah, we know it, as we know that death is coming and that love requires imagination and that humility is endless and that nothing human is alien to us and that power tends to corrupt. What good poetry often does is reanimate what we already inertly "know."

Our complicity in off-camera evils is an obsession for Hoagland. There is a haunting passage in "Candlelight," in his 1998 book *Donkey Gospel,* that ponders how

> in this world

> you have to decide what
> you're willing to kill.

It reads:

Saving your marriage might mean
dinner for two

by candlelight on steak
raised on pasture
chopped out of rain forest
whose absence might mean

an atmospheric thinness
fifty years from now
above the vulnerable head
of your bald grandson on vacation

as the cells of his scalp
sautéed by solar radiation
break down like suspects
under questioning.

Still you slice
the sirloin into pieces
and feed each other
on silver forks

under the approving gaze
of a waiter
whose purchased attention
and French name

are a kind of candlelight themselves,
while in the background
the fingertips of the pianist
float over the tusks

of the slaughtered elephant
without a care,

as if the elephant
had granted its permission.

Hoagland said in an interview with Miriam Sagan: "There was a time when I looked at a scene and saw a man and a woman kissing. Now I am aware that the man has a credit card in his pocket and that just behind the woman a beer commercial is on the TV, interrupting war coverage from Afghanistan." The spirit of this perspective is not cynical because, as Hoagland knows, cynicism is too comfortable—it is an inverted form of sentimentality.

In *Unincorporated Persons,* the sensation of painfully half-voluntary complicity in political and cultural harm comes across in many good poems, though what the poems express is not simply limited to that sensation. Such poems include "Food Court," "Big Grab," "Hard Rain," "Confinement," "'Poor Britney Spears,'" "Expensive Hotel," "Complicit with Everything," "Hinge," "Foghorn," "Disaster Movie," "The Allegory of the Temp Agency," "Snowglobe." There is plenty to say about those, and critics should write about them carefully enough to move past simply categorizing them as "political poems." A long article waits to be written about their endings and how, in a poem's closing lines, Hoagland twists the knife, to make the poem disturb you after you felt sure you knew where he was going. An example is "The Allegory of the Temp Agency," which, thanks to the machete slash of its last lines, manages to become both a satirical critique of banal polemical art and a startling reminder that banal political protests against global capitalism arise from horrible inequities that suave mockery cannot remove.

So I admire those poems, and I say that if Tony Hoagland had written only those, he'd already be an important poet, doing something decisively that other poets do winkingly, evasively, or banally. However, in a way I now half-regret having focused on poems like "Dialectical Materialism" simply because they are the most noticeable poems in Hoagland's work and the ones most convenient for reviewers writing short reviews.

Hoagland also writes about love relationships, family bonds, the formation and deformation of one's identity according to gender roles and gendered tendencies of desire—and about our efforts (including poetry itself) to use language to attain a calm grip on experience. In the latter category, *Unincorporated Persons* begins with "Description," a poem that would be worth discussing alongside many poems by Wallace Stevens, as it ponders our constant need to imbue natural phenomena with human meaning and the question of whether in doing so we imprison ourselves away from reality. The same theme is more comically engaged in "Cement Truck," which mainly succeeds, via boyish zest, in dodging the tremendous magnetic pull of metaphor—though, of course, Hoagland knows we will say that his desire to let the cement truck be just a truck is a metaphor for any poet's hunger for concrete celebration of the world. "Personal" is a funny poem about being someone who has always been driven toward language by fundamental bafflements and damages and longings. "My Father's Vocabulary" painfully meditates on the long-lasting cost of acquiescing in the impoverished and demeaning language wielded by a particular social group or class or generation. A lighter poem, "Address to the Beloved," responds with hilarious cluelessness to a woman who has told our man to get real. For a postmodern protagonist, that injunction is the doorway to dervish whirls of ambivalence. The half-misery, half-excitement of constant self-consciousness is explicitly the subject of another funny poem, "I Have News for You."

I say those are all good poems. Of course, I can quibble with a phrase here and there, and occasionally, I wish Hoagland would push farther into complications. Here, though, I want to stress the consistency of achievement in *Unincorporated Persons*—achievement inseparable from Hoagland's explicitness. Take it or leave it. Readers come to poetry with many different wishes, some of them irreconcilable. (Charles Harper Webb usefully outlined this in his article "Apples and Orangutans: Competing Values in Contemporary Poetry" [*Writer's Chronicle*, October–November 2004], in which he listed sixty-two qualities that poems are asked to evince.) Tony Hoagland will never be able to please those readers who are infected by ICFU. This syndrome—Instant Contempt for the Understandable—is always active in people worried about establishing that in poetry they are doing something difficult and mysterious that your aunt and uncle, and your average students, can't do. People afflicted with ICFU (including even a few of my quasi-friends) act condescending and disdainful toward a poem immediately upon realizing that it makes sense, coheres, and can be paraphrased (with a paraphrase more specific than "Life is so weird!"). To be consistent, ICFU readers should be disdainful of all the great poets in English (including even Blake and Hopkins) up to and including Yeats, Frost, and Stevens—or else they have to claim that paraphrasability was okay "back then" but that now, since, oh, 1970, our world is so atom-smashed, the only artistic response is gaudy messes. In the ICFU-ist aesthetic, Frost's hope for a momentary stay against confusion has been ditched for the sake of a momentary grooving *in* confusion.

The question that matters is: How much truth about life does a poem illuminate, express, waken us to? All sorts of lyrical and rhetorical felicity should be subordinate to a poem's depth of insight. Verbal dexterity and mellifluousness (names like Merrill and Muldoon flash on the screen) count for very little if the poem is shallow. (Note: a truly funny poem whose meaning is inseparable from the relief of laughter can bring a kind of insight; hilarity has a truth in it, whereas the poetry of Watch-me-being-exceedingly-clever doesn't.) Meanwhile, depth of insight has a splendid way of coming to seem felicitous; thus, many of Hardy's gnarly, seemingly awkward poems turn out to be beautiful.

Plenty of contemporary poets have conveyed the truth of the misery of divorce. But there are other truths involved in divorce—new solitude becoming possibility becoming chilly new hope. Hoagland expresses this with his usual directness in "In Praise of Their Divorce." The poem begins with the word *And,* as if replying to someone who has just murmured sadly that some marriages should not be saved.

> And when I heard about the divorce of my friends,
> I couldn't help but be proud of them,
>
> that man and that woman setting off in different directions,
> like pilgrims in a proverb
>
> —him to buy his very own toaster oven,
> her seeking a prescription for sleeping pills.

The poem would already be worth something if vivid, convincing sympathy for both wife and husband were its whole purpose. But Hoagland has more on his mind; "In Praise of Their Divorce" is also a meditation on metaphor. We need metaphorical ways of thinking about any frightening experience—thus, the divorcing spouses, or their friends, might need to see the divorce as an earthquake that wrecks the surface but allows new energy to flow. Like most metaphors, this one is only satisfying for a moment (since the earthquake image doesn't guarantee that renewal and rebuilding will ensue), so the poem drops it after a few lines and moves on to improvise other metaphors in the effort to accept the divorce as something more than a disaster.

Because if marriage is a kind of womb,

divorce is the being born again;
alimony is the placenta one of them will eat;

loneliness is the name of the wet-nurse;
regret is the elementary school;

endurance is the graduation.

What do you think of those lines? I wouldn't like them if they struck me as self-pleased would-be brilliance from a writer wanting to be compared with John Donne. But Hoagland's lines, instead, want to sound makeshift, as if improvised after a few beers; the bluntness, the candid vulnerability of the metaphors, is *itself* a kind of meta-metaphor for the way we need, under stress, to knock together a framework of ideas that will help us get through the day—or through the first year of a divorce.

That is why it would be a harmless shot if some snarky experimentalist were to mock that passage as a series of "workshop metaphors." They are hammered together for a needful purpose like boards in the kind of (carpenter's) workshop that provides a non-ridiculous (though inevitably partial, provisional) metaphor for a poetry workshop. Candidly emphasizing his focus on metaphor, on the way metaphor is a good servant but a dangerous master, Hoagland in the poem's next sentence produces three examples that he says should be refused:

So do not say that they are splattered like dropped lasagna

or dead in the head-on collision of clichés
or nailed on the cross of their competing narratives.

Beware of metaphors whose cleverness might trap us into unwanted implications. ("War on terror," for instance.) Hoagland is a poet intuitively skeptical of elaborately artful figuration; he knows we need metaphor, but he feels strongly that prettiness of metaphor is not the point and may pull us away from the point. So he typically deploys metaphors in the frank provisional manner—as if saying *Let's try this one out*—displayed in "In Praise of Their Divorce," which ends as follows, with two more metaphors, which manage to be hopeful yet not exactly comforting about the splitting of spouse from spouse:

> It is like a great mysterious egg in Kansas
>
> that has cracked and hatched two big bewildered birds.
> It is two spaceships coming out of retirement,
>
> flying away from their dead world,
> the burning booster rocket of divorce
>   falling off behind them,
>
> the bystanders pointing at the sky and saying, *Look.*

Describing a relative lack of rhetorical adornment in middle-period Yeats, Richard Ellmann wrote: "It is as if the poet had an agreement with his readers to get on with the essentials." Hoagland writes in a similar spirit of urgency, for readers who will trust him to grip a subject tenaciously. When I said his metaphors have a quality of being composed on the spot, as if improvised after a few beers, I didn't mean to imply casualness; beer can foster intensity, after all. The Hoagland voice is the voice of someone trying hard to say the sharp-edged necessary thing in the pressure of the moment, as if his chance to address the reader before the evening ends (or before we get sick and die) may be brief. The mood is not frantic, nor is it grim, but it's not relaxed and easygoing either. This distinguishes Hoagland from comic-discursive poets such as David Kirby, Albert Goldbarth, and Denise Duhamel, for whom Ultra Talk is a more useful categorization than it would be for Hoagland. They seem to assume we have hours available for listening to them; he expects only minutes.

It is true that a person speaking urgently, under pressure, is tempted to boil down his meanings, simplifying them for FedEx delivery. I don't say Hoagland never does this, but I see it happening much less often and less expensively than his detractors do. Reviewing *Unincorporated Persons* in the May 2010 issue of

Poetry, Peter Campion argued that the poems too readily "can be summed up by pat phrases." Campion supported the complaint by quoting the endings of four poems, all of which use the word *that* to set up a closing comment on something described earlier in the poem. It's true that the four endings give a feeling of decisive thematic closure, but I think Campion succumbs to reviewer glibness when he says that Hoagland "points you to the meanings of his own poems with all the rigid authority of a traffic cop." I could remark that sometimes we want to encounter agents who exert firm (if not rigid) Miltonic authority; in a street situation where troubling and angry thoughts have been bashing into each other, we may want a traffic cop of ideas. But really, that point could apply only to "Love" among the four poems whose endings Campion picks out. "Love" is about a man and a woman who try to keep their sexual romance alive though age and disease have made it much more difficult. "All that talk about love, and *This* / is what that word was pointing at." The poem tries to respect the courage of people who have been unlucky but persist in being each other's good fortune. I actually think "Love" is one of the weaker poems in *Unincorporated Persons* because it doesn't think its way far into the relation between desire and love, but still I resent Campion's quick dismissal.

And in any case, the other three poems ("Jason the Real," "Jazz," "Voyage") whose endings Campion quotes are less easy to summarize than he implies. Their effect is not traffic coppy. It's the effect of someone who wants to have gotten somewhere in his poem and cares about our getting there too. Moreover, Campion is disingenuous when he pretends that the four endings are "a nearly random sample." That is false. Hoagland's endings do tend to be decisive, stark, but they are syntactically and rhetorically various.

I will try another big rebuttal of Campion's review. But first, let me say that in one respect, I emphatically approve of it: Campion is willing to express a strong preference for one book over another book. He does not shy away from evaluation. Few intelligent poetry reviewers have the guts to say that a book is bad. Ironically, Tony Hoagland as an essayist specialized in unthreatening taxonomies that allow him to imply that various uninteresting poets are all somehow interesting. The courage I attribute to Hoagland as a poet is much less apparent in his criticism.

What really bothers me in Campion's review is his resorting to the most dubious and subjective criterion for poetry—how sound should enhance sense—

and asserting (with a traffic coppy air) that Hoagland's poetry suffers from "the almost total lack of music." To back this up, Campion quotes the first six lines of "Foghorn":

> When that man my age
> came towards me in the fast-food restaurant
> with his blue plastic cafeteria tray
>
> and stood next to the table where I sat alone
> (there was no place else to sit),
> I looked up at him in welcome—

Now, those six lines are straightforwardly narrative, and I'm not about to call them beautiful. But they catch our interest by being ominous in an understated way—a frequent effect in Hoagland, one that Campion wittily but unfairly acknowledges by likening the voice to that of Eddie Haskell, the manipulative hypocrite in *Leave It to Beaver.* Haskell's tone is ominous because he has hidden selfish intentions; Hoagland's is ominous because we sense he is going to bring something out into daylight that we tend to keep decorously concealed or half-concealed by circumlocutory metaphors or "music."

The whole issue of music in poetry is much more mysterious than Campion pretends. If you wanted to complain about those first six lines of "Foghorn" (setting aside, for the moment, the way they work in the context of the whole poem, which concerns how citizens of different races are alienated from each other by their racist assumptions), you could say they don't contain a fresh turn of phrase or a particularly vivid image, and you'd be right—though you wouldn't have established anything about the value of the whole poem. There are many reasons why a poem might need a patch of simple, flatly stated phrases. Campion, who admires Louise Glück, must know this. But if what you seek in poetry is language loaded with poetic effects—every rift with ore—and you get along well with people who say (about Derek Walcott, perhaps, or Anthony Hecht), "Oh, the language!" as if self-evident glory is being recognized, you're on much firmer ground praising passages for their density of reference, their elevated diction, their syntactical complexity, or their vividness of sensory description, than if you proclaim the favored passages are good due to their music.

If I were a certain kind of critic, I could defend those six Hoagland lines on "musical" grounds. Hear the tense, almost frightening inhuman harshness of "blue plastic cafeteria tray." Hear the acceleration-toward-crisis in the anapests of "and stood next to the table where I sat alone." Et cetera. Hoagland, master of music! But I always find that kind of "analysis" unconvincing and professionally pompous.

Probably what Campion really feels, when he decides to call Hoagland's six lines unmusical, is that they are not different enough from everyday speech. (Actually, though, it's hard to imagine a real conversation in which someone would say exactly, "When that man my age came towards me in the fast-food restaurant"). How different from everyday speech does a poem need to be? Any answer to this question gets exploded by the next good poet—Horace, Wordsworth, O'Hara—who wants a new way to find poetic power in the moves of daily talk.

Like you, and like Hoagland, and like Campion, when I write a poem, I care a lot about how it sounds. Getting this right is complicated in ways that are not encompassed by pieties about music. Pace, tone, consistency or variety, grace, momentum, lexical register, roughness or smoothness—there are many factors. For me, a crucial factor is convincingness of voice: the seeming reality of the implied persona. This, too, is hard to define. A lonely Jesuit priest, half-crushed by tedious labor and desperate for spiritual fulfillment, throbbing with obsessive awareness of his desires and fears, created the convincing voice (though it certainly doesn't sound conversational) of Hopkins's late sonnets. It is certainly possible to write a bad poem in a convincing voice. I've done it, and one's more naive students do it. But it is even easier, and much more common, to write a bad poem in an unconvincing voice.

Music? Reader, suppose you are asked to "hear" the following set of eight examples and decide which passages have the best music:

I   It's a year exactly since my father died.
     Last year was hot. At the funeral, people talked about the weather.
     How hot it was for September. How unseasonable.

     This year, it's cold.
     There's just us now, the immediate family.

2   Come the marrow-hours when he couldn't sleep,
the boy river-brinked and chorded.

Mud-bedded himself here in the root-mesh; bided.
Sieved our alluvial sounds—.

3   There are the suppressed reports. There is
a captain telling of villagers he befriended.
How he returned to find them kneeling in a line.

How a sergeant from another unit opened fire.
How his superior held the captain back
with his clipped, bureaucratic "no can do"

as the shots and pleading ripped the air.

4   I am very happy to be here at the Villa Hügel
and Prime Minister Nehru has asked me to greet the people of Essen
and to tell you how powerfully affected we in India
have been by Germany's philosophy, traditions and mythology.

5   I walked into the room.
There were objects in the room. I thought I needed nothing
from them. They began to speak,
but the words were unintelligible, a painful cacophony . . . .

6   From his desk your father asked for you
that Christmas morning. He explained. Last night

your mother ". . . passed." You would be leaving now
for boarding school. The silence of that ride

across Ohio echoed down our family.

7   Always the story-man lights lard-lamps in a circle and tells.

A boy scrapes and ever-graves for likeness with a stick.
Two girls croodle corn-songs cane-songs back and forth unbroken.
Once-bent bodies leap (in chorus) leg and whirl.

8   Finally, in middle age,
I was tempted to return to childhood.

The house was the same, but
the door was different.
Not red anymore—unpainted wood.
The trees were the same: the oak, the copper beech.
But the people—all the inhabitants of the past—
were gone: lost, dead, moved away.
The children from across the street
old men and women.

The correct answer? The correct answer is to refuse this ridiculous quiz! There is nothing useful to say about the music of those passages without a view of the whole poems they belong to. You may like this or that phrase, for its sheer sound or for a more serious reason, but everything important depends on how the lines contribute to a poem's whole effect.

The most blatant attempts to offer music are in #2 and #7. Those passages are by Atsuro Riley, from his poems "Chord" and "O." Campion, in the same review in which he deplores Hoagland's unmusicality, enthusiastically praises Riley's "beguiling music." If you love the lush sentimentality of Dylan Thomas or the baroque prose of Cormac McCarthy, maybe you're attracted by the Riley lines I've quoted. For me, they evoke a sensation that I'm being sold a box full of trinkets labeled "Americana." But again, what matters is the working of whole poems.

The other six passages in the Music Quiz are all notably plain in their phrasing; in some cases, the flatness serves to generate a hint of foreboding—as in the opening lines of Hoagland's "Foghorn." We might observe that the writer of #8 sounds unaware that most middle-aged persons in America have had the same experience. We might wonder how the writer of #3 will be able to justify such simple appropriation of a sensational atrocity. We might consider whether the un-idiomatic phrase "echoed down our family" improves the (musical?) effect of #6. We may be curious how the chatty pomposity of #4 can serve a poetic purpose. But the point is, *all* of these passages (excepting perhaps the two Riley quotes, which to me seem irredeemably hokey) could exist in very good poems. Their arguable lack of music is not what counts.

Passages #1 and #8 are from poems by Louise Glück ("Labor Day" and "Unpainted Door"). Passage #5 is from "To My Father" by Frank Bidart. Campion, in the review that has provoked my last several pages, cites Glück and Bidart as "the modern masters" of a music involving "perfect timing of statements." Well, I say that *Unincorporated Persons* is full of perfectly timed statements, but I don't ask you to appreciate them as musical—because the notion is too mysterious, as I've tried to show. Passages #3 and #6 are from "Protest" and "The Great Divide" by Peter Campion. Passage #4 begins a funny satirical poem by Frank O'Hara, "Image of the Buddha Preaching." You can bet there were New Critic types in the 1960s well prepared to explain that such O'Hara lines ("I am very happy to be here at the Villa Hügel"—nice alliteration!) lacked poetical music.

The statements in Tony Hoagland's poetry—observations, illustrations, reflections, speculations, laments, bits of narrative, direct addresses to the reader—all come from a man determined to stay calm, to think aloud, and to speak clearly. It's not that he lacks complicated emotions; it's that he wants to reflect on those emotions in the half-tranquility of composition. We hear the effect, for instance, in the opening lines of "Phone Call," in *What Narcissism Means to Me:*

> Maybe I overdid it
> when I called my father an enemy of humanity.
> That might have been a little strongly put,
> a slight overexaggeration.

(Some exaggeration, the son feels, would be excusable under the circumstances but maybe not overexaggeration.) Behind Hoagland's poems, we often sense rage, humiliation, frustrated desire, disgust, guilt, dejection—but the voice of the poems is never frantic or sweaty or upset-in-the-moment. It is not a midnight voice.

Hoagland pays a price for his evenness of voice and his concomitant effort to discuss specified real-life situations directly with the reader. Obviously, he pays the price of losing ICFU readers, but more important, he pays the price of doing without much strangeness and potentially losing readers who feel that the baffling contradictions and intermixings of life should be met with a strangeness in poetry. Now I've often argued that shallow strangeness (for instance, in some of James Tate and most of Joshua Clover) vitiates much contemporary poetry. Still, some wonderful poetry achieves a combination of strangeness with understandability. Dickinson. Stevens. Kenneth Fearing. Claire Bateman. Kevin Prufer.

Since Hoagland has many poems energized by his sense of American society being terribly screwed up, it's interesting to compare *Unincorporated Persons* with Kevin Prufer's *National Anthem* (2008), a book obsessed with capitalism's future apocalypse. In a way, Prufer's book is the midnight dream-steeped version of Hoagland's book. In *National Anthem,* the protagonists are helplessly caught in violent nightmarish breakdowns of civilization, breakdowns so total that they can barely endure and grope toward pale vestiges of love. Such a vision could be Hollywood-cheesy, but Prufer explores it with such intelligence and resourcefulness that *National Anthem* is an outstanding book, giving us a picture of the awful world we seem to be drifting toward while we sleep. When we wake up each morning, though, we have to live in the banal folly (and comfort) of capitalism today, and we need to live as if it is still possible to make moral and compassionate choices. Tony Hoagland writes poetry for that part of our lives.

Readers crave many more things than any one poet can give. Moreover, any one poet can only write a few of the poems that float along on currents in his or her brain. Hoagland's poem "Requests for Toy Piano" expresses ambivalence about which poems he should write among those that seem desirable to him or to some audience. The voices in the first and third stanzas ask the performer to provide cozy sweet images, of the beauty of Nature (a charming family of ducks) or the beauty of romantic love (lovers ready for their first kiss). But the performer, answering in the second and fourth stanzas, feels obliged to address grimmer realities, such as terrorism or the economic forces behind romance:

> No, I should play the one about
> the hard rectangle of the credit card
> hidden in the man's back pocket
> and how the woman spent an hour

plucking out her brows, and how her perfume
was made from the destruction of a hundred flowers.

In the next stanza, the requester voice unexpectedly capitulates and asks for further moralizing exposure of dark truths behind romantic scents.

Then play the one about the flower industry
in which the migrant workers curse their own infected hands,
torn from tossing sheaves of roses and carnations
into the back of the refrigerated trucks.

The performer, however, instinctively refuses to give the audience what it expects.

No, I must play the one about the single yellow daffodil
standing on my kitchen table
whose cut stem draws the water upwards
so the plant is flushed with the conviction
that the water has been sent
to find and raise it up
from somewhere so deep inside the earth
not even flowers can remember.

This daffodil in a vase is actually dying—its egotism is deluded—like yours and mine if we feel that our individual vitality can overcome the social and economic forces pulling our society toward injustice and massive suffering. Nevertheless, we live better—more morally as well as more happily—if we can feel a deep worthiness in our lives, as the daffodil feels. By letting "Requests for Toy Piano" end with that affirmation, Hoagland is allowing us to feel its beguiling restfulness. At the same time, the poem is organized to remind us how much that feeling depends on the repression of knowledge and perception that would spoil the feeling.

To appreciate "Requests for Toy Piano," it's important to notice that Hoagland has written all the stanzas—both the requests and the responses—in a manner that satirizes the easy familiarity of each attitude. Marxist cynicism about credit cards and commodities can be as banally lazy as romantic piety about Nature or love. Apparently, the poet has to be like someone hopping across burning sand, trying never to put his full weight on one spot. However, when a poet's hopping becomes too chaotic or too crazed or too postmod-trendy, we get an indeterminate goulash in which nothing can be cared about and nothing will be seriously thought about. That is the fate Hoagland's poetry boldly, sometimes bluntly, avoids. What I admire about "Requests" is that Hoagland manages to satirize the attitude in each of the six stanzas (three requests, three responses) without simply demolishing any of them. They remain intact and clear and indeed attractive despite their limitations. Some contemporary poems offer you a handful of debris with a twenty-first-century shrug: What can you do? Tony Hoagland insists on taking What can you do? seriously. On guard against poet pomposity, he accepts "toy piano" as one metaphor for his instrument. But he is also on guard against the sly pleasure of self-deprecation, which is why the bulky title *Unincorporated Persons in the Late Honda Dynasty* is finally better than the funny title of his previous book, *What Narcissism Means to Me.* The newer title, though, has a tensely provisional quality, like so many of Hoagland's metaphors: "Let's look at it this way, and see where it gets us." That truth-seeking energy, with its defiance of ICFU and its willingness to barge into subjects that make us nervous, is rare—and rarer still when combined with such non-evasive intelligence. Tony Hoagland is a poet to be grateful for.

TONY HOAGLAND
AND SECOND THOUGHTS

Tony Hoagland tried many moves in his poetry, which is more various and more odd and sometimes more mysterious than readers who summarize too quickly may realize. My focus here is on poems that unexpectedly call upon both the speaker and the reader to reconsider an attitude or judgment. Such poems can be found in Hoagland's first three books, but for this discussion, I draw examples from four later collections: *Unincorporated Persons in the Late Honda Dynasty* (2010), *Application for Release from the Dream* (2015), *Recent Changes in the Vernacular* (2017), and *Priest Turned Therapist Treats Fear of God* (2018). At or near the end of each of the poems I've gathered, a shift or swerve arrives, with a tone different from the tone that has prevailed earlier and sometimes with a strong implication that the preceding attitude or judgment was unwisely shallow or biased or sour. Even if what came earlier in the poem seemed smart, appealing, commendable, the effect of the "second thought" is to leave us with a refreshed, albeit perhaps uneasy, sense of the true complexity of experience.

The outline thus described may call to mind the way the final couplet of a Shakespearean sonnet sometimes reverses or repairs the feeling expressed in the preceding twelve lines, but this effect is so traditional in a sonnet as to seem planned and predictable (even if still powerful) rather than discovered and unexpected.

One reason why this second thought move in Hoagland's poetry seems particularly worth noticing is its relevance to Hoagland's reputation: it invites the reader to allow in herself an openness to nuanced perception and a resistance to facile generalization about life—while Hoagland himself deserves from readers such openness and such resistance to generalization about him. Thanks to his insistence on writing with what I've called courageous clarity—a quality felt by some readers to be too simple or too confrontational—Hoagland's poetry is always in danger of being too easily summed up. It makes sense that a good poet who will deserve some reconsidering sometimes writes poems that dramatize delayed or belated reconsidering.

Of course, there is a sense in which all good poems summon us to some sort of reconsidering, causing us to perceive or ponder an aspect of life in a fresh way. But I'll try to justify sorting my selection of Hoagland poems into a special category. I suggest that usually a good poem, even though it surprises us in various ways (through tonal shifts and metaphorical changes and structural maneuvers, for instance) as it proceeds, seems in retrospect to display a continuity of impetus and energy, to embody one continuous undertaking by the speaker, to constitute a meditation or exploration that has evolved but not reversed itself. Not that the poem simply reiterates one idea or feeling but that we sense—on rereading if not on first reading—the links that carry the poem across its junctions and that make its ending, even if startling or surprisingly forceful, seem in retrospect a fulfillment of a pursuit that has developed since the opening line.

True? I should be wary here because one of my favorite ways to praise a poem has been to call it a truth-seeking poem, truth seeking rather than truth declaring, with a claim that we see the speaker searching for a truth he or she does not possess yet at the start or at the middle of the poem and indeed may still not possess at the end. That's a way of describing countless poems I've loved, including some by Hoagland, but the particular move I hope to distinguish in this essay is more narrowly definable, and often simpler, since it usually shows up just in a poem's last several lines. The difference is like the difference between listening to someone struggling throughout a speech to figure something out and hearing someone who has been talking confidently or boldly suddenly pause and say, "No, wait—on second thought . . . ."

How common is this second thought move? Perhaps more common than I am inclined to imply in my desire to praise the Hoagland poems I've picked out. No doubt the move can be accommodated within the catalog of types of poetic turns developed so usefully by Michael Theune and his collaborators in *Structure and Surprise: Engaging Poetic Turns* (2007). The move can be considered an instance of ironic structure, as analyzed in that volume by Christopher Bakken; Bakken focuses on poems in which "what is first proclaimed is suddenly or systematically undermined by what follows" and in which the effect of a poem's ending is to invoke a corrective skepticism, "to disclaim any absolute, positive certainties about life or love." At the same time, the second thought move can be seen as a case of concessional structure, as analyzed by Mary Szybist in her contribution to *Structure and Surprise:* "The structure provides poets ample opportunity to renovate the subjects they initially disparage, diminish, expose, or otherwise play down."

One stark example is Frank Bidart's poem "For Mary Ann Youngren"—my short essay about how this poem presents an impressive thought and then argues decisively *against* that thought appeared in 2013 as a contribution to online discussion of poetic turns, at *Voltage Poetry* (https://voltagepoetry.com). The Hoagland poems I will look at present second thoughts less emphatic and urgently frontal than Bidart's poem; what they share with Bidart, though, is a strong inclination to *show,* rather than to fix or conceal, the way a tempting view can on reflection come to feel inadequate, one-sided, misleading.

Most of Hoagland's second thoughts tilt toward tolerance, forgiveness, sympathy, and away from complaint or sarcasm. This kind of shift acquires special resonance in the context of Hoagland's oeuvre of seven books because quite often he has been an abrasive, unrelaxing poet pushing against propriety and taboos. Thus, when a poem's ending is unexpectedly gentle, there is an impression that this poet is himself trying to learn gentleness. Examples of this kind of reconsidering will be the most affecting Hoagland poems considered here.

First, however, a few examples in which it is the edgy, edge-seeing tendency in Hoagland's personality that produces the second thought.

"Spanish Ballad," in *Recent Changes in the Vernacular,* is one of many Hoagland poems about male heterosexual desire. (Recent examples include "Moment in the Conversation" and "The Wetness" and "A History of High Heels.") These poems tend to deliberately tease the reader's sense of decorum through candor about lust, but usually they culminate in rueful self-deprecation, acknowledging the stupidity that seems built into male desire. "Spanish Ballad" seems at first destined for that meaning, as it describes a young, attractive, and majestically bored barista in a coffee shop. If we were to predict a turn for this poem, it would be a turn toward either I-am-a-fool-to-want-her or she-is-a-human-with-her-own-problems; both of these turns could be worthwhile. Instead, "Spanish Ballad" ends like this:

She scares me speechless with desire
but I would give a million, uncle,

to see her smile
and even more to tell a joke
that would make her actually
choke in laughter

and send the spray
of that eight-ounce energy drink
uncontrollably bursting
from her beautiful nose.

This ending chooses one of the possible feelings in the situation—resentment of the power that the desirable other holds (even if unwittingly) over one's imagination—and lets it own the poem's vivid last image. Hoagland escapes writing another typical Older Guy Lament that re-realizes the absurdity or folly of desiring a much younger woman. Not that such laments are not called for (I've written my share!) but that on second thought, this time, the poem can accentuate another truth. If the attractive barista were to laugh convulsively with droplets of her beverage flying from her nostrils, the moment would in one way reflect her humanity, as someone with an inner life, but she'd be divested of her scary haughtiness—she'd be rendered helpless for at least a few seconds, and the male joke teller would have controlled her experience just then. Of course, *one* of the things we want in sexual romance is to render the beloved (or the desperately admired) helpless in passion. A sort of nasal orgasm for the barista would be a messy and un-sublime substitute for an actual orgasm, but it would be a feat by the man who caused it, a brief transcending of the normal dreariness of admiring someone from afar. There's a streak of hostility in Hoagland's imagining of this, true. At the same time, though, if a person laughs suddenly and wildly at another person's joke, a human connection in humor (instead of in sexuality) has occurred.

"Spanish Ballad" is nonetheless too simple to be one of Hoagland's best poems, relying too heavily on its slapstick ending; the poem's simplicity is signaled by its title and its short-line quatrain structure and its address to "uncle," all of which distance the poem from Hoagland's typical discursive meditative mode. Still, I like it as an example of his changing direction away from an attitude (in this case wistful and respectful) that seemed to be the poem's destiny.

Hoagland's poems about sexual desire overlap with a larger category of poems about gender. Hoagland aspires, more openly than most poets, to register and ponder currents in contemporary culture vectored by gender, race, and class. This is a serious ambition (with precursors including Pope, Byron, Whitman, Lowell, Rich), though it tends to import a texture of time-bound pop sociology into poems. It pulls Hoagland toward controversy, due to his impatient boldness, his impulse to say straight out what most of us say elliptically or tiptoe around. "But the Men," in *Application for Release from the Dream,* is one of his brash gender poems. Except for its last two words, it consists of a loquaciously extended sociological generalization about men nowadays realizing the harmfulness of their traditional patriarchal privilege.

> Now they're ready to talk, really *talk* about their feelings.
> In fact, they're ready to make you sick with revelations of
>   their vulnerability—
>
> a pool of testosterone is spreading from around their feet,
> it's draining out of them like radiator fluid,
> like history, like an experiment that failed.

For the sake of the pleasure of sweeping generalization, the poem doesn't bother to associate all the apologetic and self-revealing behaviors with particular social groups; Hoagland knows we will infer that he is thinking of men with college educations and more or less liberal political leanings. We can feel that the generalizing oversimplifies contemporary society while still finding it entertaining, with a satirical force that is light and fairly gentle but real. The meaning that "But the Men" seems headed for is the sympathetic (though not heartrending) sense that it's confusing to be a man nowadays responding to feminism. That could be a decent outcome for the poem. Instead, it ends with these lines:

> So here they come, on their hands and knees, the men;
> here they come. They're really beaten.

No tricks this time. No fine print.
Please, they're begging you. Look out.

A lot depends on how we hear those last two words. If they hit us merely as a sucker punch, kept ready by a sly satirical poet who knew all along that his real point was the insincerity of male efforts to behave better toward women, the effect is rhetorical and thin, though not contemptible. I prefer to hear "Look out" as a reconsidering felt in the moment of speaking by a male speaker who has found in himself, and also seen in other men, the temptation to use apparent acceptance of feminism as a roundabout strategy for regaining some power in relation to gullible lovers and wives. The warning "Look out" arises from a fatalistic sense of how deeply ingrained gender roles are and of how seldom power is voluntarily and cheerfully relinquished. Hoagland has expressed such fatalism in other poems (such as "Not Renouncing" and "Demolition" and "Dinner Guest"), a tendency that I admit makes the last two words of "But the Men" seem more a deft surprise for the reader than a presently reflective reconsidering by the speaker, but the latter reading is possible.

The same choice between two ways of reading a poem's ending is presented by "Aubade," in *Application,* a poem whose title calls to mind romantic sweetness but whose observations can't ignore that the pleasant morning illuminates a world of contingencies and difficulties.

Just off stage, the rooster someone keeps illegally
in the city crows its magnificent cry,

blessing, who knows, maybe the child
just conceived inside a woman's body.

Such tranquility—the neighbors haven't started fighting
yet, nor their loud hyena laughter.

Despite the flaws in tranquility, "Aubade" might be headed for a sweet celebration of love in an imperfect world. Instead, the poem ends with one of the scariest words in English. Here are the last six lines.

And we still love each other, in a way that makes us
tolerant, alert, perhaps a little vain

but also, we are getting older.
Come over here, darling,

and put your hand on my head
and tell me if you think this is a tumor.

The emergent meaning in this ending is about ineradicable self-concern, fear
for oneself, even in the midst of an affirmed love relationship. The poem does
not ironize or discredit the love—the love is mature and enduring and is even
a source of pride, but it has to exist alongside self-worry, and indeed, it entails
engaging with the self-worry of the beloved (which may or may not be reasonable); it will be tested by mortality.

A more elaborate and more dramatized final turn comes at the end of "The
Story of the Mexican Housekeeper," in *Application,* a relatively long poem in
which Hoagland can't stop trying to understand his father's enjoyment of a
story about a Mexican woman being virtually enslaved for many years by a
white couple in El Paso. Hoagland has published several bleak bitter poems
portraying his father as a cruel man, a bigot, a man indoctrinated by the clichés
of reactionary patriarchal culture. The poem fretfully works up six or seven
hypotheses as to his father's motivation for telling him the story of the humiliated helpless Mexican woman; the most disturbing hypothesis is that his father
implies a parallel between the woman and his son Tony—"someone paralyzed
by life, / willing to take whatever I am given // in exchange for being safe." Thus,
the poem seems headed toward some effort to resolve, or at least to attain a re-
vised perspective on, the pain of being the son of this father.

Instead, "The Story of the Mexican Housekeeper" launches into a meta-
poetic critique of Hoagland's whole meditation:

But here she is, suddenly in front of us—
her brown face wrinkled after years immersed inside my father's mind,

it's Rosalina, making her return appearance,
wearing a dusty apron, holding a rolling pin in her left hand,

and she's tired, and scared, and she's mad as hell,
not at my dad, but me—

Rosalina is imagined raging not against her real-life servitude in El Paso but
against her literary service as a handy figure in the son's emotional negotiation
with his father—"she doesn't want to be in this poem for one more minute"; she
demands release back into her separate self-defining life. We see that Hoagland
has, on second thought, detected something too facile in his appropriation of
the tale of hardship in the life of someone much less fortunate than himself.

This meta-poetic ending is striking, especially coming from a poet who
has seldom resorted to the tempting reflexivity of referring to "this poem" in
a poem. It's an interesting ending, rendering the poem even more thought-
provoking than it already was. I feel uneasy about it. I wonder if this ending may
itself be too facile. It moves the poem into the category of complicity poems—
one of Hoagland's obsessive specialties—poems that painfully acknowledge
how "we," the poet and his likely readers, cooperate with and profit from the social and political follies we mock or deplore. There's an ironic liability that hovers over complicity poems: the poet may finally come across as too comfortable
in his or her role as exposer of complicity, complacent about the rightness of
exposing complacency. The trouble with confessing complicity is that it *could*
foster enervated abstention from social criticism: we're all capitalists, after all,
so maybe we should shut up about the harm of capitalism.

Still, I like many of Hoagland's complicity poems, and I respect the moral
discomfort that prompts him to write such poems more candidly and un-
dodgeably than most poets today. In the second-thought poems I turn to now,
though, the final movement is not toward a more inclusive condemnation but,
rather, toward some awakening of tolerance and sympathy and perhaps hope.

"Summer," in *Application*, gets going as one of Hoagland's numerous poems
of sociological satire, describing tourists shopping for things they don't really
need.

People like to buy. They just do.
They like the green tissue paper.

They like extracting the card from its tight
prophylactic sheath, handing it over,

and getting it back.
They like to swing the bag when they stroll away.

We sense snarkiness looming, and we may suspect the poem is going to remind us of migrant workers or refugees or prisoners who can't afford any of this retail therapy. But "Summer" ends on a note of empathy rather than of chastisement or of shared guilt, with one more example of a shopper:

     a woman with a henna rinse
holds a small glass vase up to the light

to see the tiny turquoise bubbles trapped inside.
As a child she felt a secret just inside her skin,

always on the brink of bursting out.
Now the secret is on the outside,

and she is hunting it.

That woman may be a Republican, and she may have bad taste, but she shares with Wordsworth and you and me the intuition that something crucial is missing from life. It may have been stolen by culture or by the attrition of time, but she feels it must exist somewhere, and she hasn't given up the search. (Maybe she should read poetry!) Her way of searching may be unwise, but the poem does not prompt us to laugh at it; instead, we recognize the woman as our sister or mother, and her searching strikes us not only as touching but for a moment as heroic.

"Romance of the Tree," in *Priest*, invites us to feel revulsion for humanity's stupidly self-indulgent misuse of Nature, through the comic gambit of specifying that the book to be made using the pulp of a certain "enormous spruce tree" is "a seething hot romance novel / called *Summertime Nurses*." The poem has fun summarizing scenes in this novel, but as it does so, we're pretty sure the poem's point is about forest preservation, a great tree being "worth more than a paperback"—however, the poem's final phrases discover a new meaning whose freshness feels like a second thought.

> When the tree was cut down and hauled away to the mill
> to be turned into *Summertime Nurses,*
> we lost part of our Eden

> worth more than a paperback;
> the tree, swaying all day in the sun,
> rocked and pushed by the wind,

> yielding and tousled under the white clouds,
> with all of its arms outstretched,
> all of its mouths wide open.

That tree wants to live! Doesn't it? It *seems* to desire to live and to feel alive—and we feel a kinship with it in this way, as many poems about trees (and flowers) have suggested. (Though I love Whitman's Louisiana live-oak poem for Whitman's rueful realization that he is *not* like the tree.) The tree is a needy organism, as are the writers and readers of romance fiction; our sexual fantasies and sexual adventures are expressions of our natural vitality, even when delusory. It's true that the tree did not destroy innumerable other organisms, as we do (though it probably did prevent a few other plants from flourishing nearby), but instead of leaving us with a sense that humanity is contemptible, "The Romance of the Tree" leaves us with a quite different sense of natural human desires being some mixture of pathetic and sweet.

We are what we are. We make our choices within constrictions of culture, history, and biology. We should try to be better citizens, better persons, and we do need poems that criticize and cry out against our follies, our imperialism, our racism. Blake's "London" is still great. Hoagland has written many poems of social critique, more bluntly than most good poets. But condemnation *and* self-condemnation can both be awfully easy; sometimes the more thoughtful thing, the more interesting thing, is to try a poem that reaches (not blindly) toward some tolerance, or even forgiveness.

"Invitation to the Future," in *Recent Changes,* plays in an amusing but thin way with our fear that the insidiously tentacular power of global capitalism will redesign and control *every* aspect of our lives, including our names. Hoagland imagines a wedding invitation some number of decades in the future announcing that Jessica Exxon Mitsubishi will marry Noah Coca-Cola in a ceremony performed by Reverend Walmart at the Microsoft chapel on Zoloft Hill. The shtick of this could be extended for many more lines to entertain a listening audience pleased to get the joke, and there are poets who would cheerfully offer this as a tour de force. Hoagland does run with the routine for almost a page, but then sympathy on second thought rescues the poem from easy satire, as we saw happening also in "Summer" and "Romance of the Tree."

> And when they are used and bruised,
> weather-beaten and dented,
> when life has disenfranchised them,
>
> may they find a place to hide
> under the world of merchandise,
>
> as we did, their ancestors, so long ago,
> who lived in a cave now vaguely known,
> just dimly remembered
> as the private sector.

I find those lines moving. They constitute a second thought through which Hoagland not only rescues the poem from the formulaic quality of its protest against corporate culture but also rescues himself from a misanthropic current that could have taken over the poem. That latter possibility was audible in these lines:

> From here I can almost guess
> the logo on their bathroom towels,
>
> what they will call their children; her silly names for his thingamajig.

Having myself once published a poem that veers from dismay toward disgust contemplating the too-predictable perkiness of upwardly mobile young couples, I sense that that meaning was on the table when Hoagland drafted "Invitation to the Future." It's not a worthless meaning, but it is less complicated and less interesting than the ending Hoagland wrote. He thought, on second thought, of the helplessness of young Jessica and Noah—corporate affiliations ultimately will not insulate them from being "disenfranchised" by life; like us, they will need to take refuge from global capitalism in the non-monetized intimacies and commitments of personal life.

Those last nine lines of "Invitation to the Future," are they corny? I don't feel so. "And when they are used and bruised." What about the last five lines of *Paradise Lost,* are they corny? Both passages, I feel, are deeply humane.

And that's what I will say about the last passage in "Disaster Movie," in *Unincorporated Persons.* This is one of the poems in which Hoagland takes on the task—foolhardy, fraught with likely glibness—of addressing American culture as a whole. "You were a jumbo jet, America, / gone down in the jungle in my dream." The poem doesn't really try to convince us that Hoagland had this dream while sleeping. Hoagland is by and large a daytime poet, not claiming to swim down into the weirdnesses of wee-hours phantasmagoria. The title of "Disaster Movie" (not "Disaster Dream," thus preemptively shifting the conceit) implicitly acknowledges that the poem's governing conceit is a conscious project.

The poem develops the conceit—American culture having crashed like a giant airplane in the jungle—for half a page. Then Hoagland expresses surprise at the violence of his imagining—"that my disgust with cell phones and beauty pageants would drive me to // ram it headfirst into the side of a hill." This is a possible second thought for the poem, which would turn from jeremiad toward self-criticism; Hoagland does start through that door for a minute: "And sure I knew that this apocalypse was a thin disguise / for my pitiful fear of being no good at ordinary life." This is an interesting thought, but the poem doesn't do anything with it—because on *third* thought Hoagland finds himself more interested in imagining the survivors of the plane crash. No matter how foolishly "American" and materialistic they may have been, he's not inclined to mock them.

> But what was sweet in the dream was the quiet
> resilience of those little people:
>
> someone using duct tape to make beds out of flotation cushions;
> the stewardess limping past on crutches, as night seeped in. . . .

An AA meeting in progress by one of the enormous, flattened tires.
And a woman singing in the dusk,
as she tended a fire
fed with an endless supply
         of safety manuals and self-help books.

Kindness for humankind is the chord struck there—we keep trying to cope, even in absurdly baffling circumstances; the singing woman is a figure for the poet in her effort to create new sustenance by "repurposing" the inadequate guidance offered by popular culture.

That meaning strikes me as sweet while not at all saccharine. But if it strikes someone—perhaps a reader enraged by American hustles more obviously harmful than cell phones and beauty pageants—as too soft, I call that reader's attention to another poem in *Unincorporated Persons,* "Hard Rain." This poem amounts to an extended second thought about Hoagland's strong inclination—which he shares with any of us who can keep caring about poetry—to find, on second thought, that there is *something* admirable and even lovable in our responses to being fortunate American taxpayers. "Hard Rain" is about realizing that capitalism works insidiously to co-opt everything that we might cherish as a resistance to its enveloping force. Even Bob Dylan's great song of vocation about perceiving and finally crying out against social injustice, "A Hard Rain's A-Gonna Fall," can be transformed into background music for shoppers at a mall—and so, Hoagland feels, "there's nothing / we can't pluck the stinger from," "nothing we can't turn into a soft-drink flavor or a t-shirt." Even sympathy can be commodified—as by a TV show in which a killer expresses remorse:

And everybody in the audience claps and weeps a little,
because the level of deep feeling has been touched,
and they want to believe that
the power of Forgiveness is greater
than the power of Consequence, or History.

The poem ends with Hoagland acknowledging how un-separate he is from the tremendous temptation to feel that we—we sensitive ones—can be innocent Americans. Thus, "Hard Rain" is in the main vein of Hoagland's complicity poems.

Still, it coexists with the second-thought poems I've been discussing that turn toward tenderness and sympathy. That woman we glimpsed at the end of "Summer" might be shopping at the same mall where Hoagland hears Dylan's song divested of its meaning, and for her the song might conceivably reawaken her sensation of "a secret just inside her skin," a value not measured in dollars.

The world of poetry readers will always be fractured—inevitably, naturally—by disagreement about the competing values of clarity versus obscurity, accessibility versus difficulty, understanding versus mystery. Some readers want paraphrasable illuminations of life; some readers at the opposite extreme want unparaphrasable evocations of life's mystery. (Let's note that this debate is often conceived in terms of discursiveness versus disjunctiveness, but that as a stylistic matter is actually a different issue: there can be a discursive poem that is nonsensical, and there can be a disjunctive poem whose meaning turns out to be clear.) And of course, many of us feel we "kind of" want both at once—we quote Stevens saying, "A poem should resist the intelligence almost successfully." On a given day, faced with someone's new poem, you can argue with a friend, or enemy, about the value of the poem's clarity or obscurity, but before long, you realize that you've hit a wall, the wall of personality. For some personalities, including Hoagland's and mine, life feels so wildly jumbled—emotionally, spiritually, morally—that art should offer an alternative, a relief, a way of grasping some thread in the tangle, a momentary stay against confusion (in Frost's crucial phrase). For other personalities—including those of some people I like!—life in a way makes too much sense (the truths of mutability and mortality whacking us over and over), and art should offer an escape *into* uncertainty, the electricity of kaleidoscopic unknowing. (Let's pause here to remember that this latter craving is relatively new in the history of poetry appreciation—since 1922, as it were.)

Tony Hoagland's poetry has always inclined decisively—and in my eyes bravely—toward accessibility. All along, he has been well aware of the academically popular view (which was already boring by the late 1980s) that accessibility is corrupt (because coherent discourse reinforces capitalist orthodoxy) or at least that it is false (because we can't really understand anything!). But his sense of poetic power has impelled him to try to make sense to "the reader" who is not a professor of postmodernism. In a *Fence* symposium, Hoagland said: "The shattered glass is an eloquent emblem for our time, but it does not hold water and I am thirsty." Thirsty, that is, for meanings more pointed and more useful than the monotonous "eloquence" of saying, in effect, shattered, shattered, shattered. To me (with my personality), it seems as if all interesting persons are thirsty for meaning, though some may seek it not in poetry but in religion, mythology, philosophy, politics, or love.

Nevertheless, poetry as such attracts people who feel life is mysterious, and so they tend to resist clarity—paraphrasability—to some extent. This is why, in poetry world, it takes a kind of courage to keep writing accessible poems. You forfeit the constituency infected with what I've called, in my essay on Hoagland's *Unincorporated Persons,* "ICFU: Instant Contempt for the Understandable." As a working definition, we may say that an accessible poem is one that can be presented to college freshmen and they—the bright ones at least—will feel fairly sure they understand it, without coaching. Most of Hoagland's poems—like most of Frost's—meet that criterion. It's a criterion I see as generous and anti-elitist. Obviously, the peril is always that the poem will collapse like a soufflé into nothing-but-the-paraphrase. Frost deploys many sly strategies to render a poem's meaning more ambiguous and complex *on second thought* than it seemed on first reading. Hoagland's second-thought move is just one of the strategies he deploys for the same purpose.

We don't feel the same way every day. I love poets who honestly show this, including Dickinson, Hardy, and Stevens. Our days are peppered with second thoughts and third thoughts. Hoagland has written a few poems that contemplate this phenomenon as a continuous truth about our life. "Note to Reality," in *Application,* cites several experiences in which an expected or probable perception has been changed or superseded by an odder and more particular perception. Then Hoagland says (addressing Reality):

> I speak now because experience has shown me
>   that my mind will never be clear for long
>
> and I have given up
> on getting back to the sky where I started.

I am as thick-skinned and selfish and male, as jealous and afraid
            as I have ever been.

I float on your surface; your nets and tides entangle me.

There is ruefulness in those lines, but in context, there is also equanimity. Hoagland is in a mood here to accept the inevitability, the naturalness of endless reconsidering that never solves central problems. The same acceptance is gently affirmed in "Instead," in *Recent Changes,* in which he sees "How there is always a truth, and then underneath that / another somehow / more elusive truth"—and advises us:

So praise instead;
praise the word *instead* like a treetrunk
that falls across your path.

Like a bridge that leads
away from your destination.

Considered as a whole, I think "Instead" is a good poem, in the desirable (even if abusable) category of advice poems, though I would admit that the lines I've just quoted drift a little close to the easy-chair Zen of poetry that dishes out tranquilizing therapy too easily.

Whereupon I am glad to remember that restlessness, rather than calm, is the keynote of Tony Hoagland's poetry. He won't settle into a final thought, not even the idea of accepting second thoughts and altered perceptions. His inveterate un-tranquility is directly confronted in "No Thank You," in *Priest,* a poem that attributes the same tendency to all of us: we lurch *away* from wisdom; we

already have chosen the strange
garments of confusion
that we will die in; we love
the thrill of enemies; we burn
through beauty like it was
wrapping paper;

we breathe
the smoke of our distraction
like it was oxygen.

Those are lines by a poet who knows he won't become a reliable guru. But it's important to notice that if he says No Thank You to wisdom, it's not because he sees wisdom as false or unreal but that it scares him, since the dance of rethinking comes so naturally to him. And he expresses *this* understanding about himself with beautiful clarity. The stubbornly lucid thoughtfulness of Hoagland's restless mercurial poetry is part of why it has so often felt like oxygen to me.

LUDIC SPIRITUALISM

On Claire Bateman

In the world of contingency, the world of space and time, nothing can keep its original form. The process of mutation can be seen operating across long periods, viewed in one way—as in the evolution of a species or the gradual weakening of materials used to construct a castle in the Middle Ages. Viewed in another way, the Heraclitean way, decay is instantaneous: nothing is really what it was a moment ago, and this is particularly, flagrantly true for all expressions of spirit because every *expression* of spirit is a projection into temporal reality of an energy from a different kind of reality, and the spiritual energy— though it persists with astonishing tenacity—cannot remain pure in the new earthly medium. At the instant of crossover, it becomes distorted. This is one reason, perhaps *the* reason, why our poems (and paintings, films, dances, songs, symphonies) are never quite right, or never right enough to satisfy in the same way forever. Hence, we perpetually have to cook up new expressions. And the universe itself seems to share our hunger and frustration, constantly concocting new forms that contain or carry some spirit energy and which immediately become imperfect, inadequate conveyances for that spirit energy.

Big thoughts! What has prompted me to set forth these big thoughts? It is not Spinoza or Schopenhauer or Plato; it is the poetry of Claire Bateman.

One of the ways you can realize that a poet you've encountered is a truly powerful poet is that you feel a frowning urgency about the problem of understanding the poems. This is different from a weary slogging through fashionable obscurities and different from the bemused tolerance inspired by many moderately good poets. It's like the feeling you have reading Emily Dickinson— the sense of an important discovery awaiting you if you will ponder the poem; you may be puzzled, but you won't be merely entertained or teased.

Claire Bateman is an amazingly original poet and a poet with depth of vision. I mean to say that her vision goes deep, to the essences of experience, and that her vision seems uniquely her own—with affinities to Blake, Shelley, Dickinson, Hart Crane, and no doubt several philosophers I haven't read, but with no aura of the cobbled-up or borrowed—and that her vision drives her, seeming not like a colorful set of attitudes amusing to promote but, rather, like a great polymorphous intuition to which she feels obligations.

Bateman's vision of life is not my vision. I don't walk through the world feeling the constant presence of a transcendental reality—call it spirit—fluttering in everything, flickering forth from between molecules of matter or between words of a remark, infinitely more important than the tangible forms of earthly life. I don't, on a normal day, share the sensation of the instantaneous revision of all spirit expressions in the air of finitude. But a powerful poet can get you to see everything her way.

In this essay, I will write mostly about poems in Bateman's book *Clumsy* (New Issues Press, 2003) and then about a few of her more recent poems, from *Coronology* (Etruscan Press, 2010) and *Scape* (New Issues Press, 2016).

The poem that bumped me into the Big Thoughts of my first paragraph was "Brief Tour of the World's Back Kitchen"—it is the last in a set of twelve poems, the Fatigue poems, that comprise one of the four sections in *Clumsy*. Reading the Fatigue poems, we develop a flexible—but not emptily amorphous—sense of "fatigue" as the result when any flow of spirit, or imagination, pushes forth into the wear and tear of temporal contingency.

Brief Tour of the World's Back Kitchen

By ladle,
by teaspoon,
by batter-encrusted thumb,
the chefs of creation
are sampling each other's
fatigue.

Ah, murmurs one.
Though this is exquisite,
I find it a trifle overwrought.

Might I suggest adding
a hint of poignance,
perhaps a few notes
from the promotional theme tune
of the Lost & Missing Channel?

Hmmm . . . muses another
at the next vat over.
This possesses a suitable base,
but the undertones seem somewhat
abstract—I'd correct the balance
by stirring in some plunging
humidity and a low, throbbing sensation
at the left temple.

This, declares a third,
is nothing less than
a tonal masterpiece!
I detect a trace of purely
adrenaline-induced exhilaration
just this side of hysteria,
the beginnings of a Starbucks
tremor, & the savory mixture
of intellectual fortitude &
willpower stripped quite raw.

Such finesse,
such a sense of tradition!
And before you exit,
be sure to inspect
the shining bottles where they've preserved
the extinct fatigues of history, including
fatigue induced in the archeopteryx by preliminary genetic adaptions,
the fatigue of metals in medieval Saxon drawbridges,
& so on.

"Brief Tour of the World's Back Kitchen" satirizes the fickleness of some literary criticism while, more importantly, reaching toward its implication that all imaginative concoctions (like poems) must fall prey to the devastating critique of time itself.

As always, an abstracted statement of the poem's theme can seem (or indeed be) trite, while the poem lives and breathes as a unique embodiment of that theme. The great power of Claire Bateman's poetry is (of course) not in its ideas as such but in the personality-charged strangeness of the lines and of the speakers—often giddy, occasionally desperate (like any sensitive person strained toward exhaustion)—implied by, and between, the lines. That's why Bateman is a poet rather than a preacher or mystic or guru. Her poems, though their concerns are intensely philosophical when you ponder them, come at you like someone in a scarlet dress, someone whose eyes you can't glance away from.

And I would argue, ultimately, that this embodied humanness of the poems constitutes the crucial critique—inherent, a critique from within—of the transcendental yearning that Bateman's poems so often dramatize. The issue of whether we should think of our love—when we say we love someone—as dedicated to some "higher" magical force that moves *through* the person or to the colorful flawed mixture that is the person as a whole—this issue is beautifully caught in the poem "A Passing Stranger Who Falls Briefly in Love with Your Fatigue." The poem consists of one tour-de-force sentence beginning with the title.

A Passing Stranger Who Falls Briefly in Love with Your Fatigue

hopes it's not too wrong to love the translucence
exhaustion brings to your face, behind which
each of your thoughts floats, weightless
as the sustained note resolving a recitative,
a high A so pure the listener could almost
forget it's the work of a particular
breath that has been waiting
in line forever behind countless others
like an almost pathologically
patient child who never fidgets, but instead

exudes some secret luminosity,
as if one night at the beach
she'd managed to dogpaddle
a little distance from everyone else,
then worked herself around to face
neither the wired-up stuttering shoreline
nor her grandmother's glowing
pink-lillied swimcap & billowing magenta bathing suit,
but the open sea in the presence of whose
steadfast darkness she ducked her head to swallow
one star bobbing on a wavelet,
one amethyst from Cassiopeia's crown
gulped down on a briny wash just before she was
spotted, dragged out, smacked, & toweled down
for the long car ride home.

The child who tries to swallow a star in the ocean is a seeker of the sublime, and her romanticism is naive enough to lead to drowning—but it doesn't, and she is brusquely pulled back into the realm of contingency by pragmatic adults. In the back seat of the car going home, though, you know she has a starry gleam in her eyes. It's a look that someone—a romantic, or someone wanting to find the romantic in life—could one day fall in love with.

But wait—how did that girl get into the poem? She arrived by way of simile, her story being offered to make vivid the "secret luminosity" of the child in the preceding lines, and that patient child is herself a simile (or vehicle of a simile, if you prefer), offered to characterize the "particular / breath" that is the physical force creating a high pure musical note, and that note is itself a simile, offered to characterize the thoughts that float behind "your" face, thoughts imagined as marvelously "weightless" and "high" and "pure," thoughts that the passing stranger can—at least momentarily—discern, or intuit, through the "translucence" imparted to your face by your "fatigue." Apparently, fatigue—the stress of being spiritual in a physical world—has partly undone the opacity of your surface, of (let's say) your socialized conventional manner, enough so that the passing stranger can sense an elusive and unworldly beauty in your depths.

The passing stranger's love thus involves a discovery of something within "you" that is transcendental, ineffable—doesn't it? The way the poem's three similes blossom from one another suggests the inadequacy of any image from reality to epitomize the inner value. Yes, and yet the poem doesn't seem to want to go on forever with further similes springing from one another in endless confessed inadequacy; the poem ends quite decisively, with its wonderfully full image of the girl who went to the beach. At the end of the poem, I feel a great sense of it having found (in Stevens's phrase) what will suffice. Besides, we need to recall that what the passing stranger falls in love with is not "one amethyst from Cassiopeia's crown" nor "a high A so pure" but, rather, your fatigue and the "translucence" caused by that fatigue—translucence that is (I want to insist) a quality of the loved face—of the loved *person.*

We like tales of sudden romance—boy meets girl, and life is transformed! But we notice that the poem promises no lasting connection: the lover is a *passing* stranger and falls in love only "briefly." That seems pessimistic, and we suspect that Bateman would have us consider that we are all strangers passing briefly through this life. And indeed, Bateman's poetry mostly does not anticipate happy outcomes. To be a human container of spiritual mystery and a conduit for infinite yearning is an unrestful, frazzling existence. One speaker (in a sequence of poems addressed to "Dear Postmaster") says,

> Once you've been chased
> by a fiery swooping cloud
> singing your name with
> a thousand voices,
> you never stop running,
> whether you're running
> or not.

However, the tone of Bateman's poems is never a tone of hand-wringing lamentation or complaint. Her speakers understand their sheerly tantalized condition to be inevitable, and thus they are stoical about it, if a person vibrating with ineffable desire can be called stoical. The feeling can be bleak—notably in "Dosage" and "But Not Like This"—but more often, Bateman's speakers not only accept their hunger as necessary but embrace it as their destiny. A poem called "Harp Song" produces yet another of Bateman's rapidly metamorphosing figurations of how spiritual creations cannot remain intact in the terrestrial realm and ends thus:

But none of this is devastation,
cataclysm, catastrophe.
It scarcely even counts
as an event.
It's just how your flesh
sings the Lord's song
in a strange land.

That reference to the Lord brings up the point that there are indications in Bateman's poetry that she is some sort of Christian. But the faith does not impose any flavor of dogma on the poetry, thank heaven.

Decades ago, when I was first reading Claire Bateman's *Friction* (Eighth Mountain Press, 1998), a sensation began to come over me: Wait a second, this book is not just "partly good," like so many others—this book is *weird-original-deep.* Her book *At the Funeral of the Ether* (Ninety-Six Press, 1998) confirmed the sensation; I felt alarmed because Bateman's work didn't seem like the poetry (ironic, satiric, real-worldy; or elegiac) I tend to like. I wrote an essay about those two books for *Chicago Review* (45, nos. 3–4) and am proud to have written a short introduction to *Clumsy.*

Bateman frequently writes in short lines. Usually, I am dubious about short-line poetry, very inclined to see it as pretentious. But when Bateman's lines are short, I trust them: there's a feeling that the words are so electric with meaning for their speaker that they need to be presented in small doses lest the line overheat and burn out.

I'll discuss one more poem from *Clumsy*—not one of the strangest or hardest in the book but one I find touching and clear. "Monograph" proposes itself as a sociological summary of a period of history—say, the last phase of the twentieth century—during which living was profoundly puzzling for anyone who was really alive.

Monograph

It would later be said of our era
that even the boring parts were interesting,
& vice versa.

Without the least trace of irony,
officials christened space shuttles
after doomed & sunken
cities of yore.

Nearly all of us
constructed dashboard altars
upon which we lavished
particular & minute devotions
as we cruised past scenes
that seemed to represent disaster's aftermath
but almost always resolved
into simple sequences of yard sales—
derelict undergarments & mattresses
exposed on sullenly tilting lawns—
each just another item on the ever-growing
list of events not to be taken
personally.

For their arcane significance,
we pondered signs such as these:

IF YOU LIVED HERE, YOU'D BE HOME BY NOW!

&

GOD SEES EVERYTHING, EVEN YOU READING THIS SIGN!

Though the varieties of available lip-gloss shades
& the total number of famous people in history
were exponentially increasing
so that it became ever more difficult
to distinguish plum from maroon
or the living from the dead,
it still took approximately

the same six years
for a single exhaled breath
to become evenly mixed with the atmosphere.

For none of us was it ever clear
whether that rumbling sound we kept hearing
was static or heartfelt applause.

Everyone was professionally lonely,
yet we ceased not our shining.

Many aspired to but did not actually achieve
the office of Notary Public.

This was not considered a tragedy.

In Bateman's eyes, each of us is like Oedipa Maas, Pynchon's brave and possibly paranoid truth-seeking protagonist, moving through a world in which everything threatens to reveal itself as a clue to an overwhelming secret truth. In such a world, you can never be sure that anything is boring—maybe its dullness or routineness is only a cover for its transcendent meaning, which may lurk beneath the mundane surface or at the edge of your peripheral vision. You try to create homemade versions of meaning—"dashboard altars"—but the world keeps distracting you with signs that *might* offer revelation if only you could read "their arcane significance." You have moments when you feel you could be *the* crucial registrar of unveiled truth, but most of us fall short of such service. We persist, like Oedipa, in our puzzled search, seeking a kind of reality not at home in the terrain of our search; the fact that we all share this plight makes it seem non-tragic, but maybe it is tragic.

There is a possible moral objection to the sensibility expressed in "Monograph" and throughout Bateman's work: a person who lives constantly in such yearning, so radically aware of spiritual incompletion in this world, taking everything (in that sense) so personally, is liable to be useless to other people. A sensibility is not only inherited but cultivated, and a person who "lavished / particular & minute devotions" upon the private symbol of a dashboard altar might be too busy to ever help or connect with someone else. This is a significant worry called to mind by Bateman's poetry, and I can't dissolve it. However, I think she registers a sad consciousness of the issue when she says, "Everyone was professionally lonely"—and she suggests that a compulsive nursing of one's inner sense of essential *lack* is by no means a vocation only of poets. And I think the democratic inclusiveness of the first-person plural in "Monograph" is convincing: Bateman really feels she is characterizing the radical bafflement and frustration of "Nearly all of us" and honoring the radiance of our persistent aspiration.

Once in a long while, you encounter a poet so original, with a style so deeply rooted in unusual sensibility, that the sorting and ranking of felicities—though it is a respectable activity, one I frequently engage in—becomes an unsatisfying minor response. You feel the poetry plunges past your scorecard to a more exciting place. I will write about more favorite Bateman poems here—mostly from *Scape* (New Issues Press, 2016)—but she undoes my "A minus or B plus?" mentality: not turning it off exactly but quieting it down for the sake of absorption in the poet's accumulating vision.

Bateman shares with Wallace Stevens an awareness that if each person must live constantly in the bubble of his or her imagining, then any two persons live in different worlds; romantic love can give the illusion of transcending the gap between selves, but each self remains essentially solitary. Stevens tried to convince us that this condition is not only acceptable but desirable; in his poems, "solitude" is a necessary good thing. Bateman is more willing to admit that solitude can be lonely—but she does not want to complain. Indeed, there is less lamenting in Bateman than in any other serious contemporary poet. In "To Other People's Realities," in *Scape,* she says that the otherness of other persons has caused her "decades of disequilibrium," but we feel that she has mostly enjoyed the excitements of disequilibrium. The separation of one self from another self stimulates thrilled curiosity in her; she enthuses in the last passage of the poem about the "inexhaustible medium" of space between persons:

> the space between us,
> first of the world's invisible wonders.

> Boundlessly flexile,
> it swells and contracts,
> surges and dwindles,

fluidly self-resculpting
with even our subtlest gestures,

yet never once has it been
seen or heard, tasted or felt.

Oh, Other People's Realities,
might we come together just long enough
to raise our glasses
(overflowing with emptiness)
in honor of this inexhaustible medium,

the sparest slice of which
serves to hold us apart
no less unyieldingly
than every ounce of it
ever created,

or must we agree to consider it
all *by-product,* so to speak?

The separateness of persons is not a wondrous mystery for us to celebrate to-gether (or as-if-together!) because it is, instead, a condition inevitably entailed by our being individual human souls at all; our separateness is a permanent element of our being.

Many are the poets who cry out against this isolation or search for ways it can be at least momentarily overcome. Part of Bateman's originality is her responding to the condition not with sorrow but with fascination that is often cheerful. In this, she has affinities with Stevens and with Rilke. Meanwhile, of course, a poet devoting a lifetime to expressing in poems *for readers* the truths of our earthly existence must be someone who feels that poet and reader can con-nect through the medium of poetry as it keeps "fluidly self-resculpting / with even our subtlest gestures"—in some sense of the word *connect.*

And the relationship Bateman offers to the reader—with a crucial element of comic irony in her own hypothesizing about the universe—is a relationship of instruction; the poet is a teacher guiding us to realize or remember the fantastic flowingness of the interaction between spirit and materiality. She is (like Stevens and Rilke, and Milton and Blake) a cosmological poet: most of her poems directly, rather than mainly through images or narrative, undertake to present fundamental generalizations about how the world works. This could, of course, be a recipe for very bad poetry (as every workshop teacher knows). Bateman stays poetically good (and even, I've been tempted to speculate, great) through her combination of intelligent zest and unsettling originality.

"Of what elements is our universe composed?" The question comes in the first poem of *Coronology,* "A Pocket Introduction to Our Universe," and is answered thus:

> The first is *distance,*
> of which there are innumerable varieties,
> such as the chromatic stutter between
> forethought and aftertaste,
> and the measureless span between
> the transparent and the merely translucent.
>
> The second is *otherness,*
> that of the other
> and that of the self,
> reciprocal and ever-escalating glories.

Not miseries but glories. In many poems, Bateman displays Whitman-like joy in rhapsodic passages evoking the infinitely colorful metamorphic cornucopic vastness of our world. (In such passages, she can resemble Dean Young except that for him the whirling enormity is almost always felt to be intolerably *too much,* whereas for Bateman the dominant feeling is *Bring it on!*)

I've said that Bateman is not a complainer or a lamenter. But we should keep noticing that she does acknowledge frustration and unhappiness in our life in a world of distances and otherness. What is striking is her conviction—or her gut sensation—that unhappiness or wrongness-in-the-world is not a central truth to devote poems to. The word *conviction* reminds us of the idea that Bateman is—in some very unsectarian way—a religious poet. I've been bored or even repelled by religious poetry that pretends to be unaware that suffering is all around us. I love George Herbert, but his frustrations and regrets and unsatisfied longings are crucial to his poetry's value. Bateman is able to convince me that she honestly contemplates suffering, while at the same time she feels it is not the main thing that needs to be contemplated.

This poet who offers us a "Pocket Introduction" to the world knows that we could have benefited from an authoritative supernatural introduction to existence itself; she points out what we've missed in a poem in *Scape* called "The 'Introduction.'" Is it a complaint? Well, perhaps, but not an agonized one, as Bateman emphasizes by ending the poem with a lighthearted image of existence as a surprise party for each of us. We arrive in the world with

> no preliminaries,
> no gradually sloping ontological shallow end,
> no throat-clearing on the part of the announcer—
>
> for that matter, no announcer
> or announcement—
> only the shock of
>
> LET THERE BE.
>
> Yet if we were all going to so unprecedentedly
> *occur,*
>
> don't you think we might have benefitted
> from an introduction
> (nothing too formal or overwrought)?
>
> But there wasn't anything of the kind—
>
> not even that one goofy guy
> unable to keep from yelling
> SURPRISE!
> just before the lights flick on.

If you arrive at a surprise party for you, you are at first overwhelmed or flustered, but then you rise cheerfully to the occasion. A person in the world of Bateman's poetry does sometimes get tired amid the whirl of earthly experience— as the Fatigue poems in *Clumsy* observe—but she does not campaign for a life outside the whirl; we can hope not for great escapes but only brief imaginative respites. In "The Woman at the Stoplight," in *Scape,* Bateman empathizes with a stranger:

> I see in her face
> that oh, she needs it too—
>
> a gap in the day,
> cloistered though not
> confining,
>
> person-
> sized pocket to slip into,
>
> buffered as by a cloud's
> sheer inner lining,
>
> for a breath
> of self-replenishment,
> self-repair.

The loss and hurt implied by the wish for self-replenishment and self-repair are not expected to be fixed by any reorganization of society or any fundamental reshaping of life; Bateman only asks, on behalf of the other woman and herself, for "just / a breath" of peace, a "person- / sized pocket" of apartness:

> so with the full force
> of my small ferocity,
>
> I importune the air:

"What could it cost
you who are only
lavish, seamless,

great incorporeal sprawl
of everywhere?—

open!
And admit us."

Here again, I admit a complaint is being made, but its importuning sounds speculative and enjoyable (with her "small ferocity") rather than desperate.

Though she knows a person sometimes needs replenishment and repair, Claire Bateman is excited and proud to be an instance of human spirit riding across the turmoil of the world. One of her favorite images to evoke the rushing changefulness of experience is the image of a wave. "The Last Wave Standing," in *Scape*, attributes to the wave an attitude of self-accepting pride that Bateman aspires to and recommends; the wave may be "forever on the verge of breaking," but it is undaunted by the temporality of itself and others:

the wave itself
refrains from any utterance
resembling complaint, a mode of discourse
apparently alien to its nature.

Anatomically flawless
in ledge and trough and crest,
neither spindly and too-transparent
nor freakishly muscle-bound,
this singular surfer riding the world's rotation
seeks neither anonymity nor renown,

and, in regard to its collapsed kindred,
evinces not even the least hint of gloating
or survivor guilt

as it occupies its singular spot
on the List of Collections of One.

The pride here is charismatic—in a way that Stevens would approve of—though it also, as in Stevens, may strike us as too lonely. This "singular" wave has no relations with other waves and has no interest in elegy. Since I am the kind of poet who is almost always pulled toward elegy—for yesterday, for past phases of my life, for persons who have died—I find Bateman's contentment in wave-life alarming. My admiration for her work is admiration for a way of being a person that is so different from my own way. Bateman has raised two children to adult-hood, as I have, but she almost never writes about her sons, whereas I've had to resist writing too often about my son and daughter.

The deep thing I have in common with Bateman is love of language, love of writing and reading. Poems in each of her books are inspired by language play; for example, in the prose poem "Sidekick," in *Leap* (New Issues Press, 2005), the mishearing of *psychic* as *sidekick* prompts a reverie about how aging super-heroes should stay in touch with their assistants—Batman with Robin, Green Arrow with Speedy, and so on. "Intellectual Property," in *Coronology,* imagines the speaker's Big Idea as a huge construction project in her backyard, including "the polished oak banisters, the cupolas, the flying buttresses," and many other components, even "the mezzosopranos, the Visigoths, and the parking garage." This poem turns out to be a warning against the vanity of certainty about the value of Big Ideas.

Born in 1956, Claire Bateman grew up in the life of books, physical books, before the internet, and she loves to create images and narratives in which books are living phenomena—as in "A Few Things to Know about Reading" and "The Sinking of the Library," both in *Scape.* She depicts herself as a com-pulsively avid reader in "Self-Summary"—a person who feels responsible for keeping books intact by reading them:

Apparently, I'm here to read
everything in print at an ever-accelerating pace,
though without any aptitude
for synthesis or retention—

which is to say that I'm here
to be largely elsewhere.

The urgency she feels is not about intellectual gleaning but about the imaginative absorption she feels the books require.

I must have been displaced as an infant
from my native planet
where unread words don't lie
inertly on their pages,
but self-ignite.
Think of my birth-world now,
flash fires springing up everywhere,

with no reader to extinguish them!

She goes on to say that she weeps "for my people / choking amidst the flames" as well as for her own longing "to go home"—but the poem comes across not as sorrowful but as proudly happy about her "lone talent" for appreciating the energy in flammable books.

Spirit is alive and in motion everywhere in Claire Bateman's world, and she can make the reader feel—without requiring a religious meaning *and* without despair—the truth in this declaration, from "Seize," in *Coronology:*

To exist in this world
means that at any instant,
something hugely invisible
may visit you,
only to be instantly gone.

Like the wave she admires in "The Last Wave Standing" that "seeks neither anonymity nor renown," Bateman has persisted in being her intensely original self as poet, publishing nine collections since 1991, without seeming to worry about fame. I continue to be proud that I caught on to her brilliance and her depth in 1998—and if "the world" catches on, I want credit for having seen it first.

Claire Bateman's poetry, published by small presses, is a test of America's poetry culture: if Bateman doesn't win through to extensive national readership and recognition, this will be a dramatic proof that our poetry culture is too cacophonous for merit—I almost said *spirit*—to get its due.

DEAN YOUNG AND
THE MADDING FLOOD

*Dean Young died in 2022. This essay appeared first
in* The Hopkins Review *in fall 2021.*

The poetry of Dean Young stakes almost everything on the excitement of the unexpectedness of its metaphors. Whereas some poets seem to be satisfied if a poem includes just one metaphor that is a bit unpredictable, a bit puzzling, Young wants metaphorical surprises to come as frequently as possible—every two or three lines, or even more frequently. The reader gets used to being disoriented at many junctures in each Young poem. The irony in being *accustomed* to disorientation presents an issue to anyone who considers the cumulative effect of reading an entire book of such poems. Unlike poets who hope that individual poems can be reinforced and illuminated by other poems in the same book, Young seems to start over from scratch with each new poem. Though the experience of reading many Dean Young poems does help us infer the meaning of each particular one, this is mainly true only as regards recognizing Young's Constant Inescapable Flooding Subject, rather than as regards discerning patterns of relation among metaphors. Young's oeuvre is designed to hit us as a barrage of hundreds and hundreds of fresh starts.

Fresh starts on what? On describing—and/or evoking—the essential experience of being a living human in seconds and minutes and hours and days. For Dean Young, that is what a poem ought to be about: the overwhelming baffling exciting maddening confusion of being alive. This is his Constant Inescapable Flooding Subject.

To describe "and/or" to evoke: the tension between these two verbs may be crucial in considering the action undertaken by *any* good poem (because the poem both contemplates and gives the sensation of an aspect of life); this fundamental tension is especially noticeable in Dean Young for a double reason—

because he is radically suspicious of any poetry that can be viewed as meditation, contemplation, sober reflection; and because he wants each poem to concern not an aspect of life but all of emotional-psychological human life.

What is your life like? Does it hit you as a relentless barrage of fresh starts, so that you can never be usefully prepared for the next hour, next day? Insofar as you feel that way—while still wanting to read poetry!—you are Dean Young's appropriate reader.

My own temperamental relation to Young's project is ambivalent and often skeptical. Yet poems of his have won me over many times. My hope in this essay is to discuss two poems in his book *Solar Perplexus* (2019) carefully enough to convince a skeptical reader that they convey coherent meaning and that they do this charmingly, encouragingly, winningly, with shots of brilliance that help us perceive our lives.

Dean Young has many devoted readers whose affection for his poetry needs no boost from the kind of analytic appreciation I will attempt here. For them, I suppose, analytic appreciation of Young's work is not only unnecessary but radically inappropriate because his poems emphatically and constitutionally do not solicit, indeed they repudiate, the kind of appreciation we develop for a Well Wrought Urn, a Shakespeare sonnet, or poems by the great Moderns—appreciation supported by reasonable reflection and argument. Young has explicitly and fiercely scorned that kind of appreciation in his book *The Art of Recklessness* (2010) and in many interviews and in hilariously or disturbingly intense letters to other poets, including me.

So, in this essay, the reader I imagine is not Dean Young himself nor one of his habitual admirers but, rather, a reader who (like me) tends to want a poem to "make sense" and "add up" and "get somewhere." Readers like me feel that we already know too well that life is (mostly!) a 24/7 torrential tempest of bafflements and damages; what we want from art is a raincoat or umbrella or map or compass or windshield wipers, shelter from the storm (but not a windowless dry palace). Poems that can help us are poems that make a kind of sense—poems that can be paraphrased.

For me, it is an axiom that a good poem can be paraphrased. If the poem works by way of complicated metaphors or abstruse allusions or ironies and paradoxes, its paraphrase will need to be three or four or five times as long as the poem itself and will (of course) seem awfully clunky and pedestrian compared to the poem's delicacy and poise, and a reader who loves the poem will certainly feel that some lovable motion of spirit or nuance has not been retained in the paraphrase. But still, the paraphrasing is not only worthwhile but *necessary* for appreciation of the poem's value, necessary for any sharing of that valuing from reader to reader. I've never wanted to live among readers who essentially have nothing to say about a poem beyond *Ah* or *Wow* or *Sheesh* or *Huh.*

Most good poems, I think, not only tolerate paraphrase but anticipate it, which is to say they want to be understood, despite whatever cost in loss of nuance may come with expressible understanding. But it's an awkward challenge to paraphrase poems that don't want to be paraphrased, poems that frequently (though not in every line) athletically swerve to evade paraphrasability. It's a slow sort of task that does not make the critic feel like Zorro or D'Artagnan.

Consider how seldom we read a thorough discussion or analysis of *all* of a poem (especially a poem longer than a sonnet). Critics of poetry seldom oblige themselves to perform such a painstaking task. Critics like to affirm the integrity and organic completeness and pervasive rightness of a good poem, but they usually rely on generalizations and selective illustrations to support the claim; as for the labor of full exegesis, our servants (or our students) will do that for us. Of course, there are practical reasons why critics high-step above the stream of a *whole* poem: (1) the poem is apt to include something that doesn't neatly fit the critic's argument; (2) thoroughness requires more pages than a journal is likely to afford; (3) the imagined reader is impatient, busy, has other things to do; (4) the reader may prefer not to feel that the critic's fingerprints are on *every* line of the poem.

I am aware, O reader, of the soundness of those four points. But I also think they can provide camouflage for under-pondered irresponsible praise or disapproval. A strong case for the value of a poem requires some attention to every line—especially if the poem enjoys seeming wildly impulsive. (Examining whole poems, I hope, will help me achieve something that does not merely duplicate the insights in Tony Hoagland's smart useful essay on "The Dean Young Effect" in *Twenty Poems That Could Save America.*)

If my effort in this essay has a quixotic and faintly crazy aspect, since the poet I'm writing about will scorn it and his poems will vigorously resist it, then let us notice how brave I am!

One response to a life of ceaseless bafflement and inescapable mysterious suffering is despair. Dean Young often writes poems that point in the direction of despair; despair is fended off only by flurries of dark humor, the laughter of exposing the absurdity of hope. In another mood, though, Young also writes poems of encouragement, often in an imperative mode, advising the reader on how to persist in a frustrating universe. He himself has persisted as a poet, very energetically, never succumbing to the malady of feeling that one's poems don't matter. Thus, when he writes a poem suggesting that a livable persistence is possible, there is honesty in the poem's impulse—because persistence is more abidingly the central truth of his life than despair.

"Pep Talk in a Crater," in *Solar Perplexus,* is an example of his poetry of encouragement. Young's titles are often useful signals about how to interpret the poems. This is a notable tendency, in view of the impassioned disdain he has expressed for innumerable poems whose distinct and specifiable topics seem to him all too obvious. The usefulness of titles as pointers toward meaning is one of the ways in which Young diverges from some of his heroes in anti-narrative and anti-interpretability such as Robert Desnos and John Ashbery and James Tate and Donald Revell. This inclination toward helpful titles is one reflection of the larger truth about Dean Young's poetry, which is what Hoagland called its "essential earnestness"—that it *doesn't* merely have fun befuddling a supposed pedestrian reader, but rather, it has agenda; it wants to convince; it wants to win assent.

Do you live in a crater? If you feel you have been bombarded forever by illusions, deceptions, inscrutable metamorphoses, the radical unreliability of reality, then traces of those impacts may be said to surround you like craters made by bombs or asteroids. You might feel like giving up; you might benefit from a pep talk. "Pep Talk in a Crater" begins with this six-line sentence:

> Even though your engine light's blinking,
> your bicycle's been stolen and your heart's
> a mangle, try not to listen to the crow's
> opinion no matter your concurrence,
> no matter the frog's disquisition in its frog jar
> or the shalt-nots of dawn.

That sentence is quite paraphrasable in a broad way: "Even though your life is frustrating and painful on various levels, try not to focus on a nihilistic summation of it all, even if your own observation tends to confirm that view and notwithstanding intimations of mortality's obliteration of spirit and notwithstanding the sensation of chastisement and repression of desire that each bleak new day brings." (The paraphrase is clunky; adequate paraphrases of good poems tend to be clunky.) The poem's first sentence gets going with the piling up of jumbled complaints that is a Dean Young trademark. What offers to countervail against "the crow's / opinion"—the view that life is nothing but animal struggle for meaningless survival—is only the peppy resourcefulness of the voice.

Your car needs repair, your bicycle has been stolen, and your romantic life consists of harm that has been inflicted on you or that you've inflicted on others. (For Young, who underwent a heart transplant in 2011, the phrase "your heart's / a mangle" may also have a nonmetaphorical meaning.) Car, bicycle, heart—the refusal to confine items in a series to an obvious category is an inveterate Dean Young strategy. In his sense of life, practical problems and emotional problems are always simultaneously present and always intermingling in ways that obscure degrees of importance. The effect threatens to be disabling, but our poet's response is as earnest as it is plucky. In the poem's next five sentences, he assures us that he shares in the existential alarm we must feel and then generalizes (albeit via a series of metaphors)—"Often . . . Often . . . Thus . . . Thus . . . All we know for sure"—to establish that our condition appears everywhere, it can be seen in other people and inheres in Nature itself.

> Often I too have been chased barefoot
> by I know not what. Often a meadow
> struggles to mention itself. Thus
> someone can start out a column of flames
> and be moth-dust by afternoon.
> Thus another can collapse in on herself
> like a neutron star. All we know for sure
> is Mozart took a lot of hammering
> and all those trees had to be screwed in.

To be chased barefoot is to have been caught unprepared in a dangerous encounter with an indefinable force. Something basic in the universe tends to demolish any assertion of pastoral calm: "Often a meadow / struggles to mention itself." In such a world, we are subject to rapid calamitous transformations; versions of human glory ("a column of flames") deteriorate into the debris of lost vitality ("moth-dust") in a matter of hours. A person's outward strength may implode leaving nothing but the compacted inertness of psychological disability. Assertions of beautiful creativity (like the music of Mozart or like trees in a park) can only be achieved through extreme exertions, exertions that have their violent aspect (hammering, screwing). The same may be said of Nature's own creativity (trees in a forest).

As I go along paraphrasing a poem that wants to resist paraphrase, I bump into bits that resist more successfully, maybe too successfully. I don't want to maneuver myself into the position of implying that every move in each Dean Young poem is equally marvelous. So, for instance, I've squinted at the sentence "Often a meadow / struggles to mention itself." When I offered an interpretation of this, I worried that I might be behaving like all the second-rate English professors who have stifled the skepticism of students by implying that every line in a good poet's oeuvre is unassailably right. If Dean Young had asked me about the effectiveness of the meadow sentence, I would have expressed skepticism. (But he hated my skeptical suggestions thirty years ago, and I've tried to resist offering him any since then!)

Having given an overview of our extremely unsatisfying and exhausting world, Young's next move is to reassure us that our reaction to this world is not only understandable but in some sense quite acceptable—"it's ok" is the key phrase in this eight-line sentence:

> Once the little green wings are smashed
> from the wedding vessels, it's ok
> to feel like you're watching your own murder
> with a butterscotch in your mouth,
> like how laughing makes the coffin
> easier to carry, the usual rueful decorums
> masking the want-my-mommy,
> this-ain't-my-planet wail.

What are "wedding vessels"? Are they chalices of wine, or could they be the bride and groom themselves? They are containers of hope. Hope is associated with birds (Dickinson: "'Hope' is the thing with feathers") and also with the green blooming of spring. To anticipate the smashing of "the little green wings . . . / from the wedding vessels" is to suggest that our hopes are fragile and are apt to shatter. Okay, but the hybrid metaphor may be interpretable without being effective. Wedding vessels decorated by, or endowed with, little green wings— this does not call to mind a real-world image. The metaphor has the kind of artificially imposed hybridity that Hart Crane championed when he explained to Harriet Monroe why his sentence "The dice of drowned men's bones he saw bequeath / An embassy" should be admired.

For my taste—or rather, I prefer to say, for my sense of how poetry can help us perceive and appreciate truths of life—a poem whose originality relies on that Crane-esque kind of compacted metaphor tends not to be beguiling or lovable. Such metaphors solicit *either* an abject stunned acquiescence from the awed reader (as Harriet Monroe sensed) *or* a lawyerlike busy-bee defense by a professor determined to stay several jumps ahead of an unprofessional quizzical reader. Young's wings-vessels metaphor is not a case of the rapid hopping from one metaphor to another that is his typical activity but of two images being welded together willfully, with hyperefficient brusqueness, the images having been drawn from, as it were, different pages of a thick file labeled Hope Tropes.

Nevertheless! I confess that the momentum of Young's eight-line sentence does woo me from skepticism toward the kind of gaga acceptance that his poetry induces in some fans.

When you find that your fragile hopes have shattered, the poet says, it is excusable ("ok") for you to feel as if you've been deceived by life. You've been distracted from bitter truth by trivial pleasures ("butterscotch") and by humor ("laughing") and by social convention ("rueful decorums") so that you are not quite aware of your own desperate need to cry out ("wail") against your plight.

At the end of that long sentence (from "wings" to "wail"), it is as if Young abruptly senses that the poem has become *too* paraphrasable—whereupon he wants to throw a monkey wrench. Almost all of his poems include monkey wrench moves—because, for him, when the poem becomes openly (rather than manically and untrackably) a Coherent Statement about Life, it has betrayed its fountain source in wild bafflement. The line that follows *wail* in "Pep Talk in a Crater" is: "Dumpster in the front yard yellow." What shall I do with that? I must paraphrase! To paint a refuse container a bright cheerful color is to disguise the reality of smashing, degradation, waste. So we have another metaphor for the world's deceitfulness. Thus, we haven't been wrenched entirely out of understanding. (I realize that what I'm doing has a parallel in what Helen Vendler used to claim she could always do with Ashbery's poems, but Ashbery's poems resisted paraphrase blithely and suavely and uncaringly, whereas Young is, in my reading, caring and anxious and never nonchalant.)

Life fools us into persisting. The poem notes this while offering us a pep talk aimed at inspiring the same result. This irony is at the heart of the poem at hand and implicitly at the heart of Dean Young's entire torrential persistent oeuvre.

After the dumpster line, "Pep Talk in a Crater" continues with an eleven-line riff set up by the idea of a joke being told where people (all of us) are in mortal danger (as in an intensive care unit).

> Knock-knock joke in ICU.
> No one knows who's there
> so keep guessing. How about
> a burning scarecrow seeking blood donations?
> Another reverend of alienation soliciting
> for the latest political roller derby?
> Spaceman on a snapped cord?
> Lost dog and his kittens?
> Go ahead, invite the Witnesses in
> to poke fun at their weeny leviathan.
> You call that an apocalypse?

Who is at the door? Five guesses are tossed forth—scarecrow, reverend, spaceman, dog, and Jehovah's Witnesses—the last of these is actually a realistic possibility, even if Jehovah's Witnesses may seem absurd or even surreal when they appear at your door. There is a perpetual barrage of demands and impositions impinging on us. The barrage may include a brainless or hollow person (scarecrow) who is being destroyed by life (burning) while asking for charity that he won't be able to benefit from (blood donations). It may include a pious operative campaigning in support of a political cause not seriously distinguishable from a comically brutal sport whose effect is to render citizens more disconnected than ever. It may include someone who is lost in space, untethered to humanity. It may include someone fundamentally confused about his animal nature. . . . Okay, I admit that "Lost dog and his kittens" is rather pat and mechanical as evocation of a topsy-turvy universe, but I could argue that the voice of the poem knows this and wants for an exasperated second to parody the poem's own style. (This is a justification I'd better not resort to too often.) The barrage of life's impingements goes on—how to react? You can enjoy teasing people who claim to have life all figured out: you can "poke fun at their weeny leviathan." Their version of catastrophe is hilariously simple in its denial of the effulgent mystery of every minute—"You call that an apocalypse?"

The poet does not anticipate the evangelist's literal End of the World but does anticipate trouble, so he recommends a handy weapon for self-defense, along with sophisticated wine drinking. Here are the last five lines of "Pep Talk in a Crater"—

> While we may assume no immediate danger,
> it can't hurt but to avail yourself of the hatchet
> in the hatchery and a good red.
> Obviously god needs lots of purple
> streaks in his design.

If a hatchery is where chickens lay eggs, why is there a hatchet there? To fend off a fox? In Dean Young's world, domestic productivity (egg production) will never be safe from violence. (Mozart took a lot of hammering.) *Hatchet/hatchery* is an impulsive play on words—something Young does not often indulge in. I think he senses that too much wordplay would undermine his governing purpose, which is to express the dire absurdity of our baffled existence on earth. If a poet were to proffer a bon mot too frequently, there could be too much implication that being a writer is fun and life is cheerily amusing. Young is a playful poet, certainly, but he feels his play is for mortal stakes. In his dire world, alcohol may help us persist, and if we sometimes spill our wine, we can tell ourselves we are participating in a cosmically ordained pattern: "god needs lots of purple / streaks in his design." Such a notion is a delusion but a more livable and benign illusion than the ominous one marketed by Jehovah's Witnesses.

"Pep Talk in a Crater" is a poem intended to encourage us all in a constantly alarming world. Having worked through it, I'm not sure I've persuaded any skeptical reader of the poem's overall value, but my account of it is meant to support the hypothesis that Dean Young's poems are not just jumbles of amazing images but artistic wholes. Tony Hoagland wrote that "Young's poems, as a consequence of their deep integration, sustain a state of vulnerability and openness that anchors their ironic transmogrifications and jokester antics." Hoagland's sentence is noticeably cloudy-abstract, but he's getting at something true about Young's style being anchored by a deeply felt sense of life.

No matter how much he scorns definitions and aesthetic prescriptions, Young believes he is creating art, and his prose credo, *The Art of Recklessness,* is loaded with prescriptive remarks about how art should jolt us. Young unmistakably wants his poems to be appreciated as art (alongside Apollinaire and Gertrude Stein and Kenneth Koch)—and he thinks about this every day, as many of us do. One nearly inevitable result, for Dean Young as for many calmer and more reasonable poets, is poems about poetry—poems that are about (*about*— problematic, controversial, yet unavoidable preposition in any serious discussion of a poem) some aspect of the life of writing and reading poetry. Of course, we often feel that a poem evoking or dramatizing the activity of imagination is implicitly or "in a sense" about poetry. As Allen Grossman memorably remarked in *Summa Lyrica,* "I am always *about to say* that the poem is about poetry." But Dean Young has many poems that explicitly concern poetry, openly wanting to deepen or intensify our awareness of what poems and poets do. I'll turn now to one such poem, "My Process" (also in *Solar Perplexus*).

My way of tuning in to "My Process" was to take the title as the key. Any much-published poet has been asked in too many interviews and Q and A sessions to describe the "process" by which the poet manages to produce poems. The question is likely to be sweetly naive (do you use a pencil or ballpoint?), but it can also be exasperating if it seems to expect an orderly ten-step procedure that extrudes a poem in its final stage. Mr. Young, how do your poems get done?

> Sometimes it's like pushing a wheelchair
> of bones through high-tide sand.
> Like giving birth to an ostrich,
> an ostrich with antlers that glow.
> The sense there's something wrong and
> not giving a hoot like going to church

to see what you can steal. Experimental
turn signal, neurotransmitter's whim.

Those first eight lines of "My Process" are alive with revulsion for the So You
Want to Write a Poem tips offered by many poets who have hoped that a guide-
book will, unlike their books of poems, earn money. Real poems, Young feels,
come into being through weirdly unpredictable exertions. One's own mind may
feel like an invalid (in a wheelchair), and one's thoughts may seem to consist of
only the fleshless remnant (bones) of what was once vital and inspired. Progress
may seem absurdly difficult (as if through sand). What you generate may be un-
gainly and alien (like an ostrich) and may seem supernaturally peculiar (those
glowing antlers). Writing the poem may require defiance not only of propriety
(church) but even of one's own sense of rightness; you may need to lay claim to
language and ideas that don't officially belong to you. The operations of navi-
gating through the poem and of language production may occur in unforeseen
and capricious ways—"Experimental / turn signal, neurotransmitter's whim."

We feel sure that Dean Young could continue this series of metaphors in-
definitely. Why should this poem about the oceanic mystery of poetic creation
not flood onward for a hundred lines? Why indeed, should every Young poem
not go on for six hundred lines, or until the poet's dinnertime? Well, six hundred lines would make a poem less publishable. But apart from that practical
consideration, the question of the size of a poem, when the poem comes from
a poet gripped by one Constant Inescapable Flooding Subject, is a real question. (Ashbery's Flow Chart can be seen as a diabolically tedious response to the
question.) One answer is that Young intuitively knows that if a poem is to convey our radical overwhelmedness, it would be anathema for the reader to get
used to the poem, and even manic unpredictability can begin to feel routine
after sixty lines or more. "My Process" has twenty-seven lines; very few of
Young's poems run past sixty lines. This enables the reader to catch breath and
eat a little yogurt before the next metaphorical rollercoaster. More important,
though, the size of the poems can be justified with the thought that even if our
overwhelmedness is all-day-every-day, the truth of it rises into consciousness
in bursts, and the scope of a burst is aptly represented by a poem of fewer than
sixty lines.

Young's next move in "My Process" is to suggest that what he is characterizing is not merely his own artistic process but the archetypal experience of true poets who dare to take on the challenges of world mystery.

> Mythologically, by the time Orpheus
> gets the message, it's obscured
> by radiance having been delivered
> by a trickster god. Of course,
> the operatic head floats down the river,
> decapitation making for a better singer
> as with a praying mantis.

When we receive divine inspiration, it comes deceptively, as when Hermes arranges for Orpheus to find in the underworld an illusion that only seems to be Eurydice. (Is that a convincing paraphrase of the first sentence just quoted? Hermes, who serves as guide for Orpheus in one version of the myth, has traditionally been referred to as a trickster, although Hades and Persephone are the gods who dictate the agreement that Orpheus fails to abide by when he looks back to see his beloved. Young's quick summary of the myth is a bit hazy.) Young wants to imply that any message that is clear and reliable and useful, rather than obscured by radiance, must be a falsehood about reality, since reality is controlled by maniacally unreliable forces, trickster gods.

Most poets enjoy the idea that the severed head of Orpheus continues to sing beautifully as it floats down the Hebrus (Ovid's *Metamorphoses,* book 11)—poets want to believe in their posthumous appeal—but Young enjoys emphasizing that the magical singing comes from a *severed* head, detached from ordinary human functioning. His kind of poetry has a better chance of arising from someone with a blown mind than from someone whose head is too firmly on his shoulders.

What about the praying mantis? Some entomologists tell us that the female insect eats the head of the male during copulation so as to ensure that the convulsions causing egg fertilization will be more intense and decisive—less inhibited! It's a fact or factoid that would appeal to a poet who feels that calmness and rational mindfulness pull us *away* from interesting creativity.

The decapitations are unsettling, and as we ride bravely into the remaining lines of "My Process," there will be further difficulties in paraphrasing metaphors that are sprayed at us like shrapnel as we continue to hear the poet responding to the question of how his poems come into being.

> Zigzag
> in a plaid forest, it's like lying
> fully clothed under motel covers.
> Lavender spit, amniotic gin.
> It's like trying to be a cube of light
> undissolved in a bigger cube of light,
> like holding your own brain and
> wringing it out. The heart has nothing
> to do with it.

When you try to track your inspiration as it eludes you amid the jumble of notions in your head, is it like having to move zigzag across a wilderness of lines that run in other directions? You know it is! And if you reach a resting place—a momentary stay against confusion (like a motel)—you can't relax in your underwear because you will need to be on the road again so soon. Your alcoholic beverage will seem as crucial to your survival as the fluid that protects an embryo. And will your saliva be pale purple? Probably not. But spittle bugs secrete a foamy substance on lavender plants in the spring. (The internet—a source of information not available to my forerunners Matthew Arnold and Yvor Winters—tells me this.) I don't know that "lavender spit" metaphorically refers to the way experience uncontrollably soils or obscures the beauties cultivated by poetry, but I know that Dean Young is a poet with some knowledge of horticulture.

To be writing a poem in a Youngian spirit is to be so open to the world's constant cascade of phenomena that the border between self and world is very tenuous—after all, there's a constant cascade within you too—so, the attempt to sustain a coherent self-enclosed illumination of the world is naive: "It's like trying to be a cube of light / undissolved in a bigger cube of light." And what else is it like, when you try to write a living poem? It's "like holding your own brain and / wringing it out." You try to extract something vital from your mental life, but this might be dangerous. We murder to dissect, Wordsworth said; Young goes farther, implying that we murder even to express.

Having evoked the necessity of a dangerous cerebral operation, he next momentarily wants to slap away (as if it came from a naive interviewer) the proposition that a poem need only pour out feelings, feelings, feelings: "The heart has nothing / to do with it." But he knows that declaration is untenable, so he immediately contradicts it and charges ahead to a sudden ending for "My Process."

>   The heart has everything
> to do with it, floating like a jellyfish
> all bioluminescent sting, monkeys
> ripping the car chrome off
> while we tour the ruins.

The jellyfish simile, with its vivid reminder that the human heart is a source of harm, whether you think of it as the engine of animal vitality or more specifically of libido, could have sufficed as an ending for "My Process." But Young perhaps sensed that it was a shade too familiar, since we've all written and read so much about the heart; allowing only a comma for transition, he hits us with those wrenching monkeys. At some point during the poetic process, we may wax reflective and elegiac; we may muse rather placidly on the relation between the poem at hand and Shelley's "Ozymandias" (or another work of the past)—like tourists on safari visiting a prehistoric temple. Meanwhile, monkeys are ravaging our vehicle—we return to the poetic task to find it wrecked by wild truths that have sprung from the jungle of oneself.

Why should those wild monkeys end the poem? The metaphor is strikingly pessimistic about the chance for success in poetic composition, but the pessimism has pervaded all of the poem, and it's hard to argue that the monkeys metaphor has structural significance beyond simply being the sixteenth (or so) metaphor in a shapeless series. But it leaves us with a memorable picture of the psychological mayhem inherent in Young's version of authentic poetry.

I feel I've had to bob and weave in trying to interpret "My Process"—of course I have, since the poem seems to have originated in a bubbling rage against facile interpretation and reductive accounts of poems as products of "craft." I don't have the sensation of having built an irrefutable case for the exquisite architectural shapeliness or organic vitality of the poem. That sensation is more possible for critics of Milton, Keats, Dickinson, Frost. Still I do hope to have stimulated appreciation of "My Process" as a poem *about* the mysterious difficulty of creating vital art.

Reader, when I planned this essay, I thought I would go on from here to paraphrase, line by line, at least two more of Dean Young's many poems-sort-of-about-poetry. For instance, "Wheelbarrow with Wings" (about teaching poetry) and "Dear Decoration Committee" (about judging poetry). There's also one called "Die, English Department, Die." There would be pleasures in presenting these, as their titles suggest. But how many times in a row do we want to arrive at the idea that life is maddeningly confusing and that poetry should express this? What I have to acknowledge is that Young's poems force any critical reader to say extremely similar things over and over, paraphrasing his monkey swarms of metaphors all campaigning for wild liberty of imagination to express life's maddening confusion.

Indeed, it is an amazing thing about Young's huge oeuvre that he never gets tired of expressing that same outlook. The fabulous variety of his metaphors can't conceal the fact that he is essentially saying—meaning—the same thing over and over: life is a crazing chaos, and the only adequate artistic response to it must be dazzlingly unreasonable and unpredictable. To theorize or to argue logically obviously goes against the grain of that outlook, but so intense is Young's commitment to it, so intense is his desire to make it emotionally (not logically) persuasive, that he loves to mock-theorize and to hector imagined conventional skeptics. This happens not only in poems but in *The Art of Recklessness,* which is loaded with riffs combatively recommending surprise and impulse as against design and reflection. Here is a passage in favor of what he calls "the irreverent":

> It doesn't observe the separations that pieties and sacred ritual insist on. The irreverent mixes. What we need is recklessness and an owl-shit outburst and a good smack upside the head every now and then. I, too, am a creature of electrified lint; give me a doily and I'll blow my nose on it, and I mean that in the best possible way. The poem is here to be defied. I almost typed "deified." When I typed "goof student" instead of "good student" in a letter of recommendation, it was very very hard to change. The irreverent welcomes its own desecration; it has no obligation to the truth (because there are too many to be obligated to), only to clear a possible space where new truth may appear. Sweeping, sweeping the temple steps is all you can do when hoping the god will appear.

Such riffs want to be charismatic; the voice wants to carry us in its current. When I step back, though, I squint at (for example) *desecration.* Suppose someone were to scramble and republish Young's poems as the work of Araki Yasu-sada or Miasmo Strumazz or Joshua Clover or Conrad Aiken III—that would be desecration. Would Young welcome that? Also, we notice an ambivalence about "truth" in the passage quoted. Young wants poetry that doesn't bother about be-ing true ("no obligation"), and yet apparently it should create conditions "where new truth may appear." But falsehood could appear instead, couldn't it? If so, and if that would be regrettable, then in a dodgy way Young actually does imply an obligation to express or reveal truth about life. Do we or don't we have to think carefully, in writing poems, about what is true in human life? The meta-phor about sweeping the temple steps seems to have followed from the phrase "clear a possible space," but what it calls to mind is an abject mindless menial ritual with a broom—a pious rote activity describable by adjectives Young would prefer to attach to the composition of dutifully controlled traditional offerings such as sonnets or villanelles. As I hope to have shown in examining two poems closely, Young actually does a lot of thinking in his poems, behind their insistently (or someone could say programmatically!) wild surfaces, but his congenital antipathy to intellectual analysis ("Die, English Department, Die") attracts him to images of admirable thoughtless activity, free from the agitation of intelligence—like sweeping the steps of a temple. When you *think* about it, that's an odd metaphor for the work of an artist of irreverence.

Irreverence can be not only charming but psychologically and spiritually beneficial—as Dean Young's poetry cornucopically demonstrates in its recep-tion by readers who have found it exciting and liberating. But irreverence is only seriously interesting when it has a serious relation to reverence; irrever-ence for conventional faith or propriety (or literary tradition) can be combined with reverence for human kindness, human love, human imagination, the hu-man spirit. Though he is very wary of declaring such reverence except in hazy ways ("hoping the god will appear"), Young's poetry does evince it; this is why he wants to give us pep talks in our craters. He likes to adopt the attitude of the madcap anarchist whose only goals are to smash idols, *épater la bourgeoisie,* and amuse the jaded, but he is more centrally a counselor and encourager. This is much more visible and palpable in Young's work than in the work of playfully puzzling poets he admires like Ashbery, Tomaz Salamun, or James Tate. Sym-pathetic awareness that our lives are strangely difficult—not only when we are trying to write but every hour—shows up in flashes of comic-but-sincere lam-entation everywhere in Young's books. "Pep Talk in a Crater" and "My Process" thus have many forerunners. For an example, I'll go back to *Strike Anywhere* (1995), his third book, the book in which he decisively became *the* Dean Young of metaphorical zigzag who has flourished ever since.

"Errata" is a poem about how we keep making mistakes; our lives are rivers of error, but we persist—our courage funny but lovable—in trying to stay afloat. Instead of settling for mockery, instead of listening too long to the crow's opinion, we keep trying to be clever in building a viable raft or boat for our voyage. To say so on this level of generalization sounds sweet-trite, but the poem lives in its dance from metaphor to metaphor; we can feel the poet trying to fortify our courage as well as his own. I'll quote just the last two of the eleven stanzas of "Errata."

> Still, one tries to go on making, following
> instructions. It is best to assemble first
> without glue as practice, then disassemble,
> glue and reassemble but who has patience
> for that? One fucks up and regrets but
>
> sometimes not too terribly because they've
> included extra screw blocks, extra screws.
> Plethoras of putties. Everyone will understand
> why you arrive so late, so barehanded.
> The swans are back on the lake.

Since that ending comes from this poet devoted to surprise, the reader won't be surprised to hear that those swans and that lake have not appeared anywhere earlier in "Errata." The swans arrive unforeseeably and beautifully, like good poems, like our chances to thrive in the purple-streaked design (or undesign) of the world. The encouraging sensation being offered to us belongs in the tradition of encouragement that includes Yeats's swans at Coole Park and Hardy's darkling thrush. But the particular shot of bemused hope delivered by Dean Young depends on the way it seems to have surprised him while writing as much as it surprises us. Now and then, I'm grateful for a shot of vitamin Y; it has helped me persist.

DEAN YOUNG,
PRINCE OF OUR LOSTNESS

Dean Young died on August 23, 2022, in a hospital in Cincinnati, at the age of sixty-seven. He had lived eleven years with a heart transplant; suddenly, in late July, he became ill, with a severe cough, and his symptoms got worse, and by the time he reached the Emergency Room, it was too late; his kidneys and liver failed as his heart could not pump enough blood.

I met Dean in June 1992 at a summer conference at Indiana University. We were drawn to each other's humor, and we found we enjoyed arguing—and we went on arguing, mostly in letters, all through the years. I have in my files dozens of letters in which Dean passionately explained how wrong I was in my basic ideas about what poetry should do. And I have copies of many letters in which I explained how wrong he was.

The oversimplified version would be to say: I wanted poems to be clear intelligent meditations; Dean wanted poems to be amazing unforeseeable adventures.

The debate went on and on, and we loved it. Our correspondence diminished during the worst years of his heart trouble, before and after his heart transplant in 2011. Then, in 2021, though, Dean realized he was miserable at the University of Texas, where he had been the Livingston Chair of Poetry since 2008. We wrote to each other more often, and then he quit the Texas job, and in November 2021, he moved to Cincinnati. His downtown apartment was about 150 miles from my home in Athens. We managed to see each other, either in Cincinnati or in Athens, almost every month over the last nine months of his life.

And we emailed each day. An email from Dean often included a riff that seemed halfway to becoming one of his poems. In April 2022, he wrote his "plan" for the season: "Here's my spring plan. Buy a suit. Get new glasses. Change my name to Burnt Geezer. Finish *Creature Feature*. Burn it. Start looking around for an asylum. Give most of my art supplies to Melanie who is an art teacher and certainly would want them. I will keep the splendid attachment of colored pencils of course. I will address my closet. Still I'll just go on being the burning scarecrow who walks into a bar and is the only one who doesn't get the joke. Keep throwing the world through the window of myself." Optimism, self-mockery, self-worry, a hint of despair balanced by humor, a flash of surrealism—this mix from Dean was occasionally disturbing but mostly delightful.

Until July 2022, I believed that Dean's predictions of his early death were melodramatic or somehow rhetorical. When his friend the poet Matt Hart finally took Dean to the Emergency Room, I knew it was necessary, but I assumed the doctors would be able to save him.

Your best friends should not die before you. We should live to be very old in good enough health.

Dean published at least thirteen books of poems (or more if you count chapbooks). He must have published more than six hundred poems. His posthumous collection *Creature Feature* will be published by Copper Canyon Press.

In our arguments, I used to say that individual poems of his often did not show enough reason-for-being as independent works; I said they were often too similar to each other. I still do think this. But now I look at his books in the light cast by his early death and with vivid memories of his intense and urgent and often hilarious arguments in favor of poetry of wild intensity and mysterious urgency.

Several times I heard him say that one of his best books was *Fall Higher* (2011). It was a book I had not read carefully.

So, now I want to write about some poems in *Fall Higher*—to show how vigorously they present his vision of human life and to consider how their qualities connect with my sensibility, so different from Dean's.

In real life—that is, in the daily life of the job and the car and the shopping and the meals—Dean Young was competent and often impatiently efficient. But his inner life every day pulsed with a sense of the world being fantastically unmanageable—absurdly confusing, monstrously overstimulating. Friendship and romantic love offered some relief—real, though anxious and vulnerable—from the vast too-muchness. But for him the essential human condition was overwhelmedness, and he felt compelled to express this in every way he could imagine. His many books of poems, at least since his third book, *Strike Anywhere* (1995), are bursting with metaphorical declarations of our overwhelmedness. His work is a case of consistent dedication to a central theme. This consistency could seem to contradict the wildly discordant inconsistency of his daily experience, but his poetic style prioritized kaleidoscopic unpredictability of metaphor.

Here is the first half of "Scarecrow on Fire," a poem in *Fall Higher* that presents its vision of life as a twenty-three-line run-on with many commas but no period until the end:

> Everything is brushed away, off the sleeve,
> off the overcoat, huge ensembles of assertions
> just jars of buttons spilled, recurring
> nightmare of straw on fire, you the scarecrow,
> the scare, the crow, totems gone, rubies
> flawed, flamingo in hyena's jaws, noble
> and lascivious mouth of the gods hovering
> then gone, gone the glances, gone moths,
> cities of crystal become cities of mud,
> centurion and emperor dust, the flower girl,
> some of it rises, proof? some of it explodes.

I do not ask myself to explain the series of images; I only say that they are samples in a catalog of frightening disappearances. The move of presenting a catalog—that is, a sequence of five or more examples of an aspect of life, examples not selected according to any clear plan—is a move necessary to Young's style, and I will quote several more catalog passages.

Let me acknowledge that some of Young's poems do stay on a track that can be followed. In the preceding essay, "Dean Young and the Madding Flood," I tried to show the argumentative coherence of two poems in *Solar Perplexus* (2019); doing so required thousands of words, but it was doable. As I wrote that essay, I kept realizing that the poet himself would feel instantly skeptical of such analysis. Most of his poems not only risk incoherence but embrace it or at least veer vigorously into it here and there so as not to become poems that pretend to have understood or controlled reality.

"Scarecrow on Fire" is for me not among Young's best poems because it is (ironically) too comfortable in being an ungoverned outpouring. Yet I do enjoy the poem as a gush from a seething mind; what matters is whether the reader believes that the pour of nominal phrases comes authentically from the state of mind that impelled the poem to be written. Not governed, we may say, but shaped by a true psychological reality.

Is that enough, though? I need to remind myself (for the hundredth or thousandth time) that "psychological reality" is not in itself the sufficient substance of a good poem. (I hear in my head the voices of my best teachers.). We want more—we want insight, or at least depth of inquiry; we want to feel the engagement of a vigorous intelligence. Further, we want to feel that everything in the poem counts, everything contributes to its pursuit of understanding—understanding or calm. (This value—everything counts, everything contributes—is what I like to advocate *instead* of the value of "compression" that has been over-celebrated by many readers.) As I've already admitted, Young's poems often prefer not to display resolutely this unity of purpose; but I do almost always feel a vigorous intelligence at work in them.

Are you a scarecrow? A scarecrow is a simulation of a competent human worker that is actually helpless, made by forces it can't comprehend, very liable to burning. This was one way Dean Young saw himself. (And indeed earlier in *Fall Higher* there is another poem called "Scarecrow on Fire," though it makes even less use of the scarecrow metaphor. I can imagine Dean in a mood saying that *all* his poems should have this title.)

Are you a flamingo in the jaws of a hyena? "Aren't we all?" Dean, in conversation, would reply to such a question. Each of us is mysteriously delicate and charming like a flamingo and horribly vulnerable in the carnivorous world. We are beautiful and bizarre and helpless. How many times should a poet say this—through metaphors but still with a palpable claim to authoritative sweeping vision of all human life? "Never possibly enough times" is the answer I imagine Dean giving. Our fundamental lostness-and-helplessness is the core perception driving the vast majority of his poems.

What good is it to declare or evoke lostness and helplessness over and over? Does the poetry in any way stave off disaster or surrender? Surrender may be postponed, but disaster is not to be escaped, in the Dean Young cosmos. Romantic love offers a comfort but ultimately a terribly limited comfort amid the violence of reality—as in these closing lines of "Alternating Current":

Do not
forsake me darling though we be carried off.
Every instance has its day and night,
every inkling is full of blinks,
the power going on and off so fast
we can hardly think until here comes a storm,
poor dog scuttled under the bed, poor dream
we recall almost not at all no matter
how we cling because throbbing is the sea
and we be torn apart.

He does not say there that his love poems or poetry as such or art provides any compensation for being swept away in the flood of change. He and his "darling" may cling together for a while, but the poem ends decisively with their being torn apart. In a universe of "throbbing," there are forces that will overwhelm our romance; earlier in "Alternating Current," he asks, "Is life just intervals of pulses[?]" and the poem can't find a way to refute this. In one sense, obviously this is sternly anti-sentimental. In another sense—if *sentimental* means comfortably oversimplified—the simplicity of "we be torn apart" can be called sentimental. But to Dean Young, it seemed horribly true—a truth that deserved to be bravely faced and expressed.

And he enjoyed the expressing. There is playfulness throughout his poetry, on the same page and indeed in the same sentence with desperation; ultimately, playfulness is for him the reliable answer to desperation—more reliable than romantic love. He mostly tried to avoid explicit references to poetry in his poems, but they did come, since he obsessed about the art every day, and occasionally, he came out openly with gratitude for it. The striking case of this in *Fall Higher* is "Non-Apologia," a poem that celebrates the fun of language and then launches into advocacy:

poetry delights if you want not
the humdrum quotidian gist,
rather a sudden brain-spinning love
for a stranger wearing a coral necklace like the sea.
Even spiders sing. We all are arpeggios
make that archipelagoes but oh, the butter

of your utterance unbanishing me
from the island of myself. Poetry is dandy
at supplying figurative language
which some find frustrating and evasive.
Why doesn't he just say outright
he wants to kiss her instead of going on
about butter? Well, screw you, to be sick
of metaphor is to be sick of the otherness
of life, in life which is like preferring
masturbating to the team sport or forms
without their depth-giving shadows.

The phrase "screw you" is a trace of the bellicosity Dean readily flourished in arguments, but the passage also offers amusement (arpeggios/archipelagoes, butter/utterance, team sport) as well as earnestness about the value of metaphor, as it gives depth to experience that might have seemed humdrum, by revealing the "otherness" that is inherent (when we realize it) in the strange complexity of experience.

Earnestness is not the quality we're most likely to expect in a Dean Young poem. For one thing, it goes against the grain of his ferocious contempt for poems that affirm safely admirable views, including poems that solicit praise for recommending social justice. As a forthright declaration of belief in an art that has helped him live, "Non-Apologia" is rare in his work. As I've said, on most days the belief declared or elaborately implied in a Dean Young poem is the belief that we are fundamentally lost and helpless.

Now I could proceed to show this with a dozen more examples in *Fall Higher* or a hundred more examples from his many books. This would be absurdly repetitious, yet I've felt tempted!—because I am interested in tiny variations among the expressions of overwhelmedness. And there is pleasure for the reader in watching Young work up his vision of our overwhelmedness over and over. He is a poet so reliable in presenting this basic claim about human life—ironically reliable given his stance as celebrator of surprise and recklessness. Young's ironic reliability calls to mind the effect some readers enjoy in John Ashbery's poetry—a delight in such versatile predictability: *There he goes again!*

Dean always revered Ashbery and would not tolerate my denigration of him as a brilliant seller of a designedly weightless product. For Dean, as for many other poets, Ashbery was a tremendous pioneer, opening up a world of happily hyper-loose quasi-connections and calmly defiant nonconnections. For an Ashbery aficionado, there is great comfort in the reliable refusal to build up coherent paraphrasable depictions of reality. Amid Ashbery's poetry, we can't be summoned to behave well socially or to judge morally because we exist in a perpetual buzz-fog. Dean Young's poetry is less relaxing than Ashbery's because it throbs with intensity, whereas Ashbery's work is a drug that smooths away all intensities. Still, in Young as in Ashbery, there is relief from responsibility. If you are helpless in the universe, you can feel excused from social demands.

In "Undertow," Young says that people watch the ocean because its unstoppable disturbedness "makes them feel less terrible about themselves." He gives two examples—a vice president and an analyst—sounding for six lines like a poet of social criticism:

> Comparatively, thinks one vice president,
> what are my frauds but nudged along
> misunderstandings already there?
> I can't believe I ever worried
> about my betrayals, thinks the analyst
> benefiting facially from the sea's raged-up mist.

But soon "Undertow" shifts to evoke the ocean's self-awareness:

>   Oh what the
> hell, I probably drove myself crazy
> thinks the sea, kissing all those strangers,
> forgiving them no matter what, liars
> in confession, vomiters of plastics
> and fossil fuels but what a stricken
> elixir I've become even to my becalmed depths,
> while through its head swim a million
> fishes seemingly made of light
> eating each other.

Every one of us, regardless of our moral goodness, is a walking seething ocean.

"Easy as Falling Down Stairs" is another of the many Young poems arising from and centered in his vision of universal bewilderment. He momentarily expresses gratitude for social (perhaps romantic) interaction, but the moment gives way to a catalog of forces and changes and distractions:

> No matter
> how stalled I seem, some crank in me
> tightens the whirly-spring each time I see
> your face so thank you for aiming it
> my way, all this flashing like polished
> brass, lightning, powder, step on the gas,
> whoosh we're halfway through our lives,
> fish markets flying by, Connecticut,
> glut then scarcity, hurried haircuts,
> smell of pencils sharpened, striving,
> falling short, surviving because we ducked
> or somehow got enough shut-eye even though
> inside the hotel wall loud leaks.

You would want to be well paid if you had to argue that all the items in that catalog, from the flashing to the leaks, have poetic rightness as they are placed. We feel that Young's mind can dish out such a barrage as easily as falling down stairs. And yet—and yet I love that long sentence; the only word that does not work for me (I say, speaking more as friend and belletrist than as professional critic) is *powder;* especially I love how Connecticut shows up as one more phenomenon to be perceived and survived like the fish markets. The poem's spirit turns out to be not despairing but convivial, culminating in invitation: "Who has the time, let's go, the unknown's / display of emeralds closes in an hour"—he is bedazzled but not daunted.

Bedazzled but not daunted—the implicit subtitle of each of Dean's books.

In "Song," he describes the endless instability of the mind—not just his mind but *the* mind. The title "Song" implies an inevitable recurring reality. Here are the first eleven lines:

> The mind is no evergreen steadily green
> among extremes of temperature, it's more squid

flushed with mood, one second smoochy, next
a puff of opaque ick. Oh, flying off the handle,
oh, orgasm, ice-cream headache, oh one way
then quick reversal like foot soldiers who
do not grasp the abstract concepts
that dragooned them to this field
to assault a brother who just wants like them
to see his squeeze again at harvest time
when the air is full of chaff and buzz and moo.

Our thoughts are like drafted infantry, pushed around the battlefield by inscrutable "concepts." We notice that those soldiers ought to sympathize with the
opposing thoughts; this I take as a flash of Dean's aversion to academic intellectual argument, even though he loved to argue when emotion was welcome in
the debate. And here as before, we notice his desire to make a gigantic generalization about life; the playfulness of imagery and diction can only fleetingly veil
the generalizing. "Song" ends with another world-vision summary:

> And groans the river
> to the sea, the dog to her fleas, all things,
> the known and unknown groan, it is the hocus-
> pocus gnosis of this world.

The line break of "hocus- / pocus" serves to downplay the funny niftiness of the
last phrase.

Young's gravitation toward such total generality of vision is acknowledged
at the end of "Vacationland." Unlike many of his poems, this one lets us discern
a specific occasion that has stimulated the thinking; he has spent a day at a
beach where people are on vacation, and he has walked around feeling alienated, noticing the absurdity of their activities. Then he recognizes, and apolo-
gizes for, his own tendency to leap from facts on the ground to ultimate truth.
Here are the last eleven lines of "Vacationland":

> The higher you get, the more
> the details point away from the hirsute

occasion—the marmot's golden teeth,
the divorcées playing volleyball on the beach—
to a cracked sheet of rock. Sorry
to be such an airhead downer. Out there
somewhere is the end of everything
but only the mountains are comfortable
with the idea. The rest of us paddle,
paddle between what we can't get
away from and where we don't want to go.

Nothing in "Vacationland" explains the reference to "the marmot's golden teeth"—the phrase seems to serve simply as a strangely specific thing glimpsed by the poet, who feels as remote from it as from the divorcées. If Dean were alive, I could ask him how the hell the marmot's golden teeth got into the poem, and he could laughingly tell me that something sharp and weird like those teeth is always nibbling into our field of perceptions. And I could say, "But why *this* detail here in *this* poem?" And we would argue happily for many minutes.

Dean Young's riffs on our lostness and helplessness are everywhere in his large oeuvre (a word he would mock), and so to point this out is to do the obvious easy thing. But obviously, I keep wanting to do it, and I hope to write about his posthumous book *Creature Feature* when it appears. Now I'll quote another catalog passage in *Fall Higher,* from the poem "Vintage." People keep making wine out of grapes, Dean Young kept writing poems, and I'm happy to call this passage vintage Young. We see in it the universal helplessness, *but* there is also our persistence—the insistence on living shown by readers of Proust, parkers of cars, and musicians and lovers.

It rains on the fireworks factory,
rains on the sea, the empires under
the sea, siege machines collapsed in sand,
people reading Proust, every word,
parallel parking, nudge forward, nudge
reverse but somehow no alarm. Some blues singer
plays back what he's just sung, tries again,
hungrier. A long-sequestered love

leaks out in the juicy circumstances
of an accident. She sends another letter
with an alternate destination, a meadow
instead of city, goldfinches on thistle.
The river starts an argument with itself
over rocks some kids drop from the bridge
where weeks ago someone jumped,
another week before he was found
sleeping in his car.

A man who tried suicide apparently changed his mind and is alive a week later, persisting.

Most of us mostly persist, despite feeling lost and helpless, and Dean Young wanted to persist (though at the end of his life, he was afraid that doctors might lock him into a death-in-life)—and he wanted to encourage us to persist through the vitality of imagination. In this purpose, he was kin to Wallace Stevens and other great poets not immediately called to mind by Young's zigzag swerving playful style. This point about his desire to encourage is the point I arrived at in my preceding essay, focusing on the poem "Errata" in *Strike Anywhere.* We can detect the encouraging happening in the passage from "Vintage," and "Vintage" ends with lines that I hear as honoring the stoical persistence of spirit in a world where art (such as opera) may fail to win over its audience.

Your eyes go on being the sky's,
beautiful sentiments set off to oblivion
while across town the new opera's booed.
You walk among the racks of dresses absently
clattering the hangers. So many blues.

If I do write about *Creature Feature,* I will probably—as in the present essay—pick out favorite passages rather than try to show that every line in a given poem contributes valuably to its meaning. As I mentioned earlier, in my 2021 essay I attempted unevasive every-line analysis of two poems in *Solar Perplexus;* this is an effort I believe in, and I think critics should more often accept the challenge of dealing with all of a poem. But a Dean Young poem makes this arduous—because of his inclusion of unforeseeable impulsive images (like the marmot's golden teeth) that jazz the poem in a way meant to resemble how our minds are jazzed by life's disorder.

Fall Higher contains a love poem, "Changing Genres," that I think could be praised in an every-line analysis, but here instead let me quote a few passages from a poem near the end of the book. "Winged Purposes" is a playful-yet-sincere lament about mutability, leading to a wistful hope that romantic love may somehow transcend time's ravages. Thus, the poem belongs in a huge tradition of poems through the centuries, and it reminds me that Dean felt his evocations of human lostness expressed truth that each generation of poets has to express. He loved to quote the last lines of "Ode to a Nightingale." In "Winged Purposes," he fears that we cannot keep even what we hold most dear.

> Too much flying, photons perforating us,
> voices hurtling into outer space, Whitman
> out past Neptune, Dickinson retreating
> yet getting brighter.

(I wish I could ask him what he means about Dickinson getting brighter.) The poem begins with a sentence that is simultaneously serious and parodic of a seventeenth-century style:

> Fly from me does all I would have stay,
> the blossoms did not stay, stayed not the frost
> in the yellow grass.

Soon come these lines:

> Hey, I'm real, say the dream-
> figments then are gone like breath-prints
> on a window, handwriting in snow. Whatever
> I hold however flies apart, the children skip
> into the park come out middle-aged
> with children of their own. Your laugh
> over the phone, will it ever answer me again?

I will never hear Dean's laugh on the phone again. I sit here writing about poems he published in 2011—as if to rescue an old book from oblivion. Each of us must eventually be represented by an old book.

He addresses his beloved (*Fall Higher* was dedicated to his second wife, Laurie Saurborn) in elegiac spirit:

> Remember running
> barefoot across hot sand into the sea's
> hover, remember my hand as we darted
> against the holiday Broadway throng,
> silver mannequins in the windows waving,
> catching your train just as it was leaving?

We recognize how deeply conventional those lines are; I like to imagine pointing this out to Dean and him in a noncombative mood agreeing.

"Winged Purposes" ends with lines more tinged with Dean Young idiosyncrasy:

> Sure, what fluttered is now gone,
> maybe a smudge left, maybe a delicate under-
> feather only then that too, yes, rained away.
> And when the flying is flown and the heart's
> a useless sliver in a glacier and the gown
> hangs still as meat in a locker and eyesight
> is dashed-down glass and the mouth rust-
> stoppered, will some twinge still pass between us,
> still some fledgling pledge?

Writing those lines for a book published in the year of his heart transplant, Dean knew that hearts wear out, and he knew that the rational answer to the question about communication after death is no. But his wishing is earnest. I am glad to have felt twinges of connection with his spirit while appreciating poems in *Fall Higher* and to have pledged to continue honoring Dean's work.

ACKNOWLEDGMENTS

Earlier versions of the essays in *Living Name* appeared in literary journals:

"Poetry and the Rescue of Particulars": *Literary Imagination;* "Whitman and the Rescue of Particulars": *The Hopkins Review;* "Dear Friend, Sit Down": *Pleiades;* "Damned Good Poet": *Michigan Quarterly Review;* "Kenneth Fearing and Human Lifetimes": *Literary Imagination;* "Kenneth Koch and the Fun of Being a Poet": *Pleiades;* "Kenneth Koch and Elegy": *Parnassus;* "Robert Pinsky and Forgetting": *The Hopkins Review;* "Art against Loneliness": *Pleiades;* "Courageous Clarity": *Pleiades;* "Tony Hoagland and Second Thoughts": *Literary Imagination;* "Claire Bateman's Ludic Spiritualism": *Pleiades;* "Dean Young and the Madding Flood": *The Hopkins Review;* and "Dean Young, Prince of Our Lostness": *Copper Nickel.*

My teachers Frank Bidart, Allen Grossman, and Christopher Ricks helped me (ever since 1977) to think about poetry.

My wife, Jill Rosser (the poet J. Allyn Rosser), and my daughter, Devon Rosser Halliday, helped me plan and edit this book.

INDEX

"Adonais" (Shelley), 56, 170

Agnew, Spiro, 186

Akhmatova, Anna, 126

"Alphabet of My Dead, An" (Pinsky), 184

American Heritage (magazine), 19

Anderson, Sherwood, 59

Andrews, Lee, 35, 36

"Angel Arms" (Fearing), 95–97, 105

Application for Release from the Dream (Hoagland), 225, 229, 230, 232, 239

Ariosto, Ludovico, 154, 161, 162

Armantrout, Rae, 209

Arnold, Matthew, 41, 43, 44–45, 126, 157, 272

Art of Recklessness, The (Young), 261, 269, 274

"Artist, The" (Koch), 134–36

Ashbery, John: admirers of, 209, 284; and attention, 80; and fame, 133; *Flow Chart* of, 270; and Francesco Parmigianino, 65, 68, 74, 75, 76; and "Grand Galop," 77–78; and Helen Vendler, 64, 65, 66, 73, 74, 75, 76–81, 267; and intimacy, 76–79, 80; as Koch's friend, 127, 148, 149, 151, 158, 159; language of, 76, 77–78, 80; and meaning, 77–81; and painting, 74; and "Paradoxes and Oxymorons," 76; as a pioneer, 283; as a poet, 132, 263, 275, 282, 283; poetry of, 75–82, 127, 129; and readers, 66, 68, 75–82, 135. *See also* "Self-Portrait in a Convex Mirror" (Ashbery)

"As You Leave the Room" (Stevens), 117–18, 146

"At Castle Boterel" (Hardy), 37–40, 88

Athens, Ohio, 277

"At Lulworth Cove a Century Back" (Hardy), 14–16, 17, 39

At the Foundling Hospital (Pinsky), 182–84, 185, 187

At the Funeral of the Ether (Bateman), 248

"At the Zen Mountain Monastery" (Wetzsteon), 194, 203

Auden, Wystan Hugh, 73

Australia, 43

Baldwin, Prudence, 19, 20, 21, 22, 45

Baraka, Amiri, 182

Bateman, Claire: and "A Passing Stranger Who Falls Briefly in Love with Your Fatigue," 245–46; and "A Pocket Introduction to Our Universe," 253, 254; and books, 257–58; children of, 257; and fatigue, 243–46, 247, 255; and "Intellectual Property," 257; and intuition, 243; and language, 257; and love, 245, 246–47, 251; and "Monograph," 248–51; poetry of, 242–52, 256–59; "Seize" of, 258; "Self-Summary" of, 257–58; and "Sidekick," 257; and similes, 246–47; and solitude, 251; and spirit, 243, 245, 246, 247, 248, 250, 253, 256, 258; and suffering, 254; and "The 'Introduction'," 254–55; and "The Woman at the Stoplight," 255–56; and tone, 247; and "To Other People's Realities," 251–52; and truth, 250, 253; and understandability, 222; and unhappiness, 253; vision of, 242–43, 251. *See also Clumsy* (Bateman); "The Last Wave Standing" (Bateman)

Beckett, Samuel, 118

Bernstein, Charles, 209

Berryman, John, 137, 167

Bidart, Frank, vii, 27, 28, 29–31, 33, 221. *See also* "For Mary Ann Youngren" (Bidart); "Happy Birthday" (Bidart)

Bishop, Elizabeth, 7, 73

Blake, William, 212, 234, 243, 253

Bloom, Harold, 74

Board, Lillian, 31, 32, 33

Bonnard, Pierre, 5

"Brief Tour of the World's Back Kitchen" (Bateman), 243–45

Brown, Michael, 181

Browning, Robert, 59, 145, 150

Buddha, 35, 124, 183

Burning Mystery of Anna in 1951, The (Koch), 133, 150, 156, 164

"Burnt Norton" (Eliot), 86

Bush, George W., 180

"But the Men" (Hoagland), 229–30

Byron, Lord George Gordon, 131, 154, 169, 229

Caesar, Sid, 178, 179

Campion, Peter, 216, 217, 218, 220, 221

Castile, Philando, 181

Catch or Key, Journeys to far off lands or strolls at home (Fox), 31, 33

Catullus, 17

Celan, Paul, 126

Charles I, 24

Chaucer, Geoffrey, 83, 104

Chicago Review, 248

Christ, Jesus, 67, 68–69

Cincinnati, Ohio, 277

"Circus, The" (Koch), 139, 140, 142, 143–49, 150, 160

"Circus, The" (II) (Koch), 139–51, 153, 154, 160, 161, 164, 167

"Clinic, The" (Kees), 105

Clover, Joshua, 222, 274

Clumsy (Bateman), 243, 248, 255

Collected Poems (Lowell), 33

Collected Poems of Kenneth Koch, The, 139, 146, 151, 160, 171

Columbia University, 19, 128

Complete Poems (Fearing), 83, 84, 96, 110, 112, 116

Coolidge, Calvin, 95

Coronology (Bateman), 243, 253, 257, 258

Coward, Noel, 137

Crane, Hart, 97, 126, 243, 266

"Crime Club" (Kees), 105–6

Cromwell, Oliver, 23, 24

"Crossing Brooklyn Ferry" (Whitman), 72–73, 124

Dante, 83, 104, 154

Davis, Bette, 201

"Day Lady Died, The" (O'Hara), 4–7, 18

Days and Nights (Koch), 132, 133, 135, 136, 164

"Dejection: An Ode" (Coleridge), 150

"Denouement" (Fearing), 107–8

Desnos, Robert, 263

"Dialectical Materialism" (Hoagland), 206–9, 211

"Dialogue" (Herbert), 67

Dickens, Charles, 188

Dickinson, Emily: and alienation, 69; critics of, 273; and dead friends, 41; and feelings, 239, 242; greatness of, 206; and Helen Vendler, 64; and hope, 266; and "It struck me – every Day –," 89; and joy, 138; poetry of, 138, 243, 289; and readers, 70, 72; style of, 77, 144; and suffering, 137–38; and understandability, 222

"Directive" (Frost), 171

"Dirge" (Fearing), 96, 106–7, 123

"Dividends" (Fearing), 91–93

Donkey Gospel (Hoagland), 209

Donne, John, 214

Dos Passos, John, 97

Duhamel, Denise, 7, 215

Dumas, Henry, 184

Dunne, Irene, 197

Duplications, The (Koch), 160, 163

Dylan, Bob, 137, 237, 238

"Easter 1916" (Yeats), 25–27

Easton, Emily Meader, 19

"Easy as Falling Down Stairs" (Young), 284–85

"Elegy Written in a Country Churchyard" (Gray), 23–24

Eliot, George, 124

Eliot, T. S., 73, 85–86, 93, 97, 105, 126. *See also* poets; *The Waste Land* (Eliot)

Emerson, Ralph Waldo, 180

England: and Civil War, 25; Cornwall region of, 38, 39; and Irish rebels, 26, 27; London in, 31, 158, 167, 187, 234; and Olympic runner Board, 33

"Even-Song" (Herbert), 65

"Faces" (Whitman), 54, 57–60

Fall Higher (Young), 278, 279, 280, 281, 282, 287, 289–90

"Fate" (Koch), 7, 143, 150–60, 61, 165

Faulkner, William, 59

Fearing, Kenneth: and absurdity, 119; and "American Rhapsody" (2), 96; "American Rhapsody" of, 93–95; and American society, 83, 84, 86, 90–91, 94–95, 97, 112, 116–17; and anger, 86, 90, 94, 96–97, 110; and "A Pattern," 118–20; and capital punishment, 99; and "Class Reunion," 104–5, 120, 122–24; and "Conclusion," 90–91; and cynicism, 88, 100, 102, 104, 108, 122; and "Damned Good Poet" (Halliday), 112; and death, vii, 84, 87, 88, 91, 94, 105, 107, 110–11, 115–19, 123; and depression, 86, 104, 105, 110, 112, 118, 124; and desire, 89, 90, 97, 113; and despair, 124, 125; and desperation, 104, 108, 112, 124; and egocentrism, 110; and "Engagements for Tomorrow," 106; essays on, vii; and "Evening Song," 116; "Flophouse" of, 109, 120–21; and Great Depression, 86, 90, 102, 116; and human experience, 86–89, 90, 93–95, 112–13, 119–24; "If Money" of, 108; and individual creation of meaning, 104, 112–13, 122, 124–25; and "Invitation," 120, 122; and "Jack Knuckles Falters," 97–100; life of, 84, 114, 121; and love, 84, 87, 89, 93, 100, 114, 122; and media, 95, 97, 99–100; "Memo" of, 87–88, 107, 125; and "Minnie and Hoyne," 108; and overwhelming forces, 86, 90, 93, 97; and pathos, 86, 99, 115; and poem "$2.50," 101–2; as a poet, 83–84, 86–88, 90, 99, 104, 106, 110, 112–13, 115–16; and preservation, 86–87; protagonists of, 112–13, 114, 116, 118–23; and "Radio Blues," 102–4, 105; and readers, 86, 99, 113, 119; and "Requiem," 110–11, 115; and "Scheherazade," 100, 108; "Statistics" of, 84–85, 86, 107; and "This Day," 114–15, 118, 121; and truth, 115; and understandability, 222; and victory, 87, 88; and "X Minus X," 88–90, 95, 178. *See also* "Angel Arms" (Fearing); *Complete Poems* (Fearing); "Denouement" (Fearing); "Dividends" (Fearing); "Lanista" (Fearing); *Stranger at Coney Island* (Fearing)

feminism, 229, 230
Ferrar, Nicholas, 69
Ferry, David, 110
"Filling Station" (Bishop), 7
Fitzgerald, Ella, 137
Fitzgerald, F. Scott, 97
Forché, Carolyn, 209
"For Mary Ann Youngren" (Bidart), 227
"Forgetting, The" (Pinsky), 178, 181–82, 185
Fox, Ruth, 31, 32, 33
Freilicher, Jane, 148, 149, 151, 157, 158, 159
Friction (Bateman), 248
Frost, Robert, 73, 76, 141, 171, 179, 206. *See also* poetry

Garner, Eric, 181
"Geist's Grave" (Arnold), 41–45
Genet, Jean, 5
Germany, 219
Gershwin, Ira, 137
Gifford, Emma, 38, 39
Ginsberg, Allen, 132, 208
Glück, Louise, 217, 221
Goldbarth, Albert, 7, 188, 215
"Glimpse, The" (Herbert), 65
Gray, Thomas, 23–25
Grossman, Allen, 18, 269
Guest, Christopher, 134
Gulf Music (Pinsky), 176–77, 180, 181, 182

"Hearts, The" (Pinsky), 34–37
Halliday, Ernest M., 19
Halliday, Mark, 81, 122, 205
Hampden, John, 24–25
"Happy Birthday" (Bidart), 27–31, 33, 34
Hardy, Thomas: and belated appreciation, 149; and elegies, 157; and feelings, 239; greatness of, 206; and "I Look into My Glass," 89; and images, 11, 12; marriage of, 38; and pathos, 115; poetry of, 8–17, 20, 24, 34, 37–40, 189, 213; and remembering, 44, 166; and "The Missed Train," 166; thrush of, 276; and truth, 115. *See also* "His Immortality" (Hardy)
Hart, Matt, 278
Hass, Robert, 188
Hayworth, Rita, 23
Hemingway, Ernest, 19
Herbert, George: and death, 69, 71; "Dialogue" of, 66–67; and God, 65, 66–69, 71, 73, 76; and Helen Vendler, 64, 66–68, 69, 73; and intimacy, 68–69, 71; and Jesus, 68–69; and "Love Unknown," 68, 69; as a poet, 75, 254; and religion, 69; and *The Temple*, 66, 68–69
Herrick, Robert, 2, 19, 20, 21, 22, 45
Hill, Geoffrey, 126
"His Immortality" (Hardy), 8–9, 17, 24, 34, 44
History of My Heart (Pinsky), 172, 174, 184
Hoagland, Tony: and accessibility, 238–39; and "Address to the Beloved," 212; and American culture, 236–38; and art, 211, 238; and "Aubade," 230–31; and "Candlelight," 209–11; and capitalism, 205, 207–8, 211, 222, 232, 234–35, 236, 237,

Hoagland, Tony (*continued*)
238; and clarity, 206, 209, 221, 224, 225, 239,
241; and complicity poems, 232, 237; and Dean
Young, 269; death of, 205; and "Description,"
211–12; and desire, 211, 221, 227–29, 234; and
"Disaster Movie," 236–37; and emotions, 221;
and family, 211, 231, 232; father of, 231, 232; and
"Foghorn," 211, 217, 220; and gender, 229–30,
240; "Hard Rain" of, 237; and hope, 232; and
identity, 211; and "In Praise of Their Divorce,"
213–15; and "Instead," 240; ironic mode of, 208,
232; and love, 211, 222, 230–31; and metaphor,
206, 212, 213–15, 224; and Nature, 212, 213–14,
223–24, 233–34; and "Note to Reality," 239–40;
and "No Thank You," 240–41; and "Personal,"
212; as a poet, 216, 218, 220, 221, 224–27, 239–41;
poetry collections of, 225, 227; protagonists
of, 212; and race, 205, 217, 229, 231; and readers, 207, 208, 215, 221–22, 225–27, 232, 237; and
"Requests for Toy Piano," 222–24; and second
thoughts, 225–28, 230, 234, 235, 236, 239–40; and
sexism, 205; and social class, 205, 212, 229; and
social critique, 234; "Spanish Ballad" of, 227–29;
style of, 205, 206, 208, 215; and "Summer,"
232–33, 235, 238; and sympathy, 238; and 'The
Allegory of the Temp Agency," 211; and "The
Dean Young Effect," 262; and "The Story of the
Mexican Housekeeper," 231–32; and truth, 224,
226, 239, 240; and *Unincorporated Persons in the
Late Honda Dynasty*, 239; and wisdom, 240–41.
See also "But the Men" (Hoagland); "Romance of
the Tree" (Hoagland); *Unincorporated Persons in
the Late Honda Dynasty* (Hoagland); *What Nar-
cissism Means to Me* (Hoagland)
Holiday, Billie, 4, 5, 6, 7
"Hollow Men, The" (Eliot), 86
Homer, 83
Hopkins, Gerard Manley, 70, 72, 198, 212, 218
Hopkins Review, The, 260
Horace, 2, 17–18, 110, 181, 218
Housman, A. E., 32

identity, 30, 89, 115–16, 171, 175, 177. *See also* Hoag-
land, Tony; Wetzsteon, Rachel
India, 219
"In Memory of Major Robert Gregory" (Yeats), 4

Invisible Listeners (Vendler), viii, 64–66, 68, 71, 77,
80, 81
"Invitation to the Future" (Hoagland), 234–36
Ireland, 25, 26
Italy, 15

"Jabberwocky" (Carroll), 80
"Jack Knuckles Falters" (Fearing), 97–99, 103
Jarrell, Randall, 73, 137, 150, 178, 191
Johnson, Kent, 209
Johnson, Lyndon B., 128
Jones, Jim, 186

Keats, John, 14, 15, 16, 17, 39, 123, 129. *See also* poets
Kees, Weldon, 105–6, 107, 123
Kenyon Review, 127
Kirby, David, 7, 188, 215
Ko (Koch), 160, 161
Koch, Kenneth: and "A Big Clown-Face Shaped
Cloud," 170–71; and apostrophe mode, 171; and
art, 130–31, 134, 135–36, 140, 147, 269; and *The Art
of Love*, 130, 133 and attention, 147; and autobiographical style, 150, 152, 160, 167, 171; and "Bel
Canto," 169–70; and Bollingen Prize, 133; and
creative potential, 132–33; "Currency" of, 164;
and death, 139, 146, 161, 162, 168–70; and elegies, 139, 140, 143, 148, 149, 150, 151, 156–57, 160,
164, 167, 168, 169–71; epic poems of, 160; and
Europe, 150, 151, 152–57, 160, 164–66; and Frank
O'Hara, 140, 142, 156; and "Fresh Air," 128, 131,
134; and friendship, 148–49, 152–55, 156, 158–59;
and fun of poetry, 126–27; and greatness, 139,
164; and happiness, 136, 142, 147, 152–56, 159,
161; and "Hearing," 135; and inspiration, 169;
and Janice, 140, 142, 144–45, 147, 149, 160, 162,
163, 164, 168–69, 170; and joy, 138, 139, 154, 155;
and loss, 169, 170; and love, 148, 161; and "Memoir," 168–69; and memory, 142, 143–44, 145, 147,
151–53, 155–59, 164, 168; and mortality, 170–71;
and New York, 142, 169; and Paris, 140, 142, 150,
169; and "Passing Time in Skansen," 164–66,
170; poetry of, 7, 127, 128–36, 137, 145, 151, 153,
154–57, 161, 164–65, 168–70; protagonists of,
170; and readers, 131, 132, 135, 142, 143, 151, 161,
166–67, 171; real-life voice of, 141–42, 147–48,
150, 152, 154; recognition of, 133; and satire, 135,

136; self-questioning of, 139, 140, 145–46, 151, 160; and suffering, 136; and "Time Zone, A," 127; and "To My Fifties," 167–68; and "To My Old Poems," 167; and truth, 166; and variety, 152, 168, 171; and "When the Sun Tries to Go On," 127; and Whitney Museum, 142; and youth, 161, 164–66, 169. *See also* "A Time Zone" (Koch); *Collected Poems of Kenneth Koch, The; Days and Nights* (Koch); "Fate" (Koch); *New Addresses* (Koch); *Possible World, A* (Koch); "Seasons on Earth" (Koch); *Thank You* (Koch); "The Artist" (Koch)
Ku Klux Klan, 186

"Lanista" (Fearing), 117, 118
"Last Wave Standing, The" (Bateman), 256–57, 258
Lawrence, D. H., 94, 97
"Lawyers on the Left Bank" (Wetzsteon), 195–96, 200–201
Leaves of Grass (Whitman), 47, 49, 51, 54, 58, 61, 66. *See also* Whitman, Walt
Léger, Fernand, 140, 141
Levine, Philip, 7, 188
Lincoln, Abraham, 124
Liuzzo, Viola, 186
Living Name (Halliday), vii, viii
"Louie Louie" (Pinsky), 178–81, 182, 185, 188
"Love Song of J. Alfred Prufrock, The" (Eliot), 85
"Love Unknown" (Herbert), 65
Lowell, Robert: and autobiographical style, 167; and culture, 229; and "Dunbarton," 7; life of, 119, 161; and "My Last Afternoon with Uncle Devereux Winslow," 7; poetry of, 1, 7, 31–34, 73, 161; striving of, 137. *See also* "Remembrance Day, London 1970's" (Lowell)
"Lycidas" (Milton), 56, 170

MacFarquhar, Larissa, 80
McCarthy, Cormac, 220
Mercer, Johnny, 137
Metamorphoses (Ovid), 271
Mill, John Stuart, 77
Millay, Edna St. Vincent, 199
Milton, John, 24, 56, 253, 273. *See also Paradise Lost* (Milton)
Mozart, Wolfgang, 264, 265, 268
Music of What Happens, The (Vendler), 79

Napoleon, 23
National Anthem (Prufer), 222
Native Americans, 52, 53, 60, 183, 207
New Addresses (Koch), 139, 143, 156, 166–68, 171
New Orleans, Louisiana, 49, 51
New Republic, The (magazine), 199
New York City, New York, 49, 191–92, 194, 196–97, 198
New Yorker, 84
New York Times, 19
Nixon, Richard, 128
Norton Anthology of Poetry, The, 20

O'Hara, Frank: and daily talk, 218; and "Day and Night in 1952," 168; death of, 126, 142, 153, 156; and "Image of the Buddha Preaching," 221; as Koch's friend, 142, 148, 149, 150–51, 152, 154–55, 156, 158, 159; life of, 126; and loss, 126; as a poet, 126, 127, 132, 137; and "The Day Lady Died," 4–7, 18
"Old Salt Kossabone" (Whitman), 61–63
Old Testament, 101
"Once I Pass'd through a Populous City" (Whitman), 48–51, 54, 56, 61
One Train (Koch), 127, 164
ottava rima, 160, 164, 169

Paradise Lost (Milton), 236
Pepper, Art, 35
"Pep Talk in a Crater" (Young), 263–69, 275–76
Perloff, Marjorie, 6, 7
Petty, Tom, 113
Pindar, 184, 185
Pinsky, Robert: and "Antique," 176–77, 178, 185, 188; and art, 185; and autobiography, 187; and beauty, 177; and death, 174, 184; and despair, 185; and elegies, 176, 184; and forgetting, 172–78, 180, 181–83, 185, 187, 188, 189; and "Glory," 184–85; and individual creation of meaning, 175, 180; and "In the Coma," 185–87; and loss, 184; and love, 176–77; and memory, 172–76, 181–87; and names, 175, 179–80, 181, 187; and panoptic awareness, 183, 186; poetry of, 7, 34–37, 172–75, 177, 181, 185–89; and social injustice, 180; and "The Founding Tokens," 184, 187–88; and "The Garden," 172–73, 176, 182; and "The Living," 184;

Pinsky, Robert (*continued*)
  and "The Orphan Quadrille," 182–83, 187; and
  "The Questions," 7, 174–75, 176; and "The Want
  Bone," 89; and time, 172–73, 177, 181; and truth,
  186, 188. *See also* "Alphabet of My Dead, An"
  (Pinsky); "The Forgetting" (Pinsky); *Gulf Music*
  (Pinsky); "Hearts, The" (Pinsky); "Louie Louie"
  (Pinsky)
Plath, Sylvia, 126
Plato, 124, 242
"Pleasures of Peace, The" (Koch), 128–32, 133, 135
poetry: and "90 North" (Jarrell), 178; about poetry,
  269, 270, 273–74; and absurdity, 1–2, 153, 155,
  180, 267, 268; and accessibility, 238–39; and
  afterlife, 8, 45, 46; and American culture, 259;
  and Americans, 57–58, 179–80, 182, 186; and
  apostrophe mode, 167; and art, 6, 7, 22, 27, 33,
  34, 36–37, 45, 75, 81–82, 83, 93, 100, 101–4, 118,
  177, 183, 242, 269, 273; and beauty, 25, 27, 37, 54,
  75, 88, 129, 135, 146, 177, 213, 240; and "Bells for
  John Whiteside's Daughter," 21–22; and bodies,
  47, 191, 199, 220; and categories, 2, 57, 61, 65, 90,
  184, 215, 226, 240, 264; and children, 133, 187–88,
  219, 220, 235, 245–46, 247, 289; and clarity, 238,
  239, 241, 277; and class, 18, 21, 91–93, 205, 212,
  229; and comedy, 192, 213, 215, 221; and dance,
  182–83; and dates, 3, 6, 7, 9–10, 11, 12, 14, 33, 34,
  38, 39, 40, 44; and death, 5, 7, 9, 18–19, 23–27,
  30, 32, 33–34, 38, 40, 41–48, 52, 54–56, 57, 61–63,
  65, 84–85, 94, 98–99, 105, 106, 107, 110–11, 123,
  146, 174, 184, 186, 209, 218, 219; and depression,
  28, 29–30, 56–57, 85–86, 197; and desire, 34–37,
  38, 48, 114, 168, 169, 216, 218, 227–29, 234, 247;
  and despair, 105, 112; and drama, viii, 35, 112, 114,
  150, 158, 192, 198, 201; and egomania, 134; and
  elegies, viii, 4, 9, 17, 19, 21–24, 41, 43, 50, 54, 55,
  56, 131, 139, 140, 143, 148, 149, 150, 153, 156, 157,
  164, 168, 169–71, 248, 257, 273, 290; and English
  poetry, 7, 10, 14, 16, 20–21, 23–27, 37–45, 56, 73,
  158; and epitaphs, 20, 22, 24; essays on, vii–viii,
  65–66, 79, 183, 227, 243, 248, 260, 261, 262, 279;
  and eulogies, 55–56, 57, 106; and fame, 23, 24,
  25, 26, 27, 28, 32, 44; and fear, 191, 198, 218; and
  forgetfulness, 31, 33, 54, 57, 62, 122, 182, 183; and
  the future, 52, 60, 65, 69, 70–73, 75, 115, 201–2,
  234–35; and glory, 184–85, 194, 253, 264; and
  God, 24, 35, 36, 46, 65, 66–68, 92, 97, 120, 138,
  162, 207, 248, 249, 268, 271, 275; and greatness,
  84, 253; and hope, 118, 119, 232, 265–66; and human experience, viii, 1–4, 10, 13, 14, 15–17, 19, 28,
  30, 31, 34–40, 43, 46, 57, 74–75, 77–79, 83, 106–7,
  111, 113–15, 117–19, 142, 147, 157, 169–70, 173–75,
  178, 188, 209, 213, 222, 225–27, 234–36, 248–52,
  254–57, 260, 274; and "Hysteria" (Eliot), 178; and
  imagery, 33, 83, 148, 217, 222–23, 247, 253, 256,
  269, 279, 286, 289; and imagination, 269; and
  immortality, 8–9, 17–18, 20, 24–25, 32, 34, 37, 55,
  129, 156; and individual creation of meaning,
  123–25, 173; and intimacy, 68–72, 74, 76–79, 81,
  152, 170; and joy, 107, 128, 140, 154, 253; and language, 53–54, 70, 71, 76–78, 80, 81–82, 136, 141,
  183, 185–86, 198–99, 207, 211, 212, 213, 217–21,
  268, 270, 281–82; and "Lapis Lazuli" (Yeats),
  183; and "Lines Written in Dejection" (Yeats),
  182; and "London" (Blake), 234; and loneliness,
  69–70, 214, 250, 251, 257; and loss, 1, 2, 18–19, 46,
  136, 139, 140, 145, 183; and love, vii–viii; 1, 4, 6, 7,
  13, 18, 20, 23, 25, 30, 39–40, 42, 43, 44, 45, 49–51,
  53, 56, 64, 65, 66, 67, 68, 72, 74, 83, 100, 103, 111,
  122, 166, 176–77, 190–91, 204, 209, 216, 222, 227,
  230–31, 239, 240, 246, 265–66; and lyric poetry,
  13, 17, 65–66, 72, 76–77, 81, 88, 100, 107; and
  Marxism, 107, 108, 223–24; and meaning, 77,
  104, 106, 107, 109, 117–19, 168, 213, 238–39, 250,
  263, 277, 288; and media, 99–100, 102–4; and
  memory, 6, 8, 9–10, 20–21, 31, 33, 34, 44, 46, 49,
  50–51, 60, 62, 143–44, 145, 151–53, 172–76, 181–85,
  201–3; and metaphors, 192, 193, 196, 197–98, 199,
  205, 206, 217, 226, 260, 261–62, 264–66, 275; and
  monologues, 106, 150; and mortality, 1, 8, 9, 22,
  31, 32, 33–34, 42, 46–47, 56, 231; and music, 136,
  168, 181, 183, 197, 202–3, 207, 208, 209, 210, 217–
  21, 238, 246, 265; and names, 1, 2–3, 4, 6, 11, 12,
  17–18, 20–29, 32, 33, 36–37, 38, 51–52, 60, 148–49,
  179, 181, 186, 234–35; and nostalgia, 140, 142–43,
  146, 149–50, 155–57; and odes, 17–18, 150, 156,
  184, 185, 193, 289; and "Ode to the West Wind,"
  193; paraphrasing of, 261–62, 264–67, 271–74,
  284; and *Poetry*, 215–16; and political poetry,
  86, 90–91, 206, 208, 211; and popular literature,
  100–101, 233–34, 237; and preservation, 1–3, 8,
  14–16, 18, 19, 22, 26–27, 30, 34, 44, 47, 52, 157;
  "Rabbit as King of the Ghosts, A" (Stevens), 116;
  and readers, 3, 4, 13, 16, 17, 19, 27, 29, 31, 32, 33,

65–82, 86, 104, 113, 119, 132, 142, 143, 171, 178, 181, 198, 206, 208, 212, 221–22, 232, 233, 237, 238–39, 248, 252–53, 258–59, 261–63, 268–69, 275, 280; and religion, 61, 65, 66–68, 183, 248, 253–54; and representation, 1–2, 13, 33, 52, 53, 62, 74, 117–19, 177; and rescue of individuals, 51, 53, 57, 61–63; and rescue of particulars, viii, 2–4, 8, 9–10, 14, 16–20, 22, 24, 25, 29, 30, 33, 34, 37, 40–41, 43–45, 53, 54, 59; and Robert Frost, 213, 238, 239, 273; and Romantic lyrical protagonist, 107; and salvation, 66–67; and second thoughts, 237–39; and sexual play, 195–96; and Shakespeare's sonnets, 225, 261; and short poems, 3, 12–13, 14, 18, 20, 34, 40, 41, 45, 49, 87, 88–89, 170; and social critique, 234, 237; and songs, 35–37, 114, 181, 185; and soul, 47, 55, 84, 85, 100, 157, 252; and spirituality, 218, 242; subjects for, 2, 12, 13, 28–29, 30, 33, 34, 37, 41, 68, 84, 136, 227, 260, 261, 270; and sunlight, 111, 159, 160; and supernatural beings, 65, 271, 279; and time, 15–17, 39–41, 52, 54, 57, 71, 73, 92, 93, 115, 188, 245; and truth, viii, 2, 13, 29, 33, 40, 57, 58, 62, 68, 69, 71, 80, 93, 114, 115, 136, 146, 153, 155–57, 162, 168, 186, 188, 213, 226, 240, 258, 263, 266, 270, 273, 274–75; and the "universal," 2, 3–4, 11, 34; and visibility, 70–71; and voice, 218, 221, 264; and whole poems, 262, 288–89; and William Yeats, 212, 215, 276. *See also* "Louie Louie" (Pinsky); ottava rima

Poetry of George Herbert, The (Vendler), 67

Poetry Review, 167

poets: and American poets, vii, 60, 73, 83–84, 124–25, 132, 137, 141, 205, 206, 208, 209; and autobiographical poets, 167, 173; and class, 24, 205; and contemporary poets, vii, 64, 73–74, 209, 213, 248, 251; critics of, 64, 73–74, 105, 132, 217, 218; and depression, 127, 192; and desperation, 126, 256, 281; and egotism, 137; and elegies, 188, 257; essays on, vii, viii, 90, 112, 143; and fame, 45, 258; in Ghana, 4, 23; greatness of, 73–74, 83, 129, 139, 144, 206, 253; and happiness, 138; and hope, 115, 116; and imagination, 63, 74, 111, 197, 236, 251; and inspiration, 167, 271–72; and internet, 137; and John Keats, 273; and joy, 126, 128, 138, 204; and loneliness, 204; and loss, 171; and love, 115; and Ludovico Ariosto, 154; and lyrical voice, vii; and male poets, 37; and meaning, 73, 78–81; and memory, 115; and Moderns, 125, 261; and names,

2–3; obsessions of, 191; parallels between, 71, 73, 81, 82, 119, 157–58; poetry about, 132, 133; and readers, viii, 23, 81–82, 205–6; and recognition, 115; and religion, 46, 47, 60; and representation, 2; and Shakespearean comedy, 192; and social injustice, 81; and Stanley Kunitz, 141; and synoptic perception, 173–74; as teachers, 253; and truth, 206, 289; and T. S. Eliot, 127, 131, 136, 150, 157; of the twentieth century, 2, 136–37

Pope, Alexander, vii, 64, 141, 229

Porter, Cole, 137

"Portrait" (Fearing), 119–20, 121

Possible World, A (Koch), 168–70

"Postcard from the Volcano, A" (Stevens), 111

postmodernism, 79, 97, 137, 224, 239

Pound, Ezra, 131

"Powers" (Goldbarth), 7

"Progress of Poesy, The" (Arnold), 41

Presley, Elvis, 137

Priest Turned Therapist Treats Fear of God (Hoagland), 225, 233, 240

Prufer, Kevin, 222

Pynchon, Thomas, 250

Rakosi, Carl, 104

Ransom, John Crowe, 21

Recent Changes in the Vernacular (Hoagland), 225, 227, 234

"Rejected Member's Wife, The" (Hardy), 10–14, 17, 34

"Remembrance Day, London 1970's" (Lowell), 31–34

Revell, Donald, 263

Rice, Tamir, 181

Rich, Adrienne, 126, 229

Riley, Atsuro, 220, 221

Rilke, Rainer Maria, 126, 252, 253

Rivers, Larry, 148, 149, 150, 153, 158–59

"River Song" (Kees), 106

Robinson, Jackie, 184

Roethke, Theodore, 137

"Romance of the Tree" (Hoagland), 233–34, 235

Ruth, Babe, 100

Ryley, Robert M., 83, 84, 107, 112

"Sad Strains of a Gay Waltz" (Stevens), 101–12

Sakura Park (Wetzsteon): diction and idioms of, 199; and disappointment, 191; and emotion, 203–4; "Flaneur Haiku" of, 194–95; and lone-

Sakura Park (continued)
 liness, 190, 196; and love, 190, 191–92, 195;
 and "Sakura Park," 197–98; and unhappiness,
 191–92, 196
Salamun, Tomaz, 275
"Salts and Oils" (Levine), 7
Scape (Bateman), 243, 251, 254, 256, 257
"Scarecrow on Fire" (Young), 279–80
Schopenhauer, Arthur, 242
Scott, Walter, 181
"Seasons on Earth" (Koch), 160–64, 167, 169
"Self-Portrait in a Convex Mirror" (Ashbery), 65,
 74–75, 77
Sexton, Anne, 191
Shakespeare, William, 35, 59, 83, 124, 131, 141, 177.
 See also poetry; poets
Shelley, Percy Bysshee, 56, 126, 154, 193, 243, 273.
 See also "Adonais" (Shelley)
Silver Roses (Wetzsteon), 190, 191, 198, 201, 202, 203
Sinatra, Frank, 124, 137
"Sixteen Dead Men" (Yeats), 25, 26
slavery, 231
Smith, Stevie, 178
Solar Perplexus (Young), 261, 263, 269, 279, 288
"Song of Myself" (Whitman), 47–48, 52, 61, 70
Spenser, Edmund, 141
Spinoza, Baruch, 242
Spoon River Anthology (Masters), 22
Springsteen, Bruce, 121, 122
Stein, Gertrude, 269
Sterling, Alton, 181
Stevens, Wallace, 87; and American Romantics,
 125; and "Farewell to Florida," 162; and feelings,
 239; greatness of, 206, 288; and "Gubbinal,"
 182; and Helen Vendler, 64, 70; and intimacy,
 81; "Latest Freed Man, The" 119; and meaning,
 124, 247; and the mind, 87; and music, 101, 102;
 "Planet on the Table, The," 146; as a poet, 70,
 117–18, 251, 253, 257; poetry of, 212; and sep-
 arateness, 252; and sunlight, 111; and supreme
 fiction, 102; and understandability, 222, 238. *See
 also* "As You Leave the Room" (Stevens); poetry;
 "Postcard from the Volcano, A" (Stevens); "Well
 Dressed Man with a Beard, The" (Stevens)
Stevens and the Interpersonal (Halliday), 81
Stranger at Coney Island (Fearing), 114, 117
Structure and Surprise: Engaging Poetic Turns
 (Theune et al.), 226–27

Summa Lyrica (Grossman), 18, 269
"Supermarket in California, A" (Ginsberg), 208
surrealism, 79, 278
Szymborska, Wisława, 205

Tate, James, 222, 263, 275
"Teardrops" (song), 35–36
Temple, Ralph, 27, 29, 32
Temple, The (Herbert), 66
Tennyson, Alfred, 97, 157, 198
Thank You (Koch), 134, 139, 171
Thatcher, Margaret, 23
"Time Zone, A" (Koch), 7, 143, 164
Theune, Michael, 226
This Is Spinal Tap (film), 134
Thomas, Dylan, 220
Thomson, James, 7
"To a Stranger" (Whitman), 72
Tolstoy, Leo, 83
"To Think of Time" (Whitman), 54–57, 60, 188
transcendental humanism, 66

Ulysses (Joyce), 2, 152
Unincorporated Persons in the Late Honda Dynasty
 (Hoagland), 205, 211–12, 215–16, 221–22, 224, 225,
 236–37. *See also* Hoagland, Tony
United States, 97, 104, 236
University of Texas, 277
"Unnamed Lands" (Whitman), 60–61
"Upon Prew His Maid" (Herrick), 19–21, 22

Vendler, Helen: and colloquy, 71, 74; human voice
 of, 64; and intimacy, 65, 67, 68–71, 73, 74, 76,
 77–79; and *Invisible Listeners*, viii; and loneli-
 ness, 70; and modern poets, 74; and readers,
 72–73, 75–76, 80; and sexual desire, 73; and
 visibility, 68. *See also* Ashbery, John; Herbert,
 George; *Music of What Happens, The* (Vendler);
 Whitman, Walt
Verlaine, Paul, 4, 5
Vietnam War, 128
Virgil, 104
Voltage Poetry, 227

Walcott, Derek, 217
Warhol, Andy, 23
Waste Land, The (Eliot), 85, 86, 97
Welk, Lawrence, 178, 179

"Well Dressed Man with a Beard, The" (Stevens), 89, 121

West, Nathanael, 96, 97

Wetzsteon, Rachel: and "Apologies to an Ambulance," 198–99; "Bluff, A" 200; and "But for the Grace," 193–94; and death, 190, 197, 199; and "Dream Vision, A," 201; and "Evening News," 192–93; and "Gusts," 196, 201; and happiness, 197, 198, 199; and identity, 194; and "Listening to the Ocean," 192; and love, 192, 193, 194, 195, 196, 200–202, 204; and "Love and Work," 195, 196; and memory, 201–3; and "Midsummer Night's Swing," 201–22; and New York, 191–92, 194, 196–97, 198; and readers, 193, 198; and "Rosalind in Manhattan," 191–92; and "Skater's Waltz," 196–97; and sonnets, 196; and suffering, 198–99, 203; suicide of, 190, 196; and unhappiness, 191, 193, 194. See also "At the Zen Mountain Monastery" (Wetzsteon); Sakura Park (Wetzsteon); Silver Roses (Wetzsteon)

What Narcissism Means to Me (Hoagland), 205, 221, 224

Whitman, Eddie, 58, 59

Whitman, Walt: and afterlife, 46; and American people, 51, 52, 72–73; and benevolence, 175; and brother Eddie, 58, 59; and "Burial Poem" or "To Think of Time," 54–55, 56, 57; catalogs of, 183; Civil War poems of, 70; and culture, 229; death of, 62; demotic phrases of, 90; and depression, 61, 62; essay on, vii; and "Full of Life Now," 71–72; greatness of, 206; and happiness, 161; and heaven, 60; and Helen Vendler, 64, 65, 66, 70, 72; and humanity, 47, 48, 53, 58, 60–61; and individuality of voices, 48; and intimacy, 70, 71, 73; and joy, 60, 253; and language, 59; and "Lawyers on the Left Bank," 195–96; and Leaves of Grass, 173; and male lover, 50; and memory, 173; and mortality, 47; Native Representations of, 53; and nature, 200, 234; and New York, 72–73; and "O Tan-Faced Prairie Boy," 70; and outer space, 289; poetry of, 75, 104, 184; and project of keeping, 2; and religion, 66; and rescue of individuals, 51, 53, 59, 61–63; and rescue of particulars, 46, 57, 60–62, 63, 184; and "Respondez!," 178; as a Romantic, 125; and "Salut au Monde!," 124;

and salvation, 58; and sexual longing, 73; and "Starting from Paumanok," 47; and time, 188; and "To a Stranger," 72; and transcendentalism, 2, 58; and visibility, 70. See also "Crossing Brooklyn Ferry" (Whitman); "Once I Pass'd through a Populous City" (Whitman); "Song of Myself" (Whitman); "Unnamed Lands" (Whitman)

Williams, Bert, 179–80

Williams, William Carlos, 100

Wishes, Lies, and Dreams (Koch), 133

Wordsworth, William: and bridge over Thames, 14; and daily talk, 218; and human experience, 233; and immortality, 156; and lyrical voice, vii, 141, 144; and meaning of experiences, 157–58; and murder, 272; and mythic youth, 120; and Prelude, The, 157–58; "Tintern Abbey" of, 150

World War II, 84

Yakusada, Araki, 274

"Year Zero" (Wetzsteon), 202–3

Yeats, William Butler, 4, 25, 26, 64, 73, 109, 162. See also "Easter 1916" (Yeats); poetry

"Yonnondio" (Whitman), 51–53, 54, 60

Young, Dean: and "Alternating Current," 280–81; and "Changing Genres," 289; and Creature Feature, 277, 278, 287, 288; and death, 260, 277, 278, 288; and despair, 263, 278; and emotion, 261, 264, 272–73, 274, 286; and "Errata," 276, 288; and friendship, 278; heart transplant of, 277, 290; and hope, 276, 289; and human experience, 253, 260–61, 264, 266–69, 276, 278–79; and irreverence, 274, 275; letters of, 277–78; life of, 277–78, 288; and love, 278, 280–82, 287–88, 289, 290; and meaning, 261; and metaphors, 260, 264–67, 270–75, 279–80, 282; and the mind, 285–86; and "My Process," 269–73, 275–76; and Nature, 264, 265–66; and "Non-Apologia," 281–82; as a poet, 272–74, 277–82; and readers, 260, 261, 280, 282; and similes, 273; "Song" of, 285–86; and spirit, 288, 290; and Strike Anywhere, 276, 279, 288; and truth, 270, 274–75, 281, 286; and "Undertow," 284; and "Vacationland," 286–87; and "Vintage," 287–88; and vision of overwhelmedness, 282, 287; and "Winged Purposes," 289–90. See also Hoagland, Tony